De Luxe Color Plates

中國食譜
CHINESE COOKBOOK

潘佩芝 編著

by

Pei-Chih Pan

名江書局印行

序

　　編者酷愛我國烹飪藝術，近十餘年開辦『也恬烹飪補習班』，精心研究，絡續編稿印成『潘佩芝食譜』，全套四冊包羅萬象，如各種雜編等，為其他食譜所無。

　　茲應同好之請就原食譜選其香色味俱佳而易學易做者菜肴一百八十色（含有年菜、宴客菜、家常菜）及中國點心十二道改編為『中國食譜』，並分中、英文版，全部均以彩色插圖說明，以應國際人士及海外僑胞之需要，使我國特有之烹飪藝術廣播於世界各儻，亦發揚中華傳統優良之文化之一助乎。

潘佩芝

中華民國62年12月於台北

PREFACE

  Chinese cookery is a great passion of mine. It has led me to found the Yeh-I Cooking Class where I have been teaching the techniques of Chinese cooking for the past ten years. I have not only taught but experimented with new ways of making Chinese dishes. In the process my first publication, in Chinese, Pei-Chih Pan's Cookbook, was published. A set of four volumes, it encompasses a great diversity of dishes, many of which cannot be found in other Chinese cookbooks. first

  The present book has been written on the request of many friends and fellow enthusiasts. It contains 180 of the best of Pei-Chih Pan's Cookbook with respect to color, fragrance and palatability. Their superiority is further enhanced by their facility to make. They include dishes for celebrating the Chinese New Year, entertaining guests in style, or simply cooking for the family. In addition, there are twelve Chinese snacks. Illustrated by colored photographs, this collection comes in both Chinese and English editions in order to meet the needs of both Chinese at home and abroad and international friends. I also hope that this book will serve as a tool in communicating Chinese culture to the world via one of its oldest and greatest art forms - - the art of Chinese cookery.

  I wish to thank Mr. and Mrs. Sung-Si Sze, Miss An-Sun Sze and Mr. Ding-Kuo Sze for their help in translating this book and making the publication of the English edition possible.

Pei-Chih Pan

Taipei, Taiwan
Republic of China
1974

目錄 Contents

冷盆類 COLD DISHES

醉鷄醉海舌	Wined Chicken and Salted Jell-Fish	9
涼拌腰片	Kidney Slices Salad	10
燻魚油爆蝦	Sauteed Shrimps and Spicy Fish	11
麻辣腰片	Kidney Slices in Hot Sauce	12
滷鴨	Red Stewed Duck	13
涼拌干絲	Bean Curd Noodles Salad	14
鳳肝鮮魷魚捲	Chicken Livers with Squid Rolls	15
素鴨素冬菇	Vegetable Duck and Mushrooms	16
鮮果沙拉	Fruit Salad	17
鷄絲拉皮	Shredded Chicken and Bean Thread Sheets	18

炸類 DEEP-FRIED DISHES

脆皮肥鷄	Crispy Skin Chicken	19
糖醋青魚尾	Sweet and Sour Grass Carp Tail	20
蛤蜊油條	Clams with You-Tiao (Fried Dough Sticks)	21
炸排骨	Deep-Fried Pork Chops	22
炸腰果	Fried Cashews	23
炸松子	Fried Pine Seeds	24
龍鳳腿	Deep-Fried Chicken Feet with Pork	25
糖醋排骨	Sweet and Sour Spareribs	26
什錦鍋粑	Ten Precious Kuo-Pa	27
煙鯧魚	Smoked Pomfret	28
麵拖黃魚	Deep-Fried Yellow Fish	29
酥炸肫肝	Deep-Fried Gizzards and Livers	30
酥炸茄塊	Deep-Fried Eggplants	31
紙包鷄	Deep-Fried Paper-Wrapped Chicken	32
炸蝦球	Deep-fried Shrimp Balls	33
炸蝦餅	Deep-Fried Shrimp Patties	34
百角蝦球	Shrimp Balls with A Hundred Angles	35
高麗肉	Korean Meat	36
蘋果夾	Deep-fried Apples	37
炸魚片	Fried Fish Slices	38
魚丸菜花	Fish Balls and Cauliflower	39
紅扒鵪蛋	Fried Quail Eggs in Brown Sauce	40
家庭叉燒	Family Broiled Pork	41
炸鷄腿	Fried Chicken Legs	42
螞蟻上樹	Ants on Tree	43
炸響鈴	Fried Bell-Shaped Pork	44
香酥鴨	Fragrant and Crispy Duck	45

炒類 STIR-FRIED DISHES

茄汁明蝦	Stir-Fried Prawns with Tomato Sauce	46
鳳尾蝦	Pheonix Tail Prawns	47
宮爆蝦仁	Fried Shrimps with Hot Sauce	48
生菜鴿松	Stir-Fried Minced Pigeon with Lettuce	49
芥蘭魚球	Fish Balls with Chinese Broccoli	50
碗豆苗炒蛋	Scrambled Eggs with Pea Shoots	51
青椒童鷄	Young Chicken with Green Pepper	52
魚香肉絲	Shredded Pork with Fish Flavors	53
爛糊肉絲	Shredded Pork and Celery Cabbage	54
爛糊牛肉絲	Beef Shreds and Onions	55
糖醋鮮魷魚捲	Sweet and Sour Squid Rolls	56
芙蓉鷄片	Chicken Slices Foo Yung	57
碗豆炒三丁	Stir-Fried Snow Peas and Three Dices	58
鳳肝黃瓜	Chicken Livers and Cucumbers	59
鷄油雙菇	Mushrooms with Chicken Fat	60
宮爆鷄丁	Fried Chicken with Paprike	61
炒牛肝	Stir-Fried Ox Liver	62
魚香腰花	Stir-Fried Kidney with Fish Flavors	63
炒腰花	Stir-Fried Pork Kidney	64
鴛鴦蝦仁	Shrimps with Snow Peas and Lima Beans	65
鳳肝蝦捲	Chicken Liver and Prawn Slice	66
炒豬肝	Stir-Fried Pork Liver	67
金菜菱角	Stir-Fried Pickled Cabbage and Horned Water Chestnuts	68
香菇菜心	Green Cabbage Hearts and Dried Mushrooms	69
廣東咕老肉	Sweet and Sour Pork Cantonese Style	70
金鉤嫩芥菜心	Mustard Green Hearts and Dried Shrimps	71
八寶辣醬	Eight Precious Hot Sauce	72
沙茶牛肉	Stir-Fried Beef with Sa-Cha Sauce	73
蠔油牛肉	Stir-Fried Beef with Oyster Sauce	74
牛肉蘿蔔絲	Stir-Fried Shredded Beef and Turnip	75
炒臘肉	Stir-Fried Smoked Pork	76
醬炒青蟹	Stir-Fried Crabs with Bean Paste Sauce	77
生炒黃蜆	Stir-Fried Fresh Clams	78
醬爆櫻桃	Stir-Fried Frogs Legs with Bean Paste	79
滑蛋牛肉	Stir-Fried Beef with Eggs	80
蝦仁跑蛋	Shrimps Omelet	81
炒四季豆	Stir-Fried String Beans	82
火腿花菜	Stir-Fried Cauliflower and Chinese Ham	83
蟹粉芥蘭	Mustard Green and Crabs	84
肉末豇豆	Minced Pork with Kidney Beans	85

煎類 SAUTEED DISHES

蝴蝶蝦	Butterfly Prawns	86
魚肉蛋捲	Egg Rolls with Fish Meat	87
雪菜鯽魚	Bastard Carps and Pickled Mustard Green	88
辣豆瓣鯉魚	Carp with Hot Bean Sauce	89

蒸類 STEAMED DISHES

油淋乳鴿	Oil Dripped Young Pigeon	90
蛤蜊蒸蛋	Steamed Eggs with Clams	91
燻鷄	Smoked Chicken	92
清蒸河鰻	White Steamed Eel	93
汽鍋鷄	Steamed Chicken	94
臘鯗蒸蛋	Steamed Eggs with Dried Salted Fish	95
滑油蒸鷄	Steamed Chicken with Oil	96
牛肉包心菜	Beef Wrapped in Cabbage	97
紅豆腐乳扣肉	Steamed Pork with Red Bean Curd Cheese	98
龍鳳花菇	Flower Mushrooms with Minced Pork and Chicken	99
蟹味青魚	Steamed Grass Carp with Crab Flavor	100
蜜汁火腿	Chinese Ham with Honey Sauce	101
芙蓉海蔘	Sea Cucumber Foo Yung	102

蕃茄蒸豆腐	Steamed Bean Curd with Tomato	103
西湖魚	West Lake Fish	104
竹筒肉	Steamed Pork in Bamboo Mugs	105
金菜蒸鴨	Steamed Duck with Pickled Cabbage	106
粉蒸肉	Steamed Pork in Spiced Rice Powder	107
髮菜燉蛋	Steamed Eggs with Seaweed	108
富貴雞	Steamed Chicken with Stuffings	109
蒸火腿	Steamed Chinese Hem	110
金銀豬肚	Gold and Silver Pork Stomach	111
清蒸豬腦	White Steamed Pork Brains	112
清蒸鯧魚	White Steamed Pomfret	113
霉乾菜扣肉	Steamed Pork with Salted Dried Mustard Cabbage	114
冰箱風雞	Salted Chicken	115

燉類　STEWED DISHES

紅燒蹄胖	Stewed Pork Leg in Brown Sauce	116
洋葱扒鴨	Duck with Onion Sauce	117
咖哩豬舌	Pork Tongue with Curry Sauce	118
油豆腐雞	Chicken with Oily Bean Curd	119
貴妃雞	Stewed Chicken Leg and Wings	120
栗子燒雞	Stewed Chicken with Chestnuts	121
紅燒圈子	Red Stewed Pork Rings	122
紅燒羊肉	Stewed Lamb with Brown Sauce	123
紅燒鰻段	Stewed Eel with Brown Sauce	124
蕃茄燉肉	Stewed Pork with Tomatoes	125
鳳爪甲魚	Stewed Turtle with Chicken Feet	126
五香肘花	Five-Spices Pork	127
鎮江肴肉	Spicy Pork Tsen-Chian Style	128
紅燒甲魚	Stewed Turtle in Brown Sauce	129
鮮果銀耳	White Wood Ear with Fruits	130
鳳採牡丹	Stewed Pigeons and Pork Lung	131
紅燒豬蹄	Stewed Pork Foot in Brown Sauce	132
砂鍋魚頭	Fish Head in Earthenware Pot	133

燒類　SIMMERED DISHES

芋芳燒鴨	Duck with Taros	134
八寶鴨	Stuffed Duck with Eight-Treasures	135
煮干絲	Boiled Bean Curd Noodles	136
醬肉	Pork in Soy Sauce and Bean Paste	137
麻婆豆腐	Ma-Po's Bean Curd	138
紅燒烏賊	Red Simmered Cuttlefish	139
四狀元	Four Gentlemen	140
花生燉肉	Pork and Peanuts Stew	141
紅燒划水	Red Cooked Fish Tails	142
醃魚燒肉	Braised Pork with Dried Salted Fish	143
咖哩雞	Braised Chicken with Curry Sauce	144
油豆腐塞肉	Pork Meat Stuffed Oily Bean Curd	145
暈素菜	Meat and Vegetables	146
紅燜雙童	Red Braised Chickens	147
羊肉粉皮	Lamb and Bean Thread Sheets	148

羹類　THICKENED SOUPS

雞絲燴翅	Shredded Chicken and Shark's Fin	149
雞耳粟米	Minced Chicken and Corn	150
羊腰腦羹	Lam Kidney and Brain Soup	151
鮮蠔羹	Fresh Oyster Soup	152
蝦球羹	Shrimp Balls Soup	153
干貝羹	Scallop Soup	154
什錦豆腐	Ten Precious Bean Curd	155
芙蓉黃魚參	Yellow Fish and Sea Cucumber Foo Yung	156
醋溜魚片	Fish Slices with Vinegar	157
菠菜羹	Chopped Spinach Soup	158

燴類　SAUCE THICKENED DISHES

蟹粉魚唇	Shark's Lip with Crabs	159
全家福	Happy Family	160
清燴鴨掌	White Braised Duck Feet	161
清燴蹄筋	White Braised Pork Tendon	162
干貝三色球	Scallops with Tri-Colored Balls	163
燴八寶	Simmered Eight-Treasures	164
金銀荷包	Gold and Silver Pouches	165
稀露海參	Sea Cucumber with Minced Pork	166
酸辣海參	Hot and Sour Sea Cucumber	167

溜類　STIRRED DISHES

糟溜魚片	Fish Slices with Pai-Tsao Sauce	168
溜黃菜	Stirred Egg Yolks	169
溜黃豆腐	Bean Curd with Egg Yolks	170
炸溜黃魚	Stirred Fried Yellow Fish	171

焗類　OTHER DISHES

塩焗蝦	Salted Shrimps	172
塩焗雞	Pan Baked Chicken with Salt	173

湯類　SOUPS

鵪蛋豬肚湯	Pork Stomach Soup with Quail Eggs	174
淡菜雞湯	Chicken Soup with Dried Oysters	175
蛋豆腐湯	Egg Bean Curd Soup	176
金銀魚圓	Gold and Silver Fish Balls Soup	177
蓮鍋湯	Soup with Lotus Leaves	178
燕皮荷包湯	Yen-Pi Soup	179
鵲橋湯	Pigeon Soup with Winter Melon	180
柴杷鴨湯	Soup with Duck Sheaves	181
鯉魚湯	Carp Soup	182
蓮藕排骨湯	Lotus Roots and Spareribs Soup	183
酸辣湯	Hot Sour Soup	184
醃燉鮮	Salted and Fresh Pork Stew	185
蕃茄牛利湯	Beef Tongue and Tomato Soap	186
河州肉片湯	Sliced Pork and Cucumber Soap	187
龍鳳雙爪盅	Dragon and Pheonix Feet Soup	188

中國點心　14. SNACKS

蟹粉麵	Noodles with Crab Meat	189
八寶飯	Eight Precious Rice	190
片兒川	Noodles in Sliced Pork Soup	191
蓮藕粥	Lotus Root Congee	192
蝦肉餛飩	Shrimp-Pork Won-Tons	193
小籠包	Steamed Small Meat Pastries	194
芝麻湯糰	Sesame Dumplings (Chih-Ma Tang-Tian)	195
炒麵	Stir-Fried Noodles (Chow-Mian)	196
粽子	Meat Dumplings in Bamboo Leaves	197
炒年糕	Stir-Fried Year Cakes	198
桂花金子糕	Gold Cakes with Kuei-Hwa (the osmanthus fragrans)	199
蟹黃燒賣	Crab Shao-Mai	200

①海參
Sea. cucumber

②豆腐皮
Salted jelly fish

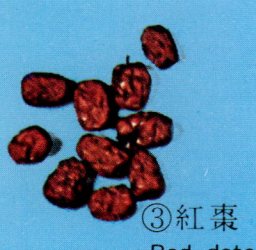
③紅棗
Red date

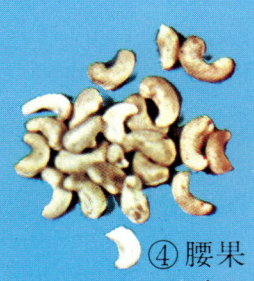
④腰果
Cashews

⑤木耳
Dried fungus

⑥青椒
Green pepper

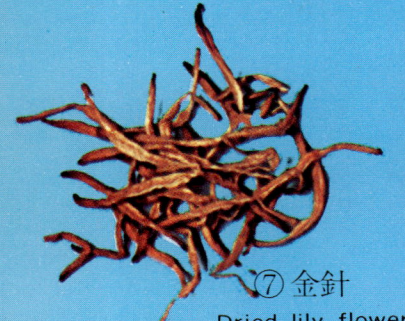
⑦金針
Dried lily flower

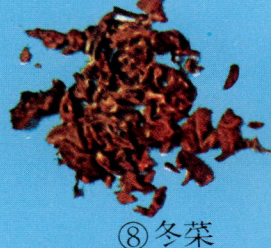
⑧冬菜
Pickled cabbage (diced)

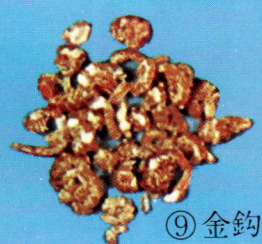
⑨金鈎
Dried shrimps

⑩蓮子
Lotus nut

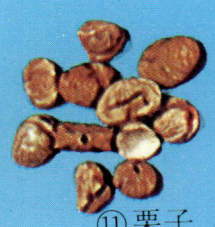
⑪栗子
Chestnut

⑫銀耳
White wood ear

⑬八角
Star anise

⑭筍干
Dried bamboo shoot

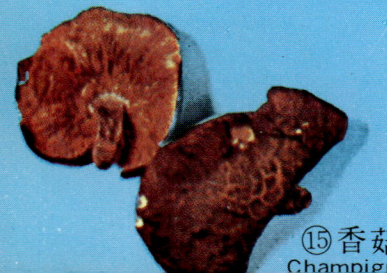
⑮香菇
Champignon

⑯淡菜

⑰松子

⑱髮菜
Seameed

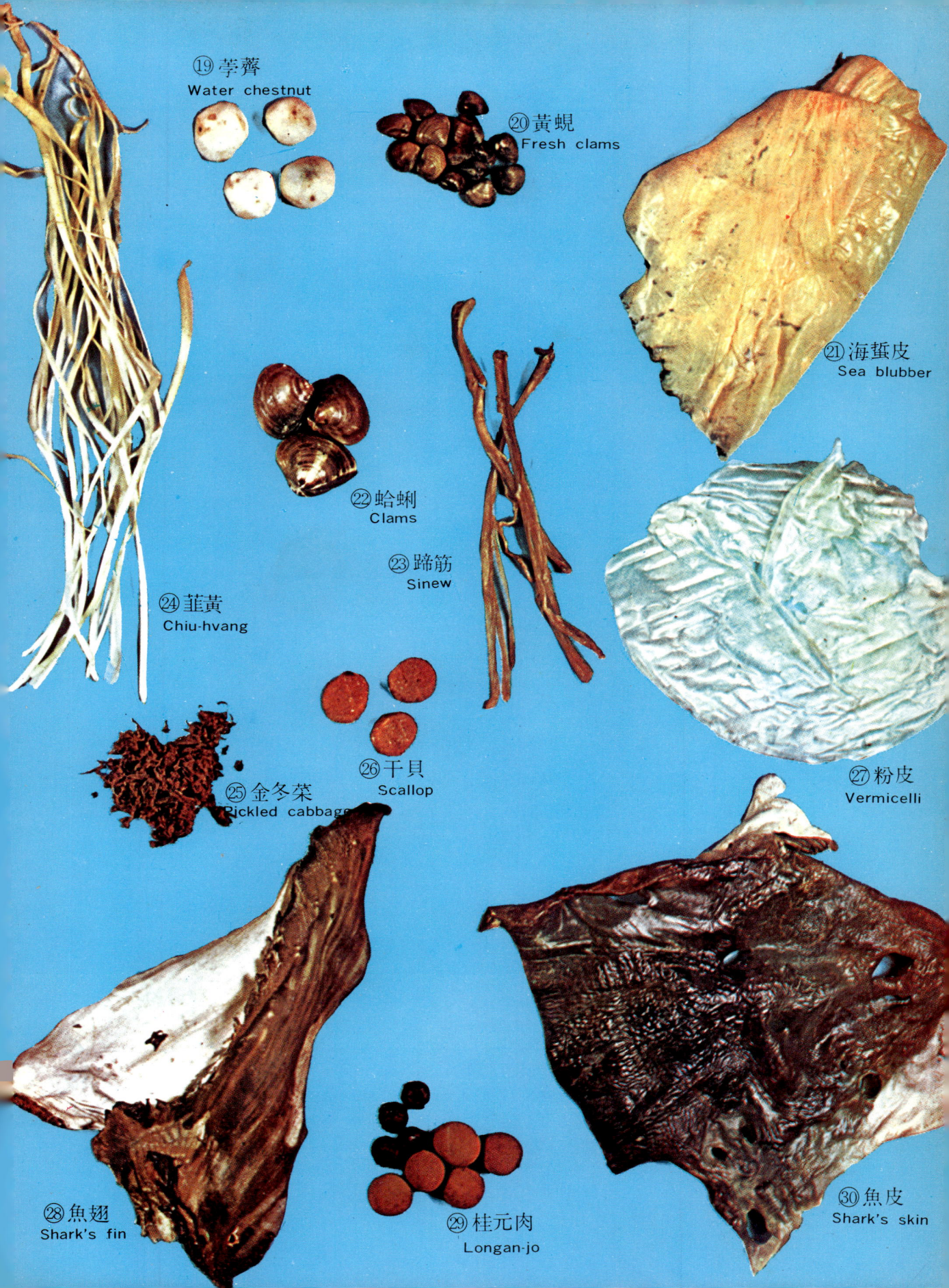

本書使用容器說明 Table of Measurements

¼ 茶匙
¼ Teaspoon

½ 茶匙
½ Teaspoon

一 茶匙
1 Teaspoon

一 湯匙
1 Tablespoon

標準容器白鐵號有售

醉雞醉海舌
Wined, Chicken and Salted Jellyfish

浙江菜　　　材料：12人份

材　料：嫩雞一隻　海舌四兩　清酒二碗　香菜三支　鹽三茶匙　蔴油一湯匙　薑二片

做　法：①將海舌先一日洗淨浸在冷水中一夜，次日洗去沙後，再以冷開水浸泡片刻瀝乾後，切細絲澆上白醬油二湯匙和蔴油一湯匙、醉雞酒汁二湯匙，再加點味精與糖拌勻，盛在拼盤中之一半。

②將雞去毛除內臟洗淨吹乾後，用一湯匙鹽擦透雞身內外約醃二、三小時，然後將雞放入碗內，面舖薑二片，以大火沸水蒸二十分鐘取出趁熱斬為四塊，放在燜碗內即傾下酒二碗浸泡四、五小時即可吃了，如要次日吃，那蒸好之雞斬塊待冷後，再倒下酒浸泡，將雞斬塊拼在冷盆另一邊，面飾香菜三支送席。

Ingredients:
- 1 young chicken
- 2 C. white wine
- 2 slices ginger
- 2 T. white soy sauce
- pinch of sugar
- 2 T. wine from wined chicken
- 4 oz. salted jellyfish
- 3 sprigs parsley
- 3 t. salt
- 1 T. sesame oil
- dash of monosodium glutamate (M.S.G.)

Directions:
1. Clean jellyfish and soak overnight in cold water. Wash off sand. Immerse in cold boiled water 3-4 min. Drain and cut into shreds. Mix well with 2 T. soy sauce, 1 T. sesame oil, 2 T. wine from wined chicken, sugar and monosodium glutamate. Place on one side of serving plate.
2. Salt chicken inside and out; let stand 2-3 hr. Put ginger on top of chicken and steam over high heat, 20 min. Cut into quarters hot and place in bowl. Pour wine over chicken; cover and let stand 4-5 hr. Cut into small pieces, 2"X1". Arrange on plate beside jellyfish. Garnish with parsley on top and serve. (If chicken is not desired until next day, let cool after quartering before soaking in wine.)

凉拌腰片
Pork Kidney Slices Salad

湖南菜　　　材料：12人份

材　料：猪腰三只　粉皮二十張　嫩黃瓜四條　蕃茄二只　葱一支　薑一片　酒一茶匙　鹽一茶匙

綜合調味：白醬油二湯匙　醋一湯匙　糖半茶匙　鹽半茶匙　蔴油一茶匙　胡椒少許

做　法：①先將猪腰對切去筋，再切斜片成大薄片洗淨浸水一小時。
②將黃瓜拍碎切長條，加入鹽醃片刻傾去水置盆四週，並加隔蕃茄片。
③將粉皮加少鹽洗二次，再拿冷開水洗一次，撈起瀝乾置盆中間。
④腰片在沸水中燙三、四分鐘，撈起再泡在薑酒葱鹽合煮之沸水中（已溫）片刻取出瀝乾水份，放在粉皮上，淋上綜合調味汁即成爲夏日之佳肴。

Ingredients: 3 pork kidneys　　20 bean thread sheets (fung-pi)　　4 cucumbers
2 tomatoes　　1 stalk green onion　　1 slice ginger
1 t. wine　　1 t. salt

Seasoning Sauce (combine):
2 T. white soy sauce　　1 T. vinegar　　½ t. sugar
½ t. salt　　1 t. sesame oil　　dash of pepper

Directions:
1. Split kidneys horizontally and remove white veins. Cut into large and thin slices diagonally. Soak in water 1 hr.
2. Beat cucumbers to flatten. Cut into strips. Add salt and let stand 10 min. To dehydrate water and arrange on sides of serving plate. Alternate with tomato slices.
3. Wash bean thread sheets with a pinch of salt twice. Rinse in cold boiling water. Drain and cut into strips. Place in center of serving plate.
4. Parboil kidneys 3-4 min. Remove to pot containing boiling water with ginger, wine, green onion and salt. Cook 1 min. Remove and drain. Place on top of bean thread sheets. Pour seasoning sauce over as dressing and serve.

燻魚油爆蝦
Sauteed Shrimps and Spicy Fish

浙 江 菜　　　材料：12人份

材　料：中段青魚一斤　葱三支　薑三片　醬油三湯匙　酒一湯匙　沸水四湯碗　花生油八湯匙　香菜三支　鹽半茶匙　活河蝦半斤　葱一支　薑一片　花生油一飯碗半

調味品：白醬油一湯匙　黑醬油一茶匙　鹽、糖各半茶匙

做　法：
① 首將河蝦剪去長鬚洗淨瀝乾裝盤內。
② 次將調味品一一倒下，並將葱薑拍碎放入，用筷子翻覆攪勻，約浸漬二三小時後再瀝乾。
③ 把油倒鍋內燒熱，將蝦全部傾入爆炸，約三四分鐘即可盛起，揀去葱薑不要，以蝦一隻隻地排列拚盤之一角。
④ 將魚去鱗洗淨對剖，然後切成三分厚之魚片放盆內加醬油、酒、鹽、葱、薑醃二、三小時取出瀝乾後備用。
⑤ 須將四湯匙糖加滾水溶化，並加下五香粉留用。
⑥ 將花生油燒熱投入魚塊，分數次炸，每次炸看魚塊呈褐色取出濾去油，放入糖水中浸片刻，候全炸好就倒出剩油，將全部炸好魚塊及浸魚之醬油、糖水倒鍋內滾燒，候汁水呈稠厚即端起離火冷醃片刻，再將魚塊裝盆拚入油爆蝦旁面飾香菜三支送席。

Ingredients for fish: 1 middle section of live grass carp (about 1⅜ lb.) 　3 stalks green onion
3 slices ginger　　3 T. soy sauce　　1 T. wine
1½ t. salt　　½ t. five-spice powder　　4 T. sugar
4 T. boiling water　　8 T. peanut oil　　3 sprigs parsley

Ingredients for shrimps:
⅜ lb. live fresh water shrimps　　1 stalk green onion (cut into 2" pieces)　　1 slice ginger
1½ bowl peanut oil

Seasonings for shrimps:
1 T. white soy sauce　　1 t. black soy sauce　　½ t. salt　　½ t. sugar

Directions:
1. Cut fish in slices crosswise, ¼" thick. Halve each slice lengthwise. Marinate in soy sauce, wine, salt, green onion, and ginger, 2-3 hr. Drain.
2. Dissolve sugar in boiling water; mix with five-spice powder.
3. Heat oil in frying pan. Fry fish slices till brown on both sides. Drain oil and soak in sugar mixture. Remove oil. Return fish to pan; add remaining marinade and sugar mixture. Simmer till sauce is thickened. Let cool.
4. Trim shrimps, clean and drain. Mix with crushed green onion and ginger. Marinate in seasonings 2-3 hr; drain. Heat oil; fry shrimps, stirring and turning constantly, 3-4 min. Remove green onion and ginger.
5. Place fish and shrimps on plate side by side. Garnish with parsley and serve.

麻辣腰片
Kidney Slices in Hot Sauce

四川菜　　　材料：12人份

材　　料：豬腰一個重約六兩　粉皮十張　葱一支　薑一片　酒鹽各半茶匙

綜合調味：黑醬油二茶匙　白醬油一茶匙　花椒粉胡椒粉各半茶匙　糖四分之一茶匙　麻油一茶匙

做　　法：①首將豬腰對剖，挖去內筋，打斜切薄片，然後浸水約一小時，粉皮切約三分闊之條，先用少鹽洗二次，再用冷開水洗一次，撈出瀝乾置小盆中間。
②腰片在沸水中，燙三四分鐘，撈起即泡在已溫之葱薑酒鹽之水中，取出瀝乾水份，放在粉皮上，淋上綜合調味汁，即為冷盆之一。

附　　註：如胡椒粉改為辣油，即為「紅油腰片」。

Ingredients:　1　pork kindey (about 6 oz.)　　　　　1　slice ginger
　　　　　　　10　bean thread sheets (fung-pi)　　½　t. wine
　　　　　　　　1　stalk green onion　　　　　　　　½　t. salt

Seasoning Sauce (combine):
　　　　　　　　2　t. black soy sauce　　　　　　　½　t. pepper
　　　　　　　　1　t. white soy sauce　　　　　　　¼　t. sugar
　　　　　　　　½　t. peppercorn powder　　　　　1　t. sesame oil

Directions:　1. Cut kidney horizontally into two halves. Remove white veins and cut diagonally in thin slices. Soak in water 1 hr. Cut bean thread sheets into about ¼" wide strips. Wash twice with salt first; then wash once in cold boiled water. Drain.
　　　　　　　2. Parboil kidney 3-4 min. Soak in warm water containing of green onion, ginger, wine and salt. Drain and place on bean thread sheets. Pour seasoning sauce and serve cold.

滷 鴨
Red Stewed Duck

杭 州 菜 　　材料：12人份

材　料：肥鴨一只（重約二斤多）　醬油八湯匙　冰糖一湯匙（碎）　薑二片　酒一湯匙
　　　　八角桂皮少許

做　法：①首將鴨子洗淨，瀝乾置大盤內，以四湯匙醬油浸漬鴨身內外，約一小時備用。
　　　　②準備較厚的炒菜鍋，放下鴨子，倒下全部醬油和一湯匙酒，薑片與八角桂皮也放下，關蓋翻覆紅透，然後加入冰糖及三飯碗沸水，密蓋後改用文火燉燒，約二十分鐘，宜翻面一次，約燒一小時半，視湯汁剩一飯碗，卽可盛起，待冷斬塊排列細瓷盆中，面澆湯汁可作自助餐的一色，亦可作小孩的便當菜。

Ingredients: 1 fat duck (about 3 lb.)　8 T. soy sauce
　　　　　　　　1 T. crushed rock sugar　2 slices ginger
　　　　　　　　1 T. wine　　　　　　　　a little antiseed and kuei-pi (cinnamon bark)

Directions: 1. Clean duck and drain. Pour 4 T. soy sauce over duck inside and out. Let stand about 1 hr.
　　　　　　　　2. Put duck in pan. Add remaining soy sauce, 1 T. wine, ginger, antiseed and kui-pi. Cook over moderate heat, turning constantly until all sides are colored. Add rock sugar and 3 bowls boiling water. Stew, covered, over low heat, 20 min. Turn duck on other side and stew about another 1½ hr. until one bowl sauce is left. Remove and let cool. Cut duck into 2"X1" pieces. Pour sauce over duck. Serve.

涼拌干絲
Bean Curd Noodles Salad

四川菜　　　材料：12人份

材　料：干絲五兩　小蝦米　銀魚干　筍絲　火腿絲各二湯匙（肉絲亦可）　蘇打粉四分之一茶匙　芹菜數支

調味品：白醬油二湯匙　蔴油一湯匙　味精少許

做　法：①首將小蝦米，銀魚略洗蒸十分鐘後切碎，筍絲也蒸十分鐘，火腿切片蒸二、三分鐘後切絲芹菜切段後燙或炒待冷後備用。
②次將干絲以蘇打沸水泡五分鐘後換沸水泡二次，瀝乾備用。
③用一中號圓盆以干絲墊盆底，面舖各色配料，然後澆上調味品，即成為一美味的涼菜，亦可為夏日請客涼盆之一。

Ingredients: 5 oz. bean curd noodles
2 T. dried white fish
2 T. shredded Chinese ham
¼ t. soda powder
2 T. dried shrimp (small size)
2 T. shredded bamboo shoots
3-4 celery stalks

Seasonings: 2 T. white soy sauce
dash of monosodium glutamate
1 T. sesame oil

Directions:
1. Wash dried shrimp and dried white fish. Steam 10 min. and cut into small pieces. Steam shredded bamboo shoots 10 min., and sliced ham 2-3 min. and shred it. Cut celery 1½" long and soak in boiling water or fry few min. Cool.
2. Soak bean curd noodles in boiling soda water 5 min.; then soak twice in boiling water. Dry.
3. Put bean curd noodles in medium sized plate and spread other ingredients on top. Pour seasonings. Serve cold.

鳳肝鮮魷魚捲　浙江菜　材料：12人份
Chicken Livers with Squid Rolls

材　　料：雞肝六付　魷魚十二兩　嫩芹菜四兩(折葉洗淨切段)　葱二支　薑二片　鹽二茶匙　酒二茶匙　香菜三支
綜合調味：白醬油一湯匙半　醋二湯匙　糖一茶匙半　鹽、麻油各一茶匙　胡椒少許
做　　法：①首將雞心對剖與雞肝洗淨瀝水，然後每個切為五片留用。
②鍋中沸水一飯碗半，先倒下芹菜段川一下撈出瀝水卽裝在盆底，鍋中之水將雞肝川一下撈出沖洗瀝乾。
③鍋中再放沸水一飯碗，同時加入葱薑鹽酒待滾，第二次將雞肝倒落川一下卽撈出瀝水，放在芹菜上，然後淋上綜合調味汁。
④將鮮魷魚去皮及內臟洗淨瀝乾對剖，然後在每塊無皮之面打斜用刀輕切粒花，再打斜切塊成為菱形狀，全部切就留用。
⑤鍋中沸水一碗半，同時加入葱薑酒待滾時，將魷魚投入川一下撈起瀝水置旁備用，此時魷魚已呈捲形。
⑥鍋中換水一碗半，同時加入葱薑及酒待滾將魷魚再入川一下撈出瀝水，拼在雞肝旁之芹菜上，淋上綜合調味汁，面飾香菜送席。

Ingredients: 8 each chicken livers and hearts　　12 oz. squids
4 oz. young celery (cut into 1½" pieces without leaves)　2 stalks green onion
2 slices ginger　　2 t. salt
2 t. wine　　3 sprigs parsley

Seasoning Sauce (combine):
1½ T. white soy sauce　　2 T. vinegar
1½ t. sugar　　1 t. salt
1 t. sesame oil　　dash of pepper

Directions for chicken livers:
1. Cut each liver into 5 slices. Split each heart.
2. Boil 1½ bowl water in pot. Dip celery in water, 1-2 min. Remove and drain. Spread over serving plate. Dip in livers and hearts 1 min. Rinse in cold water and drain.
3. Add another bowl of boiling water to pot. Add green onion, ginger, salt and wine. Let simmer. Again dip in livers and hearts 1-2 min. Remove and drain. Put on top of celery. Sprinkle ½ seasoning sauce over livers and hearts.

Directions for squid rolls:
1. Remove membranes of squids. Clean thoroughly. Half lengthwise. Score inside surface crisscross diagonally. Cut into diamond shapes.
2. Boil 1½ bowl water in pot. Add green onion, ginger and wine. Let simmer. Dip in squids 1 min. Drain water. Squids should curl up.
3. Remove old water and boil another 1½ bowl water. Add green onion, ginger, salt and wine. Bring to boil. Again dip in squids. Remove and drain. Place beside chicken livers. Sprinkle remaining seasoning sauce over squids. Garnish with parsley and serve.

素鴨素冬菇
Vegetable Duck & Mushrooms

浙 江 菜　　　材料：12人份

材　　料：半圓形豆腐衣十六張　冬菇十五只　牙籤數支
綜合調味：醬油二湯匙　蔴油和糖各四茶匙　鹽一茶匙　香菜三支　花生油四湯匙
做　　法：①首將冬菇略洗，然後放下十八湯匙之温水浸泡二小時，撈出冬菇剪去脚留用。
②將冬菇之水倒入鍋中，同時加入綜合調味滾燒片刻，倒出待冷留用。
③將豆腐衣撕去邊上硬莖，逐張塗上綜合調味，每八張摺疊約一尺長二寸許寬之長方形塊，摺至末了用牙籤插住，每疊切爲二塊裝盆內，用中火蒸約十分鐘，起鍋待冷。
④待冷除去牙籤切成鴨塊形排列冷盆之一角，又將冬菇在煎素鴨之鍋中煎一下，然後將塗豆腐衣餘下之綜合調味汁傾下，如不够水可酌加水份蓋燜之到乾，約半小時後取出待冷，小只切成一塊大只切成三塊，仍成原形排入素鴨旁面飾香菜送席。

Ingredients: 16 semi circular bean curd sheets　　15 dried mushrooms
Seasoning Sauce:
　　2 T. soy sauce (combine)　　　　4 t. sesame oil (combine)
　　4 t. sugar (combine)　　　　　　1 t. salt (combine)
　　3 sprigs parsley　　　　　　　　4 T. peanut oil
　　2 toothpicks

Directions:
1. Soak mushrooms in 18. T. warm water 2 hr. Remove stems.
2. Heat water used to soak mushrooms with seasoning sauce to boil. Simmer 3-4 min. Let cool.
3. Remove hardened edges of bean curd sheets. Moisten each sheet with diluted seasoning sauce. Fold every 8 sheets together into rectangular shape, 1'X2". Pin ends together with toothpicks and cut into half. Steam 10 min. over moderate fire. Let cool. Sauté over low fire till lightly brown.
4. Remove toothpicks. Cut vegetable duck into 2"X1" pieces. Arrange on one side of plate. Stir-fry mushrooms 2-3 min. in remaining oil. Add diluted seasoning sauce (Add water if necessary). Cook, covered, 30 min. or until liquid 1s dry. Let cool. Cut small ones in half and large ones into 3 pieces. Arrange in original mushroom shape beside vegetable ducks. Garnish with parsley and serve.

鮮菓沙拉
Fruit Salad

材　料：蘋果四只　木瓜半只　蕃石榴四只　桔子四只　香蕉二只　文旦一小個　葡萄四兩
　　　　生菜葉六張　沙拉醬一小碗　平大水果盆一隻　牛皮紙漏斗一只

做　法：①首將二隻蘋果削皮去子切丁，另二隻選色美的洗淨連皮切為眉月形，木瓜去皮去子切丁，也切幾條眉月形，蕃石榴洗淨也切丁，留幾條眉月形，桔子去皮分瓣，切為二段，另二隻不切段，香蕉去皮切丁，文旦去皮分瓣切為二段，葡萄生菜葉均洗淨留用。
　　　　②將生菜葉舖在大水菓盆中，把所有切丁之鮮菓以沙拉醬之三分之二拌勻，裝在生菜葉上，再以切眉月形之鮮菓排列其面，須裝美觀，排好後，面散葡萄，已够漂亮了，再以餘下之沙拉醬倒在牛皮紙之小漏斗內，用手擠出澆在眉月形之鮮菓及葡萄上，如網狀，這一盆『鮮菓沙拉』令賓客看了歡喜，而其味亦佳，實在令人喜愛（主人在飯後，以小盤小銅匙分給每一位客人）。

Ingredients:	4 apples	½ papaya	4 tangerines
	2 bananas	1 pomelo	4 oz. grapes
	4 guavas	6 lettuce leaves	1 small bowl mayonnaise

Directions:
1. Pare 2 apples. Core and dice. Cut other two with skin into crescents. Seed papaya. Pare. Cut in dices and make a few crescents. Dice guava and make a few crescents. Peel tangerines. Halve each piece of 2 tangerines. Leave other two intact for thin crescent shapes. Peel banana and dice. Peel pomelo. Cut each piece in half. Wash grapes and lettuce leaves.
2. Place lettuce leaves in fruit bowl. Mix diced fruits together with ⅔ bowl mayonnaise. Put on leaves. Arrange fruit crescents on top. Sprinkle with grapes. Garnish by squeezing remaining mayonnaise criss-cross over crescents and grapes through paper-made filter.

鷄絲拉皮　北平菜

Shredded Chicken & Bean Thread Sheets

材料：12人份

材　　料：鷄胸脯一個　大黃瓜半條　熟火腿絲二湯匙　粉皮二十張　芥末醬一茶匙　芝蔴醬二湯匙（用四湯匙冷開水或蒸鷄汁調和）　鹽酒各四分之一茶匙

綜合調味品：白醬油二湯匙　醋一茶匙半　蔴油二茶匙

做　　法：①首將粉皮切成四分寬之長條，加一茶匙鹽輕揉洗淨，再加一茶匙鹽輕揉再洗一次，然後以冷開水浸留，鷄胸脯敷鹽半茶匙，約十分鐘後，加入酒以大火蒸十五分鐘，待冷拆骨取肉切細絲，大黃瓜去皮除子亦切絲均留用。

②備一細瓷圓盆，先把粉皮瀝水後墊盆底，面排鷄絲火腿絲黃瓜絲，再淋上綜合調味汁，最後，在盆中間，加上芥末醬及經調和之芝蔴醬，卽成為一式好吃又好看之夏日大冷盆。

Ingredients: 1 chicken breast　½ cucumber (halved lengthwise)　2 T. shredded ham (cooked)
20 bean thread sheets (fung-pi)　1 t. mustard
2 T. sesame paste (mixed with 4 T. steamed chicken sauce or cold boiled water)
2½ t. salt　¼ t. wine

Seasoning Sauce (combine):
2 T. white soy sauce　1½ t. vinegar　2 t. sesame oil

Directions:
1. Cut bean thread sheets into ½" wide strips. Rub with 1 t. salt and clean. Repeat. Soak in cold boiled water. Rub ½ t. salt on chicken breast. Let stand about 10 min. Add wine. Steam over high heat 15 min. Let cool. Bone and shred chicken. Pare cucumber and cut in shreds.
2. Drain bean thread sheets. Place at bottom of round plate. Arrange shredded chicken, ham and cucumber on top. Sprinkle with seasoning sauce. Place mustard and sesame paste in center. Mix ingredients at table to eat.

脆皮肥鷄 廣東菜
Crispy Skin Chicken

材料：12人份

材　　　料：肥嫩鷄一隻　麥芽糖一茶匙　鹽一湯匙　檸檬半隻(直切為三塊)
綜合調味：醋一湯匙　酒一茶匙　豆粉一茶匙　蜂蜜一湯匙　醬油一茶匙
五香鹽之製法：鹽二湯匙，在鍋中炒熱後，卽加入半茶匙五香粉略炒卽可。
做　　　法：①首將鷄洗淨，斬去脚和翅，從鷄翅下開孔，取出食管和肫肝，在鷄尾開一小孔，取出腸及油，然後洗淨瀝乾片刻。
②次將熱水半鍋，加入一湯匙鹽燒滾溶化，取繩吊起鷄頭，放鹽水中燙約二分鐘，取出傾去水，再放半鍋熱水加下一茶匙麥芽糖燒溶後，重將鷄放入燙約三分鐘取出，然後在鷄肚中擦一湯匙五香鹽，鷄之外皮擦上綜合調味，卽掛在通風口吹乾，(約六小時)。
③用七分鍋油燒熱，放下鷄炸約二十分鐘，直至鷄身外皮呈金褐色卽撈出瀝油後，卽速斬塊，裝入細瓷盤中，立卽送席 (盤之一邊放五香鹽，另一邊放切開之檸檬)。

Ingredients: 1 fat and young chicken (about 2 lb. net)　　1 t. maltose
　　　　　　 1 T. salt　　　　　　　　　　　　　　　　½ lemon (cut into 3 pieces)
Seasoning Sauce (combine):
　　　　　　 1 T. vinegar　　　　1 t. wine　　　　　　1 t. soy sauce
　　　　　　 1 t. cornstarch　　　1 T. honey
How to make five-spices salt:
　　　　　　 Heat 2 T. salt over low heat in frying pan. Stir in ½ t. five-spices powder; mix well
Directions:
1. Clean chicken. Remove feet and wings. Cut under wing to remove esophagus, liver and gizzard. Cut under tail to remove entrails and fat. Clean and drain.
2. Heat ½ pot water; add 1 T. salt. Bring to boil. Suspend chicken with string tied around head and dip in pot 2 min. Drain and discard water in pot. Heat another ½ pot water; add 1 t. maltose. Bring to boil to dissolve. Dip chicken about 3 min. Rub chicken stomach with 1 t. five-spices salt. Rub skin with seasoning sauce. Suspend to dry (about 6 hr.).
3. Fill frying pan with ¾ oil. Fry chicken about 20 min. until skin is golden brown. Drain and cut into pieces (2"X1"). Place on serving plate with sliced lemon on one side and five-spices salt on the other.

19

糖醋青魚尾
Sweet and Sour Grass Carp Tail

家常菜　　　　材料：12人份

材　　料：活青魚尾一個（重約十二兩）　紅辣椒一只（不吃辣可改用甜紅椒）　葱薑屑各一湯匙　花生油二飯碗　鹽半茶匙　豆粉二湯匙

綜合調味：白醋三湯匙　白醬油二湯匙　糖二湯匙　酒一湯匙　豆粉二湯匙　鹽半茶匙　冷水五湯匙

做　　法：①首將魚尾略洗瀝水對剖後，撇去大骨，在每塊魚皮打斜切腰花形，然後用半茶匙鹽敷在每塊魚上，約半小時，臨炸時每塊在豆粉中滾一滾，即投入油中去炸，視炸呈淡黃色，即濾油撈出，裝入長盤中，把油倒出，剩下一湯匙爆炒紅辣椒、葱、薑屑，即倒下綜合調味汁，不停地溜勻，再澆在魚尾上，趁熱送席。

Ingredients:
- 1 live grass carp tail (about 1 lb.)
- 1 T. chopped ginger
- 2 T. cornstarch
- 1 red chili pepper or sweet red pepper
- 2 bowls peanut oil
- 1 T. chopped green onion
- ½ t. salt

Seasoning Sauce (combine):
- 3 T. white vinegar
- 1 T. wine
- 5 T. water
- 2 T. white soy sauce
- 2 T. cornstarch
- 2 T. sugar
- ½ t. salt

Directions:
1. Cut tail in half lengthwise. Remove central bone. Score skin crisscross diagonally. Rub with 1½ t. salt, and let stand, 30 min.
2. Before frying, dredge fish tail with cornstarch; fry in oil till light brown. Place fish tail in oblong serving plate. Leave 1 T. oil in frying pan. Saute red chili pepper, chopped green onion and ginger. Stir in seasoning sauce. Pour over fried fish tail. Serve hot.

蛤蜊油條　　家常菜　　材料：12人份
Clams with You-Tiao (Fried Dough Sticks)

材　料：	新鮮小隻蛤蜊一斤半　冷油條六條　嫩薑屑二湯匙　葱屑三湯匙　高湯一中碗
	豬油二湯匙　豆粉一湯匙（用三湯匙水調濕）　花生油一斤
調味品：	白醬油一湯匙　鹽一茶匙　味精少許
做　法：	①首將蛤蜊洗淨，用半鍋水燒沸，將蛤蜊傾入，視其殼開，立即撈起取出肉，又將油條切約五分長之段，均留用。
	②鍋中把油燒熱，將油條投入炸脆，用濾油器撈入細瓷大盤中，將油倒出，加入豬油二湯匙，把嫩薑屑爆香，即傾下高湯或燙蛤蜊之湯，待沸，即將蛤蜊肉全部倒下溜勻後，加入水豆粉，使湯汁略稠放下葱花，即刻盛在碗中與炸脆之油條同送席，立即以蛤蜊澆在油條面，亦可擠數滴鮮檸檬汁在上面，其味無窮。
附　註：	除蛤蜊以外，亦可用蝦仁、蟹粉、海瓜子、蚶子、均可隨心所欲變化為數色之菜肴。

Ingredients:
- 1⅓ lb. fresh clams (any kind)
- 2 T. chopped young ginger
- 1 bowl meat stock
- 1 T. cornstarch (mixed with 3 T. water)
- 6 pc. cold you-tiao (fried dough sticks)
- 3 T. chopped green onion
- 2 T. lard
- 4 C. peanut oil

Seasonings:
- 1 T. white soy sauce
- 1 t. salt
- dash of monosodium glutamate (M.S.G.)

Directions:
1. Scald clams in ½ pot boiling water. As soon as shells open, remove meat. Cut you-tiao into ½" pieces.
2. Heat oil in frying pan. Fry you-tiao until crisp. Remove. Heat lard. Saute chopped ginger; add meat stock or water used to scald clams. Bring to boil. Stir in clams; add cornstarch paste. Simmer 1 min. to thicken and add chopped green onion. Remove to deep bowl. Place crisp you-tiao on serving plate. Pour clams over crisp you-tiao at table and serve.

Note: Shrimps and minced crab may be substituted for clams.

炸 排 骨
Fried Pork Chops

家 常 菜　　　　材料：12人份

材　料：大排骨一斤　鷄蛋一隻　麵包粉一袋　醬油三湯匙　酒一茶匙　糖四分之一茶匙　豆粉一湯匙　五香粉少許

做　法：①首將大排骨切成十片（賣肉店可切）略洗淨瀝乾，用刀背翻覆搗爛後，置盤內每片灑豆粉、醬油、糖、五香粉，用筷子翻覆攪勻，一片一片舖放在盤內，約二小時之久。
②待炸時先將鷄蛋打碎，塗在每塊排骨上再灑上麵包粉，然後用熱油炸之，約炸三、四分鐘卽可，肉嫩可口。

Ingredients:	1⅓ lb. pork chops (make about 10 pc.)		1 egg (beaten)
	1 pkg bread crumbs		4 T. soy sauce
	1 T. white soy sauce		1 t. wine
	¼ t. sugar		1 T. cornstarch
	dash of five-spices powder		4-6 C. peanut oil
Directions:	1. Beat pork chop on surface with blunt edge of knife to crush. Marinate with cornstarch, soy sauce, sugar and five-spices powder about 2 hr.		
	2. Dip each piece in egg and dredge with bread crumbs. Deep fry on both sides in hot oil., 3-4 min.		

炸 腰 果
Fried Cashews

甜　　菜　　　　　材料：12人份

材　料：腰果四兩　蜂蜜二茶匙　棉白糖二湯匙　沸水三湯匙　花生油一飯碗

做　法：①首將蜂蜜與棉白糖放入碗中，用沸水溶化待用。
　　　　②次將腰果用乾布擦淨放入糖水中浸漬片刻然後放入炒菜鍋內以文火煮一下視糖汁已乾，即盛入盤中冷留用。
　　　　③炒菜鍋內放油一飯碗，以溫油小火倒入腰果炸之，時翻時炒，視炸成金黃色，即盛入碟中，候冷送席。

Ingredients:　4 oz. cashews　　2 t. honey　　2 T. powdered sugar
　　　　　　　　3 T. boiling water　1 bowl peanut oil

Directions:
1. Dissolve honey and sugar with boiling water in bowl.
2. Clean cashews and let dry Soak in honey-sugar mixture, 3-4 min. put in pan and cook over low heat till dry. Remove and let cool.
3. Warm oil in frying pan; fry sweetened cashews over low heat, stirring and turning constantly until golden brown. Serve cool.

炸 松 子
Fried Pine Seeds

甜　　　菜　　　　材料：12人份

材　料：松子四兩　蜜糖一湯匙　棉白糖二茶匙　花生油八湯匙

做　法：①買去松子洗淨吹乾以蜜糖棉白糖泡浸三小時。
②起油鍋以溫油小火約炸十分鐘，一面用濾油器急翻，視已炸成金褐色，即撈出冷後盛放碟中上席。

Ingredients:　4 oz. pine seeds (without skin)　　　1 T. honey
　　　　　　　　2 T. powdered sugar　　　　　　　　8 T. peanut oil

Directions:　1. Clean and dry. Soak pine seeds in honey and powdered sugar about 3 hr.
　　　　　　　2. Heat oil in frying pan. Fry in low heat about 10 min., stirring and turning to brown (use oil strainer). Remove Cool and serve.

龍鳳腿
Fried Chicken Feet with Pork

上海菜　　材料：12人份

材　料：雞脚二十隻　雞胸脯二個　猪肉半斤　網油二十小塊　雞蛋二個　洋芋一小個
　　　　麵粉六湯匙　豆粉兩茶匙　鹽半茶匙
調味品：白醬油一湯匙　酒一茶匙　鹽一茶匙　糖半茶匙　味精少許　花生油三飯碗
做　法：①首將洋芋切小片蒸爛，搗爲芋泥。雞脚斬去爪，用半茶匙鹽醃十分鐘後，下沸水中煮片
　　　　　刻，取出備用。
　　　　②次將猪肉（龍）與雞肉（鳳）斬爛，加入芋泥、蛋白及調味品拌匀，然後以逐隻雞脚包
　　　　　上肉糊，其形似腿再取網油逐隻包腿，置沸水上，蒸十分鐘。
　　　　③餘下蛋黃調入麵粉，略加水，拌匀塗於蒸熟之每隻雞腿上，即放入油鍋中炸之，視已成
　　　　　金黃色，撈出排列長瓷盤中雞脚向外，使客人易取。

Ingredients:
- 20 chicken feet
- 20 small pc. pork net fat (wang-you)
- 6 T. flour
- 2 chicken breasts
- 2 egg (separate yolks and whites)
- 2 t. cornstarch
- ⅔ lb. pork
- 1 potato (small)
- ½ t. salt

Seasonings:
- 1 T. white soy sauce
- ½ t. sugar
- 1 t. wine
- dash of monosodium glutamate
- 1 t. salt
- 3 bowls peanut oil

Directions:
1. Cut potato into small slices and steam until tender. Crush to make mash. Remove claws from chicken feet. Mix with ½ t. salt. Let stand 10 min. Cook in boiling water 3-4 min.
2. Mince chicken and pork meat. Combine with mashed potato, egg white and seasonings. Coat each chicken foot with minced meat and wrap with net fat. Steam above boiling water 10 min.
3. Mix egg yolks with flour and a little water. Dredge each cooked chicken foot. Deep-fry in hot oil until brown. Arrange on long serving plate with feet outward for easier helping.

糖醋排骨
Sweet and Sour Spareribs

杭州菜　　　材料：12人份

材　料：猪排骨一斤　鷄蛋白二湯匙　花生油一飯碗
調味品：醬油三湯匙　豆粉三茶匙　糖四湯匙　醋三湯匙　鹽一茶匙　清水二湯匙
做　法：①首將排骨洗淨，斬成似麻將牌形，加入一湯匙半醬油和一茶匙豆粉及蛋白拌匀備用，另用一碗放下醬油一湯匙半豆粉二茶匙糖與醋鹽及清水二湯匙合爲拘汁料。
②油鍋燒熱，倒下排骨約炸五分鐘，即將排骨濾起，倒出剩油，然後把拘汁的作料傾入鍋內，視滾卽將炸好之排骨倒下拌匀，盛起供食。

Ingredients: 1⅓ lb. spareribs　　2 T. egg white　　1 bowl peanut oil

Seasonings: 3　T. soy sauce　　3 t. cornstarch　　4 T. sugar
　　　　　　　3　T. vinegar　　　1 t. salt　　　　　2 T. water

Directions:
1. Cut spareribs into mah-jong shapes. Mix with 1½ T. soy sauce, 1 t. cornstarch and egg white. Mix separately 1½ soy sauce, 2 t. cornstarch, sugar, vinegar, salt and water to make paste.
2. Heat oil in frying pan. Fry spareribs about 5 min. Remove and drain. Remove oil. Pour paste in pan and bring to boil. Add fried spareribs and mix. Remove and serve.

什錦鍋粑
Ten Precious Kuo-Pa

湖南菜　　　　　材料：12人份

材　料：乾鍋粑半斤　蝦仁、海參、火腿、里肌肉、鳳肝(蒸熟)、冬菇、冬筍、荷蘭豆、胡蘿蔔、洋葱各一小碟　花生油半鍋　猪油二湯匙　高湯二飯碗半

調味品：蕃茄醬四湯匙　白醬油一湯匙　鹽糖各半茶匙　豆粉一湯匙（用二湯匙水調和）

做　法：①先將配料均切小薄片，里肌肉調下白醬油一茶匙和豆粉½茶匙拌勻，蝦仁加入豆粉鹽酒各¼茶匙攪勻留用。
②用猪油爆炒洋葱和肉片，傾下高湯燒滾，然後倒下其他配料（只留蝦仁最後川下），改用小鋁鍋滾片刻，再加入調味品，並川下蝦仁然後盛在大碗內。
③油鍋燒熱，將切約二寸見方之鍋粑投入炸黃撈在大盆內，同時將什錦燒熱，一同送席，速卽澆在炸好之鍋粑上，卽起劈拍之聲。

Ingredients: ⅔ lb. dried kuo-pa (The burned rice that adheres to sides of pot)
1 small saucer each shelled shrimps, seacucumber, ham, lean pork, chicken liver (steamed), dried mushroom, winter bamboo shoots, snow peas, carrot, and onion
½ frying pan peanut oil　　2 T. lard　　2½ bowls meat stock

Seasonings: 4 T. tomato sauce　　1 T. white soy sauce　　½ t. salt
½ t. sugar　　1 T. cornstarch (mixed with 2 T. water)

Directions:
1. Cut ingredients in saucers into small slices. Mix lean pork with 1 t. white soy sauce and ¼ t. cornstarch. Mix shrimps with ¼ t. cornstarch, ¼ t. wine and ¼ t. salt.
2. Heat lard. Stir-fry onion and pork. Add meat stock. Let boil. Add all ingredients except shrimps. Transfer contents to small pot and boil a few minutes. Add seasonings. Add shrimps. Remove immediately. Pour contents into large bowl.
3. Heat peanut oil in frying pan. Deep-fry dried kuo-pa (cut in 2" squares) until brown. Arrange on large serving plate. Heat assorted ingredients. Serve at table by pouring ten precious ingredients over fried kuo-pa, which will produce a crackling and sizzling sound.

27

煙鯧魚
Smoked Pomfret

廣東菜　　　　　材料：12人份

材　料：鯧魚一尾（重約一斤六兩）　蕃茄二只　生菜葉四張　沙拉醬四湯匙　鹽一湯匙　蕃茄醬一湯匙　葱二支　薑二片　蒜頭一粒　花生油一斤多　醬油三湯匙　糖一茶匙　酒一湯匙

做　法：①首將鯧魚剖肚，去內臟和鰓，即用半茶匙鹽敷在魚身兩面擦淨（凡是無鱗的魚應先用鹽擦魚身）然後洗淨，使魚背光亮潔淨。
②將已瀝水過的鯧魚，整條在魚身兩面劃菱形狀，放在大盆內，先敷鹽放下拍碎之葱薑蒜，約十分鐘後，再傾下綜合調味汁浸漬至少四十分鐘，並須隨時翻動。
③將花生油放下鍋中燒滾即將魚炸上二分鐘，撈起濾去油裝盆備用。
④再將木屑一飯碗紅茶半飯碗及紅糖二湯匙，放在舊鐵鍋內，上面將炸好之魚連盆放入，密蓋後先燻五分鐘，開蓋將魚翻面，塗上一點浸魚之綜合調味汁，續燻十分鐘，此時魚身已成金褐色取出放在已墊生菜葉之細瓷長盆中，一邊飾蕃茄片，另一邊放沙拉醬，趁熱送席。

Ingredients: 1 pomfret (1 ½ lb.)　　2 tomatoes
4 lettuce leaves　　4 T. mayonnaise
1 T. salt　　2 green onions (cut into 1 ½" strips and crushed)
2 slices ginger (crushed)　　1 clove garlic
3 C. peanut oil

Seasoning Sauce (combine):
3 T. soy sauce　　1 t. sugar
1 T. tomato sauce　　1 T. wine

Directions: 1. Rub pomfret inside and out with ½ t. salt. Rinse thoroughly and let dry.
2. Score crisscross both sides of pomfret. Sprinkle with salt; add ginger and green onion let stand 10 min. Marinate in seasoning sauce, 40 min., turning frequently.
3. Heat oil in frying pan. Fry pomfret 2 min., remove and drain.
4. Mix 1 bowl saw dust, ½ bowl black tea leaves, and 2 T. brown sugar in old pot; and place pomfret with plate on top. Heat pot. Cover tightly and smoke 5 min. Uncover and turn pomfret over. Baste with remaining marinade; smoke another 10 min. till golden brown. Cover oblong plate with lettuce leaves and place pomfret on top, with tomato slice and mayonnaise, each at one end.

麵拖黃魚
Deep-Fried Yellow Fish

杭州菜　　　材料：12人份

材　料：黃魚肉半斤　薑末二片　蛋白二只　上好太白粉三湯匙　花生油　麵粉一茶匙
調味品：白醬油　鹽　酒　太白粉　味精
做　法：①首將黃魚洗淨取肉，每條魚一刀不切斷，兩刀才切斷，裝在碗內，調入白醬油一湯匙、鹽一茶匙、酒二茶匙、太白粉拌勻留用。
②鷄蛋白放入碗內，用筷子打得非常發泡，再加入上好太白粉及麵粉攪勻待用。
③花生油燒熱，將魚肉放入已打發泡之蛋白汁內撈一下，即刻投入油內炸之，呈淡黃色卽可，熱吃味美。

Ingredients: ⅜ lb. yellow fish fillet (cut grainwise into 1½" sections)　2 slices ginger (chopped)
2 egg whites　3 T. cornstarch
peanet oil enough to deep fry　1 t. flour

Seasonings: 1 T. white soy sauce　1 t. salt
2 t. wine　1 t. cornstarch
dash of monosodium glutamate

Directions: 1. Blend fish meat with ginger and seasonings.
2. Beat egg whites until fluffy. Add connstarch and flour. Mix well.
3. Heat oil. Dip fish meat in batter. Fry until light brown. Serve hot.

酥炸肫肝
Deep-Fried Gizzards and Livers

廣東菜　　　材料：12人份

材　料：鮮鴨肫肝五副　蛋黃二個　薑末一茶匙　酒一茶匙　鹽一茶匙　五香鹽或辣醬油一小碟酌加麵粉

做　法：①首將肫肝洗淨，肝一切四，將鴨肫切除內外之筋皮，縱橫切花後切塊，盛在碗內加入鹽薑酒醃浸片刻再加入麵粉拌勻。
②用油燒熱炸之，熟後與五香鹽或辣醬油同送上席。

Ingredients:
- 5 duck gizzards
- 5 duck livers
- 2 egg yolks
- 1 t. chopped ginger
- 1 t. wine
- 1 t. salt
- 1 small saucer five-spices salt or hot soy sauce
- flour
- peanut oil enough to deep-fry

Directions:
1. Clean gizzars and livers. Cut liver in quarters. Remove gizzards membranes inside and out. Score criss-cross on outer surface and cut into 4-6 pieces. Blend with salt, ginger and wine. Let stand 5 min. Stir in flour Mix well.
2. Heat oil in frying pan. Deep-fry gizzards and livers until done. Serve with five-spices salt or hot soy sauce as dip.

酥炸茄塊
Deep-Fried Eggplants

家常菜　　　　材料：12人份

材　料：新鮮粗嫩茄子半斤　豬肉四兩　鷄蛋一個　葱一支　豆粉一湯匙　粗麵包粉四湯匙
　　　　油二飯碗
調味品：黑醬油二茶匙　白醬油一茶匙　豆粉一茶匙　鹽¼茶匙　味精少許
做　法：①把茄子洗淨修去皮，再切約一寸長之斜塊，然後在每塊中間劃一刀，又將碎肉加入調味
　　　　品拌勻留用。
　　　　②把茄塊裏外塗上一點豆粉，然後將碎肉夾在中間，逐塊放在已加味精和鹽打碎之蛋汁中
　　　　塗一下，然後再包上一點粗麵包粉，入油鍋中炸呈淡黃色，趁熱供食。

Ingredients:	⅔ lb. eggplant	4 oz. ground pork	1 egg
	1 stalk green onion (chopped)	1 T. cornstarch	4 T. bread crumbs
	2 bowls oil for frying		
Seasonings:	2 t. black soy sauce	1 t. white soy sauce	1 t. cornstarch
	¼ t. salt	dash of monosodium glutamate	

Directions:
1. Wash and pare eggplants. Cut diagonally into 1" pieces. Slit in center. Marinate ground pork with green noion and seasonings to make filling.
2. Rub eggplants with cornstarch, inside and out. Stuff filling in eggplants. Dip in beaten egg seasoned with salt and M.S.G. Coat with bread crumbs. Heat oil. Fry till light brown. Serve hot.

紙包雞
Deep-Fried Paper-Wrapped Chicken

廣東菜　　　　材料：12人份

材　料：二斤左右肥嫩雞一只　蛋白一個　醬油三湯匙　酒半茶匙　薑二片　糖￼茶匙
　　　　玻璃紙一大張　炸油半鍋

做　法：①把雞斬成小長方塊，用醬油、酒、糖薑屑醃浸約二、三小時，須時常翻轉，使能浸勻入味。
　　　　②把玻璃紙剪成約五寸長，四寸濶之小紙塊數十張。
　　　　③用玻璃紙把雞包成陳皮梅形，一張紙包一塊。
　　　　④下沸油鍋中炸三、四分鐘卽好，時間太長炸焦了，就不美觀。

Ingredients:　1 chicken (about 2⅔ lb.)　　1 egg white
　　　　　　　　3 T. soy sauce　　　　　　　½ t. wine
　　　　　　　　2 slices ginger (chopped)　　¼ t. sugar
　　　　　　　　cooking oil to cover half of pan　1 large sheet of cellophane

Directions:
1. Cut chicken into small rectangular pieces. about 1″X 1½″). Marinate in mixture of egg white, soy sauce, wine, sugar and chopped ginger Let stand 2-3 hr. Turn occasionally in marinade for even flavor.
2. Cut cellophane wrap into 5″X4″ pieces, enough to wrap chicken pieces.
3. Wrap each piece of chicken, envelope-style, with a cellophane wrap.
4. Heat oil in frying pan. Deep-fry paper-wrapped chicken a few pieces at a time 3-4 min. Do not over fry for color will get too dark.

炸 蝦 球
Deep-Fried Shrimp Balls

湖南菜　　材料：12人份

材　料：海蝦一斤半　肥肉二兩　荸薺十粒　蛋白一個　葱屑一茶匙　豆粉二湯匙　酒一茶匙　糖半茶匙　猪油一湯匙　炸油一斤　鹽二茶匙半（一茶匙半洗蝦仁）

做　法：①先將蝦去殼抽泥臟，用鹽水和清水洗淨吹爽，先以刀背拍碎，然後以刀鋒斬碎放置大碗內，加入打碎之蛋白豆粉、酒、鹽及一湯匙猪油拌勻片刻，又加入葱屑及肥肉粒攪勻備用。

②待炸時再下斬碎而擠出水之荸薺屑拌勻。

③起油鍋燒熱，用圓匙盛一只球形，下鍋炸之，視已成金黃色，即可起鍋供食。

Ingredients:
- 2 lb. shrimps (from sea)
- 10 water chestnuts
- 1 t. chopped green onion
- 1 t. wine
- 1 T. lard
- 2½ t. salt (1 t. salt for washing shrimps)
- 2 oz. pork fat
- 1 egg white
- 2 T. cornstarch
- ¼ t. sugar
- 3-4 C. peanut oil

Directions:
1. Shell and devein shrimps. Clean with salt water. Rinse. Crush shrimps with blunt edge of knife. Mince and mix with egg white, cornstarch, wine, salt and lard. Let stand 3-4 min. Add green onion and pork fat (chopped). Mix well.
2. When ready to fry, combine with minced water chestnuts (well drained).
3. Shape into balls with round spoon. Deep-fry in warm oil over moderate heat until golden brown. Serve.

炸蝦餅
Deep-Fried Shrimp Patties

湖南菜　　　　材料：12人份

材　料：海蝦一斤　肥肉粒二湯匙　荸薺屑八粒　蛋白一小個　葱屑一茶匙　火腿屑二湯匙
　　　　猪油二茶匙　豆粉二湯匙　酒一茶匙　糖四分之一茶匙　炸油一斤　莞荽三支
　　　　鹽二茶匙半（一茶匙半洗蝦仁）

做　法：①首將蝦去殼抽泥臟，用鹽水和清水洗淨吹爽，先以刀背拍碎，再以刀鋒斬碎，放置大碗內，加入打碎之蛋白豆粉酒鹽及猪油拌勻，然後再加入葱屑肥肉粒及已擠出水之荸薺屑攪勻備用。
②用手將蝦糊做成小餅形（約可做廿五個），面飾火腿屑，以大火隔水蒸五分鐘，取出用熱油一炸，卽裝冷盆碟中，其汁加點高湯放入鍋中滾，調下一點水豆粉，澆在蝦餅上，面飾莞荽三支，亦爲冷盆之一。

Ingredients:
- 1 & 1/8 lb. shrimps
- 8 water chestnut (chopped)
- 1 t. chopped green onion
- 2 T. cornstarch
- 1/4 t. sugar
- 3-4 C. lb. cooking oil
- 3 sprigs parsley
- 2 T. chopped pork fat
- 1 egg white (beaten)
- 2 T. chopped Chinese ham
- 1 t. wine
- 2 t. lard
- 2½ t. salt (1½ t. salt for washing shrimps)
- ½ meat stock

Directions:
1. Shell shrimps and remove black line. Clean with salt water, rinse and drain. Chop finely. Combine chopped shrimp with egg white, cornstarch, wine, salt and lard; stir in chopped green onion, fat and water chestnuts (dehydrate by squeezing).
2. Make appr. 25 patties with shrimp paste. Top each patty with chopped Chinese ham. Steam over high heat, 5 min. Fry steamed patties in deep oil 1-2 min. Heat shrimp stock with meat stock. Add a little cornstarch paste. Blend and pour over shrimp patties. Garnish with parsley and serve.

百角蝦球
Shrimp Balls with a Hundred Angles

湖南菜　　　　　材料：12人份

材　料：海蝦一斤半　肥肉二兩　荸薺十粒（削皮拍碎斬細）　蛋白一個　葱薑屑各一茶匙　豆粉二湯匙　酒一茶匙　糖四分之一茶匙　豬油一湯匙　土司麵包八片　花生油一斤　鹽二茶匙半（一茶匙半洗蝦仁用）

做　法：①首將麵包去邊皮，每片切為九條之丁，略吹乾備用。
②次將蝦去殼抽泥臟略洗後，再用鹽水一小碗用筷子攪洗，然後再用清水洗淨吹爽，先以刀背拍碎，再以刀鋒斬碎，放置大碗內，加入打碎之蛋白豆粉、鹽及一湯匙豬油拌勻片刻，又加入葱薑屑及肥肉粒攪勻備用。
③將荸薺屑擠出水份攪入蝦肉內然後用手做成球形，周圍把麵包丁輕輕黏上，逐只做完裝盤中待炸。
④鍋中燒油一斤，不待沸時即將百角蝦球投入溫油中，中火炸之。視麵包丁呈金黃色即可盛起，以醋辣醬油同送席。（此材料可做百角蝦球約四十粒）。

Ingredients:
- 2 lb. shrimps (shelled)
- 10 water chestnuts (minced)
- ½ t. green onion (chopped)
- 2 T. cornstarch
- ¼ t. sugar
- 8 slices bread
- 2½ t. salt (1½ t. for cleaning shrimps)
- 2 oz. pork fat (minced)
- 1 egg white (beaten)
- ½ t. ginger (chopped)
- 1 t. wine
- 1 T. lard
- 1⅓ lb. peanut oil

Directions:
1. Throw away crusts and cut each slice of bread into small dices.
2. Remove black lines of shrimps. Clean in bowl of salted water and rinse. Flatten with blunt side of knife and mince. mix thoroughly with egg white, cornstarch, wine, salt and lard. Add green onion, ginger and fat. Mix well.
3. Squeeze water out of water chestnuts, and mix into shrimp mixture. Shape into shrimp balls and coat with bread dices.
4. Warm 1⅓ lb. oil in frying pan. Fry shrimp balls till bread dices turn golden brown. Serve with vinegar and hot soy sauce. (make about 40 balls)

高麗肉
Korean Meat

甜食　　　　材料：12人份

材　料：紅豆半斤　白沙糖半斤　細白糖三湯匙　網油半斤　猪油二湯匙　豆粉三湯匙
　　　　花生油一斤

做　法：①先將紅豆洗淨浸水二、三小時，下鍋煮爛(乾湯)。
　　　　②將煮爛之豆冷後倒入籮內以大盆清水擦下豆殼，豆沙留入清水中，卽緩倒麻布袋中擠乾，卽爲所需之豆沙。
　　　　③起猪油鍋將豆沙炒之片刻，卽加入白沙糖炒乾卽好，豆沙做成橢圓形(如鴿蛋形大)網油切爲方形，一塊包一個豆沙，再途上乾豆粉入油鍋內炸之見呈淡黃色卽可起鍋，裝盆內上灑細白糖這是一樣別緻的甜菜。

Ingredients:
- ⅔ lb. red beans
- 3 T. powdered sugar
- 2 T. lard
- 4 C. peanut oil
- ⅔ lb. white granulated sugar
- ⅔ lb. pork net fat (wang-you)
- 3 T. cornstarch

Directions:
1. Wash and soak red beans in water 2-3 hr. Cook until soft. Let cool.
2. Strain beans through a strainer by rubbing skins off in large pot of water. Red bean granules will fill in the water. Pour slowly into sack. Squeeze out as much liquid as possible. The mash left is red bean paste.
3. Heat lard in frying pan. Fry paste and add sugar. Fry till no liquid is left. Make paste into oval shapes like pigeon eggs. Cut net fat into squares. Wrap each "egg" in one square of net fat. Dip in cornstarch to coat. Heat oil. Deep-fry until light brown. Sprinkle with powered sugar.

蘋 果 夾
Deep-Fried Apples

甜　　　　食　　　　　材料：12人份

材　料：蘋果二只　豆沙半飯碗　鷄蛋一只　棉白糖二湯匙　麵粉四湯匙　水少許　花生油二杯

做　法：①首將蘋果去皮，對剖後刮去心，打斜切片，形似眉月（一只蘋果可切十片）每二片之中以豆沙夾住，置旁備用。

②次將麵粉鷄蛋棉白糖水拌爲麵糊，將蘋果夾，一一在麵糊中滾一滾，卽投入油鍋中炸之，視已呈金黃色，卽可供食。

Ingredients:	2 apples	½ bowl sweet red bean paste
	1 egg (beaten)	2 T. powdered sugar
	4 T. flour	a little water
	2 C. peanut oil	

Directions:
1. Pare apple. Cut in half and remove cores. Slice diagonally into crescent shape (10 slices an apple). Sandwich red bean paste between two slices.
2. Mix flour, egg, sugar and water to make batter. Dip sandwiched apple in batter to coat. Heat oil in frying pan. Deep-fry until golden brown. Serve

炸魚片
Fried Fish Slices

地　方　菜　　　　材料：12人份

材　料：大鮮魚肉一斤　肥豬肉二兩　蛋白一個　葱三支　薑三片　白醬油一湯匙　酒一湯匙　豆粉一湯匙　麵粉三湯匙　五香粉四分之一茶匙　糖半茶匙　鹽一茶匙　花生油二飯碗

做　法：①先將魚洗淨，去皮直切大薄片，肥肉切小丁，蛋白打成發泡，加入葱薑末，白醬油、酒、豆粉、五香粉、鹽，放在碗內攪勻，然後再加入麵粉攪勻。
②油鍋燒熱，一片一片置油鍋內炸之，炸黃起鍋，趁熱加莞菜上桌，宜作酒菜。

Ingredients:
- 1 large piece fish meat (about ⅔ lb.)
- 1 egg white
- 3 slices ginger (minced)
- 1 T. wine
- 3 T. flour
- ½ t. sugar
- 2 bowls peanut oil
- 2 oz. pork meat with fat
- 3 stalks green onion
- 1 T. white soy sauce
- 1 T. cornstarch
- ¼ t. five-spices powder
- 1 t. salt

Directions:
1. Clean fish, skin and cut into thin slices. Cut pork fat into small dices. Beat egg white until fluffy. Add green onion, ginger, white soy sauce, wine, cornstarch, five-spices powder and salt. Combine with fish and pork fat. Add flour and mix well.
2. Heat oil in frying pan. Fry fish slices until golden brown. Garnish with parsley and serve.

魚丸花菜
Fish Balls & Cauliflower

家常菜　　　　材料：12人份

材　料：新鮮海鰻半斤　生猪油一兩　花菜半斤　胡蘿蔔一條（在高湯內煮十分鐘）　薑二片　葱二支　花生油一飯碗　豆粉一湯匙　清水四湯匙

調味品：白醬油一湯匙　鹽一茶匙　酒一茶匙　糖半茶匙

做　法：①首將鰻魚洗淨瀝乾，去皮骨取魚肉，用刀背拍碎後細細斬爛，葱薑切末斬入猪油切小粒拌入，然後將半茶匙鹽及豆粉，酒，清水攪勻，花菜依花切下洗淨，胡蘿蔔切滾刀塊均留用。
②次將油鍋燒熱，用圓匙將魚漿逐只投入油鍋中炸（約做二十粒）視已微黃堅硬即可盛起，鍋中留二湯匙油倒入花菜炒之，加下鹽與白醬油炒勻，即倒下魚丸與胡蘿蔔攪炒，然後傾下沸水一飯碗滾煮，視花菜已軟調下少少水豆粉盛起供食（無花菜時可以筍或蒿筍代替，味亦佳。）

Ingredients: ⅔ lb. fresh sea eel
⅔ lb. cauliflower
2 slices ginger (chopped)
1 bowl peanut oil (or any cooking oil)
4 T. water
1 oz. raw lard
1 carrot (cooked in meat stock 10 min.)
2 stalks green onion (chopped)
1 T. cornstarch

Seasonings: 1 T. white soy sauce
1 t. wine
1 t. salt
½ t. sugar

Directions:
1. Clean sea eel. Remove skin and bones. Crush and mince meat. Combine with chopped green onion, ginger and lard; add ½ t. salt, cornstarch, wine and water. Mix well. Separate cauliflower into flowerets; cut carrots in pieces at different angles.
2. Heat oil in frying pan. Spoon chopped fish paste one by one into oil to make about 20 fish balls; fry till light brown. Leave 2 T. oil. Fry cauliflower; season with salt and white soy sauce. Add fish balls and carrots. Turn and toss lightly. Add bowl of boiling water. Cook until cauliflower is tender; blend in cornstarch mixed with 2 T. water. Remove and serve.

Note: Bamboo shoots and garland chrysanthemum may be substituted for cauliflower.

紅扒鵪蛋   廣東菜   材料：12人份
Fried Quail Eggs in Brown Sauce

材　　料：鴿蛋二打　鮮蔴二兩　冬筍二只　青菜心十餘顆　豆粉三湯匙　花生油三杯
綜合調味：鹽一茶匙　糖半茶匙　醬油一湯匙　蔴油　胡椒少許　豆粉一茶匙　冷水二湯匙
做　　法：①首將冬筍去殼切斜塊蒸熟備用，次將青菜燙熟留用。
　　　　　②將鵪蛋煮熟剝殼後在乾豆粉上滾拌，落油鍋炸成金黃色離鍋，留少油爆炒青菜心卽下三分之一綜合調味炒數下，盛起排飾盆邊。
　　　　　③重再另用三湯匙油，爆炒筍塊及鮮蔴，卽加入半飯碗開水略煮，再下三分之二的綜合調味，繼續兜炒調勻，最後加入炸好之鴿蛋略炒卽盛菜心盆之中間，趁熱上席。

Ingredients: 2 dozens quail eggs
　2 winter bamboo shoots
　3 T. cornstarch
　2 oz. fresh mushrooms
　1 dozen hearts of any green vegetable with leaves
　3 C. peanut oil

Seasoning Sauce (combine):
　1 t. salt
　1 T. sesame oil
　2 T. cold water
　½ t. sugar
　1 t. cornstarch
　dash of pepper

Directions:
1. Clean winter bamboo shoots; cut into small pieces at different angles, and steam till tender. Scald vegetable hearts.
2. Boil quail eggs till well-done and remove shells. Coat with cornstarch. Heat oil in frying pan and fry eggs until golden brown. Remove and leave enough oil to fry vegetable hearts with ⅓ seasoning sauce, and arrange around plate.
3. Fry bamboo shoots and mushrooms with 3 T. oil. Add ½ bowl of boiling water and bring to boil. Add rest of seasoning sauce and stir in. Add eggs; cook 1-2 min. Remove contents to center of plate and serve.

家庭叉燒
Family Broiled Pork

廣東菜　　　　　材料：12人份

材　料：猪排骨肉一斤
調味品：黑白醬油各二湯匙　鹽一茶匙　糖二茶匙　酒一茶匙　紅粉少許　炸油八大匙
做　法：①先將猪肉洗淨瀝乾，交叉切長條，不要切斷，即用黑白醬油酒，鹽，糖泡浸約二、三小時，使能入味。
②在炸前將紅粉少許，加入浸肉之汁內，將肉塗勻，片刻，即放入沸油鍋內炸之，約炸三、四分鐘，即換用平底鍋加蓋烤六、七分鐘，取出待冷切薄片，外紅內白，色美味鮮，肉嫩可口，不但可供宴客之冷盆，又可給小孩帶便當，並可作叉燒包之用。

Ingredients:　1⅓ lb. pork tenderloin　　　3 sprigs parsley (for garnishing)

Seasonings:　1 T. black soy sauce　　　1 T. white soy sauce
　　　　　　　1 t. salt　　　　　　　　　2 t. sugar
　　　　　　　1 t. wine　　　　　　　　　a little red powder (for coloring)
　　　　　　　8 T. oil for frying

Directions:
1. Without severing meat, cut pork crosswise at 1 to 1½ inch intervals from both sides alternately. Each cut should go ¾ the way. Marinate in black soy sauce, white soy sauce, wine, salt and sugar. Let stand about 2-3 hr.
2. Before frying, mix red powder with pork (in marinade). Heat oil in frying pan. Fry pork on both sides 3-4 min. Transfer to flat pan and broil, covered, 6-7 min. Remove and let cool. Cut into thin slices. Serve cold.

炸 鷄 腿
Fry Chicken Legs

地 方 菜   材料：12人份

材　料：	鷄腿十二隻（每隻重約三兩多）　鷄蛋白一隻　麵粉一湯匙　鹽一湯匙　豆粉一湯匙　味精少許　生菜葉四張　花生油一斤
綜合調味：	黑醬油黑醋蜂蜜各一湯匙　酒一茶匙　豆粉二茶匙
做　法：	①首將生菜葉洗淨，以灰錳養水洗後，以冷開水沖洗吹乾備用。 ②次將鷄腿略洗瀝乾後，從小腿骨上割開，大骨旁的肉也割開，即成平扁之鷄腿，然後每隻腿加入鹽和豆粉各¼茶匙，約十分鐘後，即傾下綜合調味汁在鷄肉面，每隻塗勻，翻覆浸漬數次，最後將鷄皮向盆泡漬約一小時，再將已加味精而打發泡之鷄蛋白淋在逐隻鷄腿上，最後每隻洒上麵粉¼茶匙在鷄肉面留用。 ③油鍋燒熱，將鷄腿逐隻投入，以中火炸之，視鷄皮紅亮，即可撈起。逐隻以鷄骨向外，排列在已舖好生菜葉之細瓷長盤中，趁熱送席。

Ingredients: 12 chicken legs (each about 3 oz. or more)　　1 egg white
　　　　　　　 1 T. flour　　　　　　　　　　　　　　　　1 T. salt
　　　　　　　 1 T. cornstarch　　　　　　　　　　　　　　dash of monosodium glutamate
　　　　　　　 4 lettuce leaves　　　　　　　　　　　　　　3-4 C. peanut oil
　　Seasoning Sauce (combine):
　　　　　　　 1 T. black soy sauce　　　　　　　　　　　　1 T. brown vinegar
　　　　　　　 1 T. honey　　　　　　　　　　　　　　　　 1 t. wine
　　　　　　　 2 t. cornstarch

Directions: 1. Clean lettuce leaves by soaking in sodium permanganate water and rinse in cold boiled water. Let dry.
2. Clean chicken legs and drain. Slit from leg to thigh to flatten. Sprinkle ¼ t. salt and ¼ t. cornstarch over legs evenly. Let stand 10 min. Pour seasoning sauce over each leg. Marinate all sides, turning constantly. Soak skin side about 1 hr. Beat egg white, seasoned with M.S.G., till fluffy. Pour on each leg. Dredge with ¼ t. flour.
3. Heat oil in frying pan. Deep-fry legs over medium heat, until chicken skin is crisp red. Remove. Spread lettuce leaves over plate. Arrange legs on top with thigh inward and tarsus outward. Serve hot.

螞蟻上樹
Ants on Tree

四　川　菜　　　　材料：12人份

材　料：	瘦肉四兩　細乾粉條一捆　小紅辣椒一個　醬油一湯匙　豆粉半茶匙　高湯小半碗　蔥末半茶匙　炸油半鍋
做　法：	①把瘦肉剁成肉末，加醬油、豆粉、蔥末及碎紅椒攪勻備用。
	②把乾粉條一捆攔腰切為兩段，每段成U字形，然後把每段分開兩份共成四份U字形再把兩個U字形粉條上下一套成長圓形。
	③把弄好的兩份乾粉條下油鍋炸之，炸時油要開滾，先把一份乾粉條平放在油上，即時膨脹成一個大圓餅形，約炸兩分鐘即刻用筷子整餅翻轉，再炸一分鐘，即拿起來，再如法炸第二份，待好全裝在盆內。
	④用兩大匙油爆炒一下拌好之肉末，加小半碗開水，攪煮至成濃稠的肉汁，倒在小碗內，上桌吃時加荽菜澆在炸好的粉條上，即符合此特別之菜名。

Ingredients:
- 4 oz. lean pork
- 1 red chili pepper (chopped)
- ½ t. cornstarch
- ½ frying pan peanut oil
- 1 roll dried bean thread (fung-sze)
- 1 T. soy sauce
- ½ t. chopped green onion
- ½ bowl meat stock

Directions:
1. Mince pork. Combine with soy sauce, cornstarch, green onion and chopped red chili pepper.
2. Cut bean thread in half so that each half forms "U" shape. Separate each U into two "U"s; altogether makes 4 "U"s. Connect each 2 "U"s to make one oblong loop.
3. Heat oil to boil. Fry bean thread loops one at a time. Loops will become round and fluffy. Fry one side 2 min, and another 1 min. Place both on serving plate.
4. Stir-fry marinated pork in 2 T. oil. Add ½ bowl boiling water. Stir until sauce thickens. Pour over fried bean thread. Top with parsley and serve.

炸 響 鈴
Fried Bell-Shaped Pork

杭 州 菜　　　　　材料：12人份

材　料： 豬腿肉半斤　筍一支（小）　半圓形豆腐衣六張　葱二支

調味品： 醬油一湯匙　鹽糖各四分之一茶匙　甜麵醬四湯匙　糖三湯匙　蔴油一湯匙（蒸好調下）
五香粉四分之一茶匙（摻勻裝碗，蒸十分鐘）

做　法： ①首將豬肉洗淨瀝乾，去皮後細切細斬葱筍亦斬在內，然後加入調味品拌勻備用，豆腐皮一切六塊，以冷水淋潮，用筷子挾一點肉放在豆腐皮當中，包成小長條或整張豆腐皮包長條，炸好後切一寸長之段，可隨心所欲得形似響鈴即可。
②油鍋燒熱逐一投入鍋內炸黃，盛起裝盆與甜麵醬同送席蘸食，香穌味美。

Ingredients: ⅔ lb. pork leg　　1 bamboo shoot　　6 semicircular been curd sheets.
2 stalks green onion　　3-4 C. peanut oil

Seasonings: 1 t. cornstarch　　1 T. soy sauce　　¼ t. salt
¼ t. sugar

Dip (combine): 4 T. sweet flour paste　　3 T. sugar　　¼ t. five spices powder
1 T. sesame oil

Directions:
1. Clean pork and drain. Remove skin. Mince pork together with green onion and bamboo shoot. Mix with seasonings. Cut each been curd sheet into 6 pieces or leave sheet intact. Sprinkle with cold water to moisten. Place pork on each piece, and make rolls. (Cut whole sheet rools into 1" sections after frying.)
2. Heat oil. Deep-fry rolls one by one until brown on all sides. Serve with sweet flour paste* as dip.

Note: *Combine 4 T. sweet flour paste, 3 T. sugar and ¼ t. five-spices powder. Steam 10 min. Remove and blend in 1 T. sesame oil.

香 酥 鴨
Fragrant and Crispy Duck

江 浙 菜　　　材料：12人份

材　料：約二斤重肥鴨一隻　花椒一茶匙　鹽一湯匙　小饅頭數個

做　法：①先將鴨子洗淨，略吹乾，用鹽與花椒摻勻灑在鴨之全身內外，約醃二、三小時。
②將醃好之鴨，整隻蒸熟或煮熟（以湯收乾爲原則）要把鴨燒得非常頓。炸了才可穌。
③鴨頓後，瀝乾水份，待涼以太白粉和五香摻勻擦鴨，即置油鍋內炸之，一直炸到金黃色即可起鍋盛在大盆中，以小饅頭沿邊放着，即可上桌，香酥味美。也可備花椒末摻鹽炒後蘸食。

Ingredients: 1 fat duck (about 2⅔ lb.)　　1 t. peppercorn
　　　　　　　1 T. salt　　3-4 C. peanut oil to deep-fry
　　　　　　　10 small Chinese steamed buns (man-tou)

Directions:
1. Clean duck and let dry. Mix salt and peppercorn to sprinkle over duck inside and out. Let stand 2-3 hr.
2. Steam or boil until very tender to ensure crispness after frying. (If boiling, cook until no water is left.)
3. Drain duck and let cool. Dredge duck evenly with mixture of cornstarch and five-spices poweder. Deep-fry duck in heated oil until golden brown. Place Chinese steamed buns on side of serving plate with duck in center and serve. (Optional: Serve with fried chopped peppercorn-salt mixture as dip.)

茄汁明蝦
Stir-Fried Prawns with Tomato Sauce

江浙菜　　　　材料：12人份

材　料：明蝦一斤　葱薑屑各二湯匙　蕃茄醬三湯匙　醬油一湯匙　酒一茶匙　猪油一湯匙
　　　　酒釀二湯匙　鹽一茶匙　豆粉一茶匙（用二湯匙水調和）　花生油四大匙

做　法：①首將明蝦剪鬚洗淨，每只一切二（小的可整只）。
　　　　②次將油鍋燒熱，下薑末先炒，即下明蝦爆炒片刻，再下酒釀酒鹽油稍煮，然後落蕃茄醬
　　　　　略炒，再下水豆粉、葱、猪油一湯匙略滾即盛起送席。

Ingredients:
- 1 ½ lb. prawns
- 2 T. chopped ginger
- 1 T. soy sauce
- 2 T. sweet fermented glutinous rice
- 1 t. cornstarch (mixed with 2 T. water)
- 1 T. lard
- 2 T. chopped green onion
- 3 T. tomato sauce
- 1 t. wine
- 1 t. salt
- 4 T. peanut oil

Directions:
1. Trim and clean prawns. Cut large ones in half.
2. Heat oil in frying pan. Stir-fry chopped ginger, 30 sec. Add prawns and stir-fry 3-4 min. Add sweet fermented glutinous rice, salt and soy sauce. Cook another 4-5 min. Add tomato sauce and mix before adding cornstarch paste, green onion and lard. Cook until boiling. Serve.

鳳尾蝦
Pheonix Tail Prawns

北平菜　　　　材料：12人份

材　　料：新鮮海蝦（花殼）一斤半　嫩碗豆仁四兩　鹽二茶匙半（一茶匙半洗蝦用，另一茶匙調入蝦內）　鷄蛋白一個　豆粉一湯匙　蘇打粉½茶匙　猪油十二大匙

綜合調味：鹽¼茶匙　酒一茶匙　豆粉半茶匙　冷水一湯匙

做　　法：①首將蝦去頭殼留尾，剖背肉去泥腸，先以水洗，再以鹽水洗吹乾或擦乾。
②將蝦置碗內同時加入蛋白，鹽蘇打粉及豆粉拌勻備用。
③將猪油放鍋中燒熱，不待沸時即放下蝦仁炸炒，候蝦仁已成彎曲，即用濾油器盛起瀝乾油，鍋內留一湯匙油落鹽，爆炒碗豆仁數下，至豆仁已脫生，即倒入綜合調味及蝦仁，略加兜勻，即可盛起，趁熱上席。（蝦剝去尾即爲炒蝦仁）

Ingredients: 2 lb. prawns　　　　　　　　　　4 oz. snow peas (podded)
2½ t. salt (1½ t. for washing prawns; 1 t. for blending with prawns)
1 egg white　　　　　　　　　　　　1 t. cornstarch
⅛ soda powder　　　　　　　　　　12 T. lard

Seasoning Sauce (combine):
¼ t. salt　　　　　　　　　　　　　1 t. wine
½ cornstarch　　　　　　　　　　　1 T. cold water

Directions:
1. Shell prawns, but leave tails intact. Remove black lines. Wash first with water, then with salted water. Dry.
2. Blend prawns with egg white, salt, soda powder and cornstarch.
3. Heat lard in frying pan until hot. Stir-fry prawns till they curl up. Remove and drain. Leave 1 T. oil in pan. Add salt and peas. Stir-fry till done. Add seasoning sauce and prawns. Stir to mix. Serve hot.

宮爆蝦仁
Fried Shrimps with Hot Sauce

四川菜　　材料：12人份

材　料：	新鮮紅蝦一斤半　乾紅辣椒十只　鷄蛋白一個　薑末一茶匙　蘇打粉四分之一茶匙　豆粉一湯匙　鹽二茶匙半（一茶匙調入蝦內，另一茶匙以一飯碗水溶化，作洗蝦用）　花生油十二大匙
綜合調味：	黑醬油二湯匙　豆粉一茶匙　醋二茶匙　糖半茶匙　酒一茶匙　水一湯匙　味精少許
做　法：	①首將蝦去頭殼，用牙籤挑去泥臟，然後以清水沖洗瀝水，再以鹽用筷子攪拌，使腥味下來，再以清水沖洗潔淨，瀝水吹乾留用，如不乾，可用布擦。 ②將蝦仁置碗內，加入蛋白、鹽、蘇打粉、豆粉拌勻，乾紅辣椒用乾毛巾擦淨，每只剪為三四段，均備用。 ③將鍋燒熱，傾下花生油，不待沸時，將蝦仁投入大火溫油中炸炒，候蝦仁已成捲曲，即用濾油器盛起瀝乾油，鍋中留三湯匙油，放入乾紅辣椒段爆成黑色盛起。當即將綜合調味傾入溜勻，即刻放下蝦仁拌炒，再倒下乾紅辣椒火速盛起送席。

Ingredients: 2 lb. shrimps　　　　　　　　　　10 paprikas　　　　　　　　1 egg white
1 t. minced ginger　　　　　　　¼ t. soda powder　　　　　1 T. cornstarch
2½ t. salt (1 t. to mix with shrimps; 1 t. to dissolve in 1 bowl water to wash shrimps)
12 T. peanut oil

Seasoning Sauce (combine):
2 T. black soy sauce　　　　　　1 t. cornstarch　　　　　　2 t. vinegar
½ t. sugar　　　　　　　　　　　1 t. wine　　　　　　　　　1 T. water
dash of monosodium glutamate (M.S.G.)

Directions:
1. Shell shrimps; remove black lines. Wash with salted water and drain. Let dry.
2. Combine shrimps, egg white, salt, soda powder, cornstarch and mix well. Cut paprika into 3 or 4 sections.
3. Heat oil in frying pan. Fry shrimps in warm oil over high heat until they curl up; remove and drain. Leave 3 T. oil in pan; fry paprikas till scorched; remove. Pour seasoning sauce into pan; stir. Add shrimps. Cook 1 min., turning frequently and tossing lightly; add fried paprikas. Serve hot.

生菜鴿鬆
Stir-Fried Minced Pigeon with Lettuce

廣東菜　　　　材料：12人份

材　料：肥鴿一隻　里肌肉四兩　冬菇三隻　筍二支　荸薺十隻　甜青椒一隻　葱五支　嫩薑五片（切丁）
　　　　鷄油二兩（以上均切丁）　鷄蛋黃二粒　米粉乾一兩　生菜二十四瓣（選購有曲邊的）　花生油半鍋
調味品：醬油一湯匙　豆粉一茶匙　冷水一湯匙　鹽半茶匙　糖四分之一茶匙蔴油胡椒少許
做　法：①首將鴿子殺好去毛洗淨，拆骨取肉，與里肌肉切細斬裝碗內。
　　　　②次將生菜剝下二十四瓣洗淨，再以灰錳養水洗，冷開水沖洗吹乾，每十二張疊成圓片，盛放在二
　　　　　隻小瓷盤內備用。
　　　　③再將花生油燒熱，放入米粉炸成金黃色撈出，濾油放入盤邊。四週用筷子壓平，不使成塊。
　　　　④再將鴿肉猪肉鷄油丁盛放碗內，加入蛋黃，酒一茶匙，白醬油一湯匙，鹽四分之一茶匙，胡椒拌
　　　　　匀備用。
　　　　⑤先用一湯匙燒熱炒各色素菜丁，並加點鹽拌炒盛起。再用二湯匙油炒鴿鬆，再倒下菜丁及綜合調
　　　　　味及一湯匙熟油一兜，盛在米粉盤中心，與生菜同送席。

Ingredients (finely diced):
　　　1 fat pigeon (finely diced)　　　　　4 oz. pork fillet (finely diced)　　　3 dried mushrooms (finely diced)
　　　2 bamboo shoots (finely diced)　　10 water chestnuts (finely diced)　　1 sweet green pepper (finely diced)
　　　5 stalks green onion (finely diced)　5 slices young ginger (finely diced)　2 egg yolks
　　　1 oz. rice flour noodles　　　　　　24 lettuce leaves (edge curved)　　　2 oz. chicken fat (finely diced)
　　　peanut oil to cover half of pan

Seasoning Sauce (combine):
　　　1 T. soy sauce　　　　　　　　　1 t. cornstarch　　　　　　　　　　1 T. cold water
　　　½ t. salt　　　　　　　　　　　　¼ t. sugar　　　　　　　　　　　　dash of pepper
　　　few drops of sesame oil

Directions:
1. Kill, feather and clean pigeon. Bone and mince pigeon meat with pork fillet. Set aside.
2. Wash lettuce leaves with water first. Next wash with sodium permanganate solution. Rinse with cold boiled water. Let dry. Arrange every 12 petals on one plate.
3. Heat oil in pan. Fry rice flour noodles till golden brown. Remove and drain off oil. Put on sides of plate.
4. Combine pigeon, pork, chicken fat, egg yolks, 1 t. wine, 1 T. white soy sauce, ¼ t. salt, and pepper. Mix thoroughly.
5. Heat 1 T. oil in pan. Fry all diced vegetables; add salt. Remove. Fry Step 4 in 2 T. oil. Add fried vegetables, seasoning sauce and 1 T. cooked oil. Put in middle of plate. Serve with lettuce leaves.

芥蘭魚球
Fish Balls with Chinese Broccoli

廣東菜　　　　材料：12人份

材　　料： 魚肉一塊　芥蘭菜半斤　香菇三只　薑花片六小片　鹽半茶匙　豆粉二茶匙（用二湯匙水調和）　花生油半斤

綜合調味： 蠔油一湯匙　酒一茶匙　鹽糖各半茶匙　麻油數點　胡椒少許

做　　法： ①先將魚肉洗淨，連皮用刀輕切二刀，不切斷下去，第三刀才切斷下去，都切成每塊後加下一茶匙水豆粉及鹽拌和待用。
②將油燒熱後，先放薑片，再倒下魚塊急炒數下視魚塊已捲成球形即撈起，鍋中所留之油，即倒下芥蘭菜段及香菇爆炒片刻，再加下三湯匙清水燒片刻，調入綜合調味及一茶匙水豆粉，繼續攪炒，並落魚球略一兜炒，即刻起鍋送席。

Ingredients:
- 1 large pc. fish meat (about 1 lb.)
- 3 dried mushrooms
- ½ t. salt
- ½ cup peanut oil
- ⅗ lb. Chinese broccoli
- 6 slices ginger
- 2 t. cornstarch (mixed with 2 T. water)

Seasonings:
- 1 T. oyster sauce
- ½ t. salt
- a few drops of sesame oil
- 1 t. wine
- ½ t. sugar
- dash of pepper

Directions:
1. Cut fish meat into pieces. Mix thoroughly with 1 t. cornstarch paste and salt.
2. Heat oil in frying pan. Add ginger and fish; turn quickly few times. Remove when fish pieces curl up to ball shape.
3. Fry Chinese broccoli and mushroom in remaining oil; add 3 T. water to cook 2 min. Blend in seasoning and remaining cornstarch paste; continue stirring and turning. Add fish balls; cook another 1 min., tossing lightly and quickly. Serve hot.

碗豆苗炒蛋　　家常菜　　材料：12人份
Scrambled Eggs with Pea Shoots

材　料：鷄鴨蛋四個　火腿屑二湯匙(生熟均可)　碗豆苗一撮(洗淨切碎)　鹽半湯匙　味精少許　豬油或鷄油四湯匙

做　法：①首將蛋打在碗內加鹽與味精打散，然後加入火腿屑和碗豆苗攪勻。
②油鍋以大火燒熱，將蛋整碗倒下，用鏟子急炒，視蛋已凝固，即可盛起供食。

Ingredients: 4 eggs
pinch of pea shoots (chopped)
4 T. lard or chicken fat
2 T. chopped ham
½ t. salt
dash of monosodium glutamate

Directions:
1. Beat eggs seasoned with salt and monosodium glutamate. Then add chopped ham and pea shoots. Mix well.
2. Heat oil over high heat. Add egg mixture. Stir-fry quickly until eggs set. Remove and serve.

青椒童鷄
Young Chicken with Green Pepper

家常菜　　　　　材料：12人份

材　料： 童子鷄一隻（退毛去內臟後重約十二兩）　大青椒一只　小紅辣椒二只　葱白頭三支（切段）嫩薑六薄片　花生油三湯匙　豆粉二茶匙（一茶匙調為水豆粉）

調味品： 醬油一湯匙　白醬油一湯匙　鹽糖酒各半茶匙

做　法： ①首將童子鷄洗淨瀝水，斬為小塊放入碗內拌入豆粉一茶匙，黑白醬油各一茶匙，及糖酒攪勻，約半小時後再炒，大青椒對剖去子洗淨，直切二條後，切為三角塊，小紅椒對剖也切三角塊，均留用。

②鍋中把油燒熱，先爆香葱薑和紅辣椒，然後倒下鷄塊翻覆爆透，再放下大青椒同炒，又加入鹽及餘下之黑白醬油，翻覆炒數下，加入沸水半飯碗，關蓋略滾，即放下一茶匙水豆粉，使湯汁呈薄稠狀，即可盛起供食。

Ingredients:
- 1 young chicken (about 1 lb. net weight)
- 1 green pepper (halved lengthwise and seeded)
- 1 red chili pepper (halved lengthwise and seeded)
- 6 slices young ginger
- 3 green onion (cut into 1½" pieces)
- 2 t. cornstarch (1 t. mixed in water)
- 3 T. peanut oil

Seasonings:
- 1 T. soy sauce
- 1 T. white soy sauce
- ½ t. salt
- ½ t. sugar
- ½ t. wine

Directions:
1. Cut chicken into small pieces, and mix thoroughly with 1 t. cornstarch, 1 t. black soy sauce, 1 t. white soy sauce, sugar and wine. Marinate 30 min. Cut halved green pepper into triangular shapes. Repeat same procedure with red chili pepper.
2. Heat oil in frying pan. Stir-fry green onion, ginger and red chili pepper; add chicken, turning constantly. Put in green pepper; add salt and remaining soy sauce. Turn and stir several times. Add ½ bowl boiling water. Cook, covered, 3-4 min. Add cornstarch paste. When sauce thickens slightly, remove and serve.

魚香肉絲
Shredded Pork with Fish Flavors

四川菜　　　　材料：12人份

材　　料：	猪排骨肉或里肌肉半斤　木耳二湯匙　荸薺十只　葱薑屑各一湯匙　辣豆瓣醬一茶匙半　蒜屑一粒　花生油四湯匙
綜合調味：	醋一湯匙　醬油四茶匙　鹽糖各半茶匙　蔴油胡椒少許　豆粉一茶匙（用二湯匙水調和）
做　　法：	①首將肉略洗瀝水，橫紋切絲放在碗內，加入一半之綜合調味汁拌匀，木耳浸發後整理洗淨切丁，荸薺修皮後切丁，均備用。 ②將油鍋燒熱，倒下肉絲爆炒數下，卽撈起留下剩油爆炒木耳，荸薺，葱薑屑，蒜屑，及辣豆瓣醬炒約二分鐘，再倒下肉絲及一半之綜合調味汁炒匀，卽刻盛起供食。

Ingredients: ⅜ lb. pork fillet
10 water chestnuts
1 T. chopped ginger
1½ t. hot bean paste
2 T. dried wood ears (mu-erh)
1 T. chopped green onion
1 piece garlic (shredded)
4 T. peanut oil

Seasoning Sauce (combine):
1 T. vinegar
½ t. salt
dash of pepper
1 t. cornstarch (mixed with 2 T. water.)
4 t. soy sauce
½ t. sugar
drops of sesame oil

Directions:
1. Clean and shred pork. Marinate pork in ½ seasoning sauce. Soak dried wood ears in water to expand. Cut into small pieces. Peel and dice water chestnuts.
2. Heat peanut oil in frying pan. Stir-fry shredded pork quickly and remove. Fry wood ears and rest of ingredients in remaining oil about 2 min. Add fried shredded pork and rest of seasoning sauce; stir in. Remove and serve.

爛糊肉絲
Shredded Pork and Celery Cabbage

上海菜　　　材料：12人份

材　料：瘦肉六兩　肥肉二兩(用白醬油、太白粉先調)　黃芽菜一斤　豬油或鷄油三湯匙　鮮湯或煮菜湯一杯　豆粉一湯匙(用三湯匙水調和)

調味品：鹽一茶匙　白醬油一湯匙　糖半茶匙　酒一茶匙

做　法：① 首將瘦肉橫紋切細絲，肥肉亦切細絲，黃芽菜洗淨切絲，均備用。
② 備小鋁鍋，放下沸水二飯碗，倒下菜絲滾燒十分鐘，然後傾入竹籮中瀝水。
③ 備砂鍋或鋁鍋煮，放下沸水二杯，將肉絲及一茶匙酒倒下，以文火煨半小時，然後加入菜絲。並調入豬油、鹽糖及白醬油，同時又加入高湯或菜湯一杯，再用文火燒廿分鐘，即調下水豆粉，拘成稠汁，最後再加落一湯匙豬油，即可盛起趁熱送席(一杯爲十二湯匙)。

Ingredients: 6 oz. lean pork　　2 oz. pork fat
1⅓ lb. celery cabbage　　3 T. lard or chicken fat
1 C. meat or vegetable stock　　1 T. cornstarch (mixed with 3 T. water)

Seasonings: 1 t. salt　　1 T. white soy sauce
½ t. sugar　　1 t. wine

Directions:
1. Shred lean pork and pork fat. Clean and shred celery cabbage.
2. Fill pot with 2 bowls boiling water. Add shredded cabbage and cook 10 min. Remove and drain.
3. Fill earthenware pot with 2 C. boiling water. Add shredded pork and 1 t. wine. Cook over low heat 30 min. Add shredded cabbage. Blend in lard, salt, sugar, white soy sauce and meat stock. Cook over low heat another 20 min. Add cornstarch paste. Mix till sauce thickens. Add 1 T. lard. Serve hot.

爛糊牛肉絲
Beef Shreds and Onion

上　海　菜　　　　材料：12人份

材　料：牛肉半斤　洋葱半斤　熟花生油一湯匙　花生油五湯匙
調味品：黑醬油一湯匙　白醬油二茶匙鹽一茶匙　豆粉一湯匙　糖一茶匙
做　法：①首將牛肉略洗，橫紋切絲，加入黑醬油、豆粉、糖拌勻，臨炒前再加入熟花生油攪拌，洋葱撕皮洗淨對剖後切直絲，均備用。
②鍋中放油二湯匙。燒熱，傾下洋葱絲，加一茶匙鹽煸炒，然後放下水一飯碗半，關蓋煮爛汁少盛起。
③鍋中再放三湯匙油，以大火燒得很熱，卽倒下牛肉急炒數下，當卽倒下已爛之洋葱絲拌炒二下，卽刻盛起供食。

Ingredients: ⅔ lb. beef　　⅔ lb. onion　　2 slices ginger (shredded)
　　　　　　　1 T. cooked peanut oil　　5 T. peanut oil
Seasonings: 1 T. black soy sauce　　2 t. white soy sauce　　1 t. salt
　　　　　　　1 T. cornstarch　　1 t. sugar
Directions: 1. Shred beef against grain. Blend with black soy sauce, cornstarch and sugar. Before frying, mix with 1 T. cooked peanut oil. Peel and clean onion; cut in two and shred.
2. Heat 2 T. peanut oil in frying pan. Stir-fry shredded onion. Add 1 t. salt. Mix. Add 1½ bowl water. Cook, covered, till very tender. Remove.
3. Heat another 3 T. peanut oil over high heat. Add beef and stir-fry quickly. Return shredded onion to pan; stir and turn together a few seconds. Remove and serve.

糖醋鮮魷魚捲 家常菜　　材料：12人份
Sweet and Sour Squid Rolls

材　　料：鮮魷魚一斤　紅辣椒段二只　青蒜葉段二支　嫩薑寬絲四片　酒二茶匙　豆粉二茶匙
　　　　　花生油二飯碗
綜合調味：黑醬油四茶匙　白醬油二茶匙　醋三湯匙　棉白糖二湯匙　鹽一茶匙　味精蔴油少許
　　　　　豆粉二茶匙　清水三湯匙
做　　法：①首將鮮魷魚剝皮，洗淨瀝水，拉去魷魚頭留煮湯用，在每只魷魚無皮這面，切為粒花，然後
　　　　　　對切交叉切為三角塊，放在盤內，加入薑絲，酒和豆粉二茶匙，拌勻備用。
　　　　　②鍋中放油燒熱，不待沸時，即以大火倒下魷魚炒約二分鐘，視魷魚已呈捲形，即刻用濾油器
　　　　　　撈出，鍋中留一湯匙油，倒下紅辣椒與青蒜葉段略爆香，即刻傾下綜合調味汁，待滾，將已
　　　　　　過油之魷魚捲倒下拌勻，立即盛起供食。

Ingredients:　1⅜ lb. fresh squids　　2 red chili peppers (cut in 1" pieces)　　2 stalks garlic stalks (cut in 1" pieces)
　　　　　　　　 4 slices young ginger　 2 t. wine　　　　　　　　　　　　　　　　2 t. cornstarch
　　　　　　　　 2 bowls peanut oil

Seasoning Sauce (combine):
　　　　　　　　 4 t. black soy sauce　　2 t. white soy sauce　　　　　　　　　　　3 T. vinegar
　　　　　　　　 2 T. powdered sugar　　1 t. salt　　　　　　　　　　　　　　　　 2 t. cornstarch
　　　　　　　　 3 T. water　　　　　　 dash of monosodium glutamate (M.S.G.)　　 drops of sesame oil

Directions:
1. Remove skin and head. Save head. Score crisscross surface without skin. Cut diagnally into bite-size triangular pieces. Mix with ginger, wine and cornstarch.
2. Heat oil in frying pan till warm. Fry squids, over high heat, about 2 min. until squids curl up. Remove and drain oil. Leave 1 T. oil in pan; fry red chili pepper and green garlic, 30 sec. Stir in seasoning sauce; let simmer. Add squids; fry, stirring, 30 sec. and remove. Serve hot.

芙蓉鷄片
Chicken Slices Foo Yung

杭州菜　　　　材料：12人份

材　料：鷄肉六兩　鷄蛋白六個　香菇片兩只　蒸熟筍片半支　熟火腿片十數片　熟毛豆二湯匙　猪油六湯匙

調味品：白醬油半茶匙　豆粉四分之一茶匙　糖四分之一茶匙　酒半茶匙　鹽一茶匙

做　法：①首將鷄肉切片（家常吃可用里肌肉代替），加白醬油豆粉糖及少許不打散之蛋白拌匀，炒散待冷備用。
②蛋白加鹽打到發泡，調入酒與已冷之鷄片再打（臨炒前才打蛋）。
③以平底鍋放在慢火上，油開了再倒入已打發泡之蛋白，不要攪動，拿鍋週圍傾斜，使鍋中間的蛋流滿全鍋，以免厚薄不匀，待蛋白剛剛凝固變白後，即可用炒菜鏟子翻一個面，待生的蛋白熟了，再加上已混合炒過之配料，即可起鍋，火大了或時間長了，蛋白熟易黃老，不如白嫩的好吃，剩下的蛋黃，可作溜黃菜。

Ingredients: 6 oz. chicken breast　　　6 egg whites
2 dried mushrooms (sliced)　　½ cooked bamboo shoot (sliced)
10 slices cooked Chinese ham　　2 T. cooked fresh soy beans
6 T. lard

Seasonings: ½ t. white soy sauce　　¼ t. cornstarch
¼ t. sugar　　½ t. wine
1 t. salt

Directions:
1. Cut chicken breast into slices. (Pork fillet may be used instead if cooking just for family.) Mix with white soy sauce, cornstarch, sugar and a little unbeaten egg white. Stir-fry and set aside to cool. Stir-fry mushrooms, bamboo shoot, ham and soy beans together. Set aside.
2. Beat egg whites seasoned with salt till fluffy. Blend in wine and cooled chicken. Beat again. (Beat egg whites just before frying.)
3. Heat oil in skillet over low heat until boiling. Pour in egg white mixture. Do not stir. Tilt and rotate pan so that the mixture spreads evenly over the entire surface. When the mixture sets, turn over with spatula. Cook until other side sets too. Add combination of mushrooms, bamboo shoot, ham and fresh soy beans. Remove and serve.

碗豆炒三丁

家常菜　　　　材料：12人份

Stir-Fried Snow Peas and Three Dices

材　料：瘦肉丁四兩　大碗豆夾十兩（連殼較嫩）　洋芋一小只（去皮切丁）　胡蘿蔔一小條（刮皮對剖）
猪油二湯匙或花生油亦可

做　法：①首將瘦肉丁加入一茶匙白醬油和半茶匙糖及半茶匙豆粉拌匀，大碗豆夾剝殼取仁，略洗瀝乾，洋芋丁放一飯碗水煮軟盛起，胡蘿蔔在高湯內煮約十分鐘撈出待冷切丁，均備用。

②油鍋燒熱，先倒下肉丁爆炒，隨即將胡蘿蔔丁及洋芋丁連湯傾下，然後加入白醬油二茶匙鹽一茶匙及糖半茶匙，如湯汁太少，可酌加沸水，待滾，即倒下碗豆仁，關蓋煮燒，豆仁已軟，炒數下卽可盛起，其色之美，一想就知，其味如何？請主婦們嚐一嚐，這一道營養豐富的家常菜，希望小孩子們多吃些。

Ingredients: 4 oz. lean pork (diced)　　10 oz. large snow peas (podded)
1 small potato (pared and diced)　1 carrot (pared and halved lengthwise)
2 T. lard or peanut oil　　1 bowl meat stock

Seasonings: 1 T. white soy sauce　　1 t. salt
½ t. sugar　　½ t. cornstarch

Directions:
1. Mix diced pork with 1 t. white soy sauce, ¼ t. sugar and ½ t. cornstarch. Clean snow peas; drain. Boil potato in one bowl of water till soft. Boil carrot in meat stock 10 min. Cool and dice.
2. Heat oil in frying pan. Stir-fry pork. Add carrot, potato and meat stock. Add 2 t. white soy sauce, 1 t. salt and ¼ sugar. Bring to boil (Add water if necessary). Add peas. Cook, covered, until peas are tender. Stir-fry a few times and remove. Serve.

鳳肝黃瓜
Chicken Livers and Cucumbers

江浙菜　　　　材料：12人份

材　料：鳳肝(即鷄肝)四副　小黃瓜半斤　葱段二支　小蝦米二湯匙　花生油三湯匙　豆粉半茶匙(用一湯匙水調和)

調味品：鹽一茶匙　白醬油一茶匙　糖四分之一茶匙　酒半茶匙

做　法：①首將鷄心對剖洗去血，將肝也洗淨，每副打斜切為五六片，加入酒鹽各半茶匙拌勻，黃瓜洗淨對剖打斜切為厚片，蝦米以四湯匙溫水泡浸，均備用。

②油鍋燒熱，先爆香葱段，倒下鷄肝爆炒，再傾入黃瓜和蝦米，同時調入白醬油糖及半茶匙鹽拌炒，再傾下浸蝦米之汁，並關蓋燒片剖，即調下水豆粉攪勻，即刻盛起供食，清脆可口。

Ingredients:　4 chicken livers with hearts　　⅔ lb. cucumbers
　　　　　　　　2 stalks green onion (cut into sections)　2 T. small dried shrimps
　　　　　　　　3 T. peanut oil　　　　½ t. constarch (mixed with 1 T. water)

Seasonings:　1 t. salt　　　　　　　1 t. white soy sauce
　　　　　　　　¼ t. sugar　　　　　　½ t. wine　　½

Directions:
1. Cut chicken hearts in half; wash away blood. Cut liver diagonally into 5-6 slices. Blend with ½ t. wine and ½ t. salt. Wash cucumbers. Halve lengthwise and cut diagonally into thick slices. Soak dried shrimps in 4 T. warm water.
2. Heat oil in frying pan. Stir-fry green onion first. Add chicken livers and stir-fry, turning continuously. Add cucumbers and dried shrimps. Season with white soy sauce, sugar and ½ t. salt. Add soaking water for dried shrimps. Cook, covered, 1-2 min. Stir in cornstarch paste to thicken. Serve.

鷄油雙菇
Mushrooms with Chicken Fat

家　常　菜　　　　材料：12人份

材　料：鮮蔴菇六兩　草菇二兩　酒一茶匙　鷄油三湯匙　高湯一中碗
調味品：鹽一茶匙　白醬油一湯匙
做　法：①將草菇洗淨瀝水，鮮蔴菇把蒂修去亦用清水洗淨瀝水。
　　　　②把鷄油燒熱，先傾下雙菇加酒爆一下倒下調味品，再傾下高湯，關蓋滾片刻，卽調下水豆粉，把汁呈稠濃狀，卽可盛入深口大瓷盆中送席。
附　註：此菜之汁，最好與雙菇平。

Ingredients: 2/3 lb. fresh mushrooms　　15 dried mushrooms
　　　　　　　1 t. wine　　　　　　　　3 T. chicken fat
　　　　　　　1 bowl meat stock　　　　1 t. cornstarch (mixed with 1 T. water)
Seasonings: 1 t. salt　　　　　　　　1 T. white soy sauce
Directions: 1. Soak dried mushrooms in warm water to expand. Halve large ones. Save water. Remove stems of fresh mushrooms.
　　　　　　2. Heat chicken fat in frying pan; add fresh mushrooms and wine. Stir-fry 1 min. Add dried mushrooms; turn and toss a few seconds. Add meat stock and water used for soaking mushrooms. Simmer, covered. Blend in cornstarch paste till sauce is thickened. Serve in deep plate.

宮爆雞丁
Fried Chicken with Paprikas

四川菜　　材料：12人份

材　料：嫩雞一只或雞胸二個　油花生肉半飯碗　乾紅辣椒十只　雞蛋清一個　豆粉半茶匙
　　　　薑二片　鹽半茶匙　花生油五湯匙
綜合調味：醬油一湯匙　醋一茶匙　糖半茶匙
做　法：①首將乾紅椒用布擦清，然後用剪刀去蒂剪為三、四段去子留用。
　　　　②次將嫩雞拆骨取肉，連皮切丁，加入豆粉薑屑及鹽拌勻留用。
　　　　③油鍋燒熱、爆紅辣椒二下，即撈起辣椒將雞丁傾入爆炒十數下後，
　　　　　加下綜合調味及紅辣椒兜炒數下，最後倒下油吞花生肉炒拌一下，即盛出趁熱上席。

Ingredients: 1 young chicken or 2 chicken breasts　　½ bowl fried peanut meat
　　　　　　10 paprikas　　　　　　　　　　　　　　　1 egg white
　　　　　　2 slices ginger (chopped)　　　　　　　　½ t. cornstarch
　　　　　　2 t. soy sauce　　　　　　　　　　　　　½ t. salt
　　　　　　5 T. peanut oil
Seasoning Sauce (combine):
　　　　　　1 T. soy sauce　　　　　　　　　　　　　1 t. vinegar
　　　　　　½ t. sugar

Directions:
1. Stem and seed paprikas; cut into 4 pieces.
2. Remove bones of chicken; dice meat with skin. Mix with cornstarch, chopped ginger, soy sauce and salt.
3. Heat oil in frying pan. Fry paprikas, 1 min., and remove. Fry diced chicken in remaining oil, stirring constantly about 10-15 times. Add seasoning sauce and paprikas; stir-fry a couple of times and add peanuts. Serve hot.

炒牛肝 Stir-Fried Ox Liver

家常菜　　　　　材料：12人份

材　料：牛肝六兩　洋葱一個　木耳二湯匙（乾）　薑四薄片　花生油四湯匙　胡椒粉少許
調味品：醬油一湯匙　鹽半茶匙　糖四分之一茶匙　豆粉一茶匙
做　法：①首將牛肝洗淨瀝乾，撕去薄衣，斜切約二分厚之片，裝在碗內，調入二茶匙醬油和豆粉糖及薑片拌勻備用。
②木耳泡發檢清洗淨，洋葱撕皮對剖後切塊備用。
③用一湯匙油燒熱，倒下洋葱爆香，再放下木耳鏟炒，即落鹽與一茶匙醬油拌炒，然後傾入三湯匙水關蓋燜燒片刻盛起。
④再用三湯匙油燒熱，即倒下牛肝急炒數下，隨即將洋葱等倒下，近速拌炒視肝無血色，即可盛起供食，面洒胡椒粉熱吃味鮮而特營養。

Ingredients:	½ lb. of liver	1 onion
	2 T. dried wood ears (mu-erh)	4 thin slices ginger
	4 T. peanut oil	dash of pepper
Seasonings:	1 T. soy sauce	½ t. salt
	¼ t. sugar	1 t. cornstarch

Directions:
1. Clean liver. Cut into thin slices diagonally. Mix thoroughly with 2 t. soy sauce, cornstarch, sugar and ginger.
2. Soak dried wood ears in water to soften and clean. Cut onion into pieces.
3. Heat 1 T. peanut oil. Stir-fry onion; add wood ears. Fry, stirring and turning constantly. Sprinkle salt and 1 T. soy sauce and mix. Add 3 T. water, Cook, covered, 3-4 min. Remove.
4. Again heat 3 T. oil. Fry sliced liver quickly, stirring and tossing lightly. Add onion and wood ears. Fry till liver loses reddish color. Sprinkle with pepper and serve hot.

魚香腰花　　　四川菜　　　材料：12人份
Stir-Fried Kidney with Fish Flavors

材　　料：	豬腰三只　　乾木耳二湯匙　　荸薺六隻　　葱薑屑各一湯匙　　蒜屑粉　　辣豆瓣醬一湯匙
	花生油六湯匙　　豆粉二茶匙
綜合調味：	豬油一湯匙　　醋一湯匙　　鹽糖各半茶匙　　酒一茶匙　　豆粉一茶匙　　清水二湯匙
	蔴油胡椒少許
做　　法：	①首將豬腰對剖，披去筋後，泡在清水中，一小時後瀝水，將每半個豬腰，直割細紋後，再交叉切三角塊，又在大頭劃分二刀，每塊豬腰，形似鷄爪，炒熟後相當美觀。
	②切好之豬腰，用沸水川一下濾水後，裝在碗內，加入豆粉拌勻備用。
	③花生油入鍋燒得極熱倒下腰塊炸炒一分鐘盛起，鍋中留油一湯匙，爆炒木耳荸薺葱薑蒜屑及辣豆瓣醬，然後傾下腰塊及綜合調味汁兜勻，即速盛起送席。

Ingredients:
　3 pork kidneys　　　　　　2 T. dried wood ears (mu-erh)　　6 water chestnuts
　1 T. chopped green onion　1 T. chopped ginger　　　　　　1 T. chopped garlic
　1 T. hot bean paste　　　　6 T. peanut oil　　　　　　　　2 t. cornstarch

Seasoning Sauce (combine):
　1 T. lard　　　　　1 T. vinegar　　　　　　　½ t. salt
　½ t. sugar　　　　　1 t. wine　　　　　　　　1 t. cornstarch
　2 T. water　　　　　drops of sesame oil　　　　dash of pepper

Directions:
1. Halve kidneys horizontally. Remove white veins. Soak in water 1 hr. and drain. Score parallel lines closely lengthwise on outer surface of each half kidney. Then cut criss-cross into four triangular shapes. Make one cut at the base of each triangle, but do not penetrate, to give each a claw-like form.
2. Parboil kidneys and drain. Mix with cornstarch.
3. Heat oil in frying pan to smoking. Stir-fry kidneys 1 min. Remove. Leave 1 T. oil in pan. Fry wood ears; water chestnuts, green onion, ginger, garlic and hot bean paste. Add kidneys and seasoning sauce. Mix and serve.

炒腰花　　四川菜

Sauteed Pork Kidney

材料：12人份

材　　料：豬腰三只（重約一斤）　香菇四、五只（洗淨以溫水浸發後切塊）　筍一支（剝殼修頭切斜片蒸十分鐘）　荷蘭豆二兩（撕筋洗淨在高湯內川片刻）　豬油六湯匙

綜合調味：黑白醬油各一茶匙半　鹽半茶匙　糖半茶匙　蔴油、胡椒少許　豆粉一茶匙（用一湯匙水調和）

做　　法：①首將豬腰對剖披去筋後，切粒花，然後切成四、五分濶之腰塊，在冷水中泡浸一小時後瀝乾，鍋中燒三飯碗滾水，將腰塊川燒片刻，即撈起在冷水中川洗數次，瀝去水份留用。
②鍋中放豬油一湯匙，先倒下香菇、筍片炒數下，加入浸香菇之水二湯匙滾燒片刻，再放下荷蘭豆拌勻盛起，鍋中重加豬油燒熱，即倒下腰塊急炒一分鐘後，加下綜合調味急速炒二下再加入各配料繼續拌炒數下，即速盛起趁熱送席。

Ingredients:
3 pork kidneys (about 1⅓ lb.)　　4 or 5 dried mushrooms
1 bamboo shoot　　2 oz. baby peas (with pods)
6 T. lard

Seasonings:
½ t. black soy sauce　　½ t. white soy sauce
½ t. salt　　½ t. sugar
1 t. cornstarch (mixed with 1 T. water)　　a few drops of sesame oil
dash of pepper

Directions:
1. Halve kidneys horizontally; trim white viens. Score entire surface crisscross; cut into pieces, about 1"X½" Soak in cold water 1 hr. and drain. Soak mushrooms in warm water to expand and cut into pieces; save water. Slice bamboo shoots diagonally and steam 10 min. String pea; parboil peas in boiling meat stock 1 min.
2. Boil 3 bowls of water in pot. Parboil kidney pieces. Remove and rinse in cold water. Drain and set aside.
3. Heat 1 T. lard in frying pan. Stir-fry mushrooms and bamboo shoots, turning frequently. Pour in 2 T. soaking water and let boil. Add baby peas. Mix and remove. Heat remaining lard in pan. Stir-fry kidney pieces quickly 1 min. Add seasoning sauce. Turn and toss quickly a couple of times. Add cooked ingredients and combine. Serve hot.

鴛鴦蝦仁

湖南菜　　材料：12人份

Shrimps with Snow Peas and Lima Beans

材　　料：鮮海蝦二斤　嫩蠶豆瓣二兩(燙熟)　嫩碗豆仁二兩　雞蛋白二個　鹽三茶匙(二茶匙洗蝦仁用，另一茶匙調入蝦仁內)　豆粉四茶匙　蘇打粉八分之一茶匙　猪油一斤　蕃茄醬二湯匙

綜合材料：鹽半茶匙　酒一茶匙半　豆粉一茶匙　冷水二湯匙

做　　法：①首將蝦仁去頭剝殼，剖背肉去泥臟，先以水洗，再以鹽水攪洗，然後再以冷水沖清、吹乾或擦乾。

②將蝦仁置碗內同時加入蛋白、鹽、蘇打粉及豆粉拌勻備用。

③將猪油放鍋中燒熱，不待沸時，即放入蝦仁炸炒，候蝦仁已成彎曲，即用濾油器撈起瀝乾油，鍋內留一湯匙油加一點水放下碗豆仁，至豆仁已脫生水已乾，即倒入綜合調味之一半及蝦仁，略加兜勻，即盛在細瓷長盤之一端。鍋中重放油一湯匙，倒入蠶豆瓣略炒，再放餘下之綜合調味及蝦仁，並即倒下蕃茄醬拌勻，即刻盛盤之另一端，趁熱送席。

Ingredients:
- 2⅓ lb. sea shrimps
- 2 oz. tender snow peas (podded)
- 3 t. salt (2 t. for washing shrimps; 1 t. for blending with shrimps)
- ⅛ soda powder
- 2 T. tomato sauce
- 2 oz. tender lima beans (parboiled)
- 2 egg whites
- 4 t. cornstarch
- 4 C. lard

Seasoning Sauce (Combine):
- ½ t. salt
- 1 t. cornstarch
- 1½ t. wine
- 2 T. cold water

Directions:
1. Remove shrimp heads and shells. Devein. Clean shrimps first with water; then with salted water. Rinse and dry.
2. Mix shrimps with egg whites, salt, soda powder and cornstarch.
3. Heat lard in frying pan. Stir-fry shrimps in hot oil (not boiled) till they curl up. Remove and drain oil. Leave 1 T. oil in pan. Add water and cook snow peas until done. Add ½ seasoning sauce and fried shrimps. Stir-fry quickly and remove. Place on one side of long serving plate. Add another 1 T. oil in pan. Stir-fry lima beans. Add remaining seasoning sauce and shrimps. Stir in tomato sauce. Blend well. Remove and place on the other side of serving plate. Serve hot.

鳳肝蝦捲

廣東菜　　材料：12人份

Chicken Liver and Prawn Slices

材　　料：明蝦十隻　鷄肝六付　鷄蛋白一個　熟火腿片　碗豆夾（在高湯內川片刻）各一小碟
　　　　　洋葱丁半隻　薑粒一茶匙　鹽半茶匙　豆粉一茶匙　豬油二杯（花生油亦可）
綜合調味：鹽半茶匙，酒一茶匙　白醬油一湯匙　蔴油數滴　胡椒少許　豆粉半茶匙（用二湯匙水調和）
做　　法：①首將明蝦去殼留尾，每只切成二片（一片留尾增色）洗淨瀝乾，放入碗內加四分之一
　　　　　茶匙鹽一茶匙豆粉及蛋白拌勻備用。
　　　　　②次將鷄肝每付切成四五片，亦加入四分之一茶匙鹽及半湯匙水拌勻，然後置沸水中川
　　　　　片刻，卽撈起用淸水沖去血水瀝乾留用。
　　　　　③將豬油燒熱，倒下蝦片爆炸二分鐘撈起，重將肝片倒下泡五六秒撈起濾油，把鍋內留
　　　　　二湯匙油爆洋葱丁及薑粒，隨卽倒下蝦肝火腿碗豆夾及綜合調味略炒，卽起鍋送席。

Ingredients:　10 prawns　　　　　　　　　　　　　　　6 chicken livers
　　　　　　　　1 egg white　　　　　　　　　　　　　　 1-2 oz. cooked Chinese ham (sliced)
　　　　　　　　1-2 oz. snow peas (parboiled in meat stock 1 min.)　½ diced onion
　　　　　　　　1 t. grated ginger　　　　　　　　　　　 ½ t. salt
　　　　　　　　1 t. cornstarch　　　　　　　　　　　　 2 C. lard (or peanut oil)
Seasoning Sauce (combine):
　　　　　　　　½ t. salt　　　　　　　　　　　　　　　1 t. wine
　　　　　　　　1 T. white soy sauce　　　　　　　　　　few drops of sesame oil
　　　　　　　　dash of pepper　　　　　　　　　　　　　½ t. cornstarch (mixed with 2 T. water)

Directions:
1. Shell prawns but retain tails. Cut in half (leave one piece with tail for color). Clean and drain. Combine with ¼ t. salt, 1 t. cornstarch and egg white.
2. Cut each chicken liver into 4-5 slices. Mix with ¼ t. salt and ½ T. water. Dip in boiling water 1-2 min. and remove. Wash away bloodish liquid. Drain.
3. Heat lard in pan. Stir-fry prawns 2 min. and remove. Soak livers in oil 5-6 sec. Remove and drain. Leave 2 T. oil in pan. Stir-fry diced onion and ginger. Add prawns, livers, ham, snow peas and seasoning sauce. Fry a few minutes and serve.

炒猪肝
Sauteed Pork Liver

家 常 菜　　　材料：12人份

材　料：猪肝十兩　乾木耳二湯匙（香菇三、四只亦可）　筍一支　嫩薑十數片（洋葱亦可）
　　　　花生油四湯匙
調味品：醬油二湯匙　鹽半茶匙　豆粉一茶匙半　酒半茶匙
做　法：①首將木耳以溫水泡浸洗淨，筍去殼切片蒸熟（約十分鐘），嫩薑亦切薄片。
　　　　②次將猪肝洗淨瀝水，切約二分厚之片裝碗內。
　　　　③用少油爆炒筍片及木耳，加鹽和水略滾盛起。
　　　　④用沸水倒在猪肝碗內，立刻用筷子攪拌，見猪肝已發白色，即刻倒在濾油器內瀝水，然
　　　　　後加入調味品拌勻，再以油鍋燒極熱，先爆嫩薑片，再倒下猪肝翻炒片刻，加入配料再
　　　　　炒數下即可，熱吃鮮嫩。

Ingredients: 10 oz. pork liver　　2 T. dried wood ears (mu-erh), or 3-4 dried mushrooms
　　　　　　　　1 bamboo shoot　　10-12 slices young ginger (onion may be substituted)
　　　　　　　　4 T. peanut oil

Seasonings: 2 T. soy sauce　　½ t. salt
　　　　　　　　1½ t. cornstarch　　½ t. wine

Directions:
1. Soak dried wood ear in warm water and clean. Peel bamboo shoots; cut in slices and steam 10 min.
2. Wash, drain and slice liver.
3. Saute bamboo shoots and wood ears. Add salt and water. Let boil and remove.
4. Pour boiling water over liver. Mix thoroughly until liver turns light. Drain water. Blend in seasonings.
5. Heat oil. Stir-fry ginger 1 min. Add liver; stir and toss lightly. Add all ingredients; stir and turn a few times. Serve hot.

金菜菱角

杭　州　菜　　　　材料：12人份

Stir-fried Pickled Cabbage and Horned Water Chestnuts

材　料：鮮嫩菱角肉半斤　金菜二湯匙　花生油二湯匙
調味品：白醬油一湯匙　糖士茶匙
做　法：①首將菱角肉用冷水煮熟，取出菱角肉湯汁留用。
　　　　②油鍋燒熱，先爆金菜，倒下菱肉煸炒，然後傾入調味品及湯汁滾燒片刻，盛起供食。

Ingredients: ⅔ lb. horned water chestnut meat (ling-chiao)　　2 T. pickled cabbage
2 T. peanut oil

Seasonings: 1 T. white soy sauce　　¼ t. sugar

Directions:
1. Put water chestnut meat in pot with water to cover. Cook until done. Remove. Keep liquid.
2. Heat oil in frying pan. Stir-fry pickled cabbage first. Add horned water chestnut meat. Stir-fry to mix. Add seasonings and liquid. Let boil a few minutes. Serve.

香菇菜心

江浙菜　　　　材料：12人份

Green Cabbage Hearts and Dried Mushrooms

材　料：青梗菜一斤半　香菇五隻　高湯一飯碗　猪油或花生油五湯匙　水豆粉一茶匙
調味品：白醬油一湯匙　鹽一茶匙　糖丰茶匙　味精少許
做　法：①首將青梗菜瓣去老葉，留菜心切去菜葉整顆洗淨，香菇略洗用冷水浸發後留用。
　　　　②油鍋燒熱先爆切塊之香菇，然後將青菜傾下煸炒，加入調味品同炒，再傾下高湯關蓋滾燒，視菜梗略輭拘下水豆粉及一點猪油盛起送席。

Ingredients: 2 lb. green cabbage
1 bowl meat stock
1 t. cornstarch
5 dried mushrooms
5 T. lard or peanut oil

Seasonings: 1 T. white soy sauce
¼ t. sugar
1 t. salt
dash of monosodium glutamate

Directions:
1. Remove old leaves; keep hearts. Wash and drain. Soak dried mushrooms in cold water to soften. Cut in quarters.
2. Heat oil in frying pan. First stir-fry mushrooms. Add green cabbage hearts. Fry, stirring and turning constantly. Add seasonings. Add meat stock. Cook, covered, to boil. When cabbage is nearly done, add cornstarch paste and a little lard.

廣東咕老肉

廣東菜　　　材料：12人份

Sweet and Sour Pork, Cantonese Style

材　料：排骨肉或里肌肉半斤　大青椒小紅椒各一個　酸喬頭六個　蒜末半茶匙　白醬油一湯匙　小鷄蛋一個　炸油半鍋
　　　　藕粉豆粉各二湯匙

調味品：白醋白糖各二湯匙　醬油一茶匙　鹽半茶匙　豆粉一湯匙　蕃茄汁三湯匙　清水六湯匙

做　法：①首將猪肉略洗瀝水，切爲小塊，加入白醬油浸漬，青紅椒對剖洗淨切塊，喬頭一切
　　　　二，拘汁料一一放入碗內攪勻，均置旁備用。
②把鷄蛋加味精打開加入藕粉慢慢調打，再將肉塊放在這蛋粉糊內拌勻。
③把豆粉放盤內用筷子挾出肉塊在豆粉裏滾一滾，使黏上一層乾豆粉一塊塊舖在盤內備炸。
④將油鍋燒至開滾，移至空爐上投入肉塊，再放到文火上炸數分鐘，使肉塊不可外焦肉不熟，要注意火候
　，炸好全部撈出留用。
⑤鍋內留一大匙油，先加入蒜末喬頭及青紅椒爆香，即盛起留用，再把拘汁料倒下，用鏟子不停地攪動，
　視汁稠濃，即可傾下肉塊及已炒過之配料攪勻，即可供食。

Ingredients: ⅔ lb. spareribs or pork fillet　1 sweet green pepper　1 red chili pepper
　　　6 pickled chiao-tou　½ t. minced garlic　1 T. white soy sauce
　　　1 small egg　2 T. lotus root powder　2 T. cornstarch
　　　½ frying pan cooking oil

Seasonings: 2 T. white vinegar　2 T. white sugar　1 T. soy sauce
　　　½ t. salt　1 T. cornstarch　3 T. tomato sauce
　　　6 T. water　dash of monosodium glutamate (M.S.G.)

Directions:
1. Clean meat and drain. Cut into small pieces. Marinate in white soy sauce. Cut sweet green pepper and red chili pepper in half. Clean and cut into pieces. Cut each chiao-tou in half. Mix seasonings.
2. Beat egg; add M.S.G. Add lotus root powder. Beat to mix. Blend with meat.
3. Roll meat in cornstarch to coat.
4. Heat oil to boil. Remove frying pan from heat. Add meat; then return pan. Fry over low heat for a few minutes. Do not burn outside leaving inside still raw.
5. Leave 1 T. oil in pan. Stir-fry garlic, chiao-tou, sweet green pepper and red chili pepper. Remove. Add seasonings. Stir until sauce thickens. Add meat and other ingredients. Stir to mix. Serve.

金鈎嫩芥菜心　　家常菜　　材料：12人份
Mustard Green Hearts and Dried Shrimps

材　料：芥菜嫩心十二兩　　金鈎（蝦米）三湯匙　　花生油五湯匙
調味品：白醬油一湯匙　　鹽一茶匙　　糖半茶匙　　味精少許
做　法：①首將水燒沸，加入少許鹽，糖，味精，將芥菜嫩心川一下，瀝水留用。
②油鍋燒熱，將蝦米略沖水，放入油鍋中去爆香，然後將芥菜心倒下煸炒，速即將鹽、糖、味精、白醬油傾下同炒，放下一點沸水一滾，即可盛起供食。

Ingredients: 12 oz. mustard green hearts　　3 T. dried shrimps
5 T. peanut oil
Seasonings: 1 T. white soy sauce　　1 t. salt
½ t. sugar　　dash of monosodium glutamate
Directions:
1. Cut mustard green hearts in 1½" lengths. Parboil in boiling water seasoned with pinches of salt, sugar and M.S.G. Drain.
2. Heat oil in pan. First stir-fry dried shrimps; add mustard green hearts. Stir-fry a few times. Add salt, sugar M.S.G. and white soy sauce. Turn and toss lightly. Add a little boiling water. Let boil. Remove at once.

八寶辣醬

四川菜　　　材料：12人份

Eight Precious Hot Sauce

材　料：瘦肉丁四兩　碗豆夾半斤或毛豆二兩　洋芋一小只　筍一支（去皮剝殼均切丁蒸熟）　胡蘿蔔一條（刮皮對剖）　蝦米一小碟　豆干八小塊（洗淨切丁）　紅尖辣椒三只（對剖去子切丁，如不愛吃辣，可改用紅色大甜椒）　猪油或花生油半飯碗半茶匙　糖四分之一茶匙

調味品：鹽甜醬各二湯匙　黑醬油一湯匙　白醬油一茶匙　糖鹽各半茶匙　豆粉

做　法：①首將瘦肉丁加入一茶匙醬油及半茶匙豆粉和四分之一茶匙糖拌匀，胡蘿蔔在高湯內煮頓切丁，碗豆剝殼取仁均備用。

②油鍋燒熱後，先將肉丁略炒盛起，隨即倒下豆干及鹽煎炒，然後倒下鹽甜醬及辣椒爆香，隨即傾下洋芋丁，筍丁，胡蘿蔔丁，蝦米等拌炒，並加醬油和糖，最後加入碗豆仁及肉丁，時蓋時炒，約三四次，嚐豆仁已頓，即可盛起供食，宜作便當菜或粥菜。

Ingredients: 4 oz. diced lean pork
⅜ lb. snow peas or 2 oz. fresh soy beans
1 small potato (pared, diced and cooked)
1 bamboo shoot (peeled, diced, and cooked)
1 carrot (pared and halved lengthwise)
1 small saucer dried shrimps
8 pc. dried bean curd (diced)
3 paprikas (halved lengthwise, seeded, and diced; sweet red pepper may be substituted)
½ bowl lard or peanut oil

Seasonings: 2 T. salted bean paste
2 T. sweet flour paste
1 T. black soy sauce
1 t. white soy sauce
½ t. sugar
½ t. salt
½ t. cornstarch

Directions: 1. Combine diced pork with 1 t. soy sauce, ½ t. cornstarch and ¼ t. sugar. Cook carrot in meat stock until soft and dice. Pod snow peas.

2. Heat oil in frying pan. Stir-fry pork and remove. Saute dried bean curd and salt; add salted bean paste, sweet flour paste and paprikas. Stir-fry a few times. Add diced potato, bamboo shoot, carrot and dried shrimps. Stir-fry to mix. Add soy sauce and sugar. Add snow peas and diced pork. Cover and stir-fry alternately 3-4 times, until snow peas are soft. Serve.

沙茶牛肉　　廣東菜

Stir-Fried Beef with Sha-Cha Sauce

材料：12人份

材　料：牛肉半斤（要里肌肉）．菜心一斤　薑一片　醬油一湯匙　沙茶一湯匙　熟花生油五湯匙
　　　　豆粉二茶匙　糖十茶匙

做　法：①牛肉洗淨，把筋剔除，橫紋切絲，加豆粉及醬油、沙茶、糖、薑末熟油拌勻備用。
　　　　②菜心折好洗淨備用。
　　　　③用大火把油燒熱，加油炒菜心，略加鹽糖，熟後裝大盆內備用。
　　　　④再度把鍋燒紅熱，加四湯匙油，隨即將泡好之牛肉下鍋，即刻翻炒五、六下起鍋，舖在
　　　　　菜心上，作飯菜甚佳。

Ingredients:
- 2/3 lb. beef fillet
- 1 slice of ginger
- 1 T. sha-cha sauce
- 1/4 t. sugar
- 1 1/3 lb. green cabbage hearts
- 1 T. soy sauce
- 2 t. cornstarch
- 1 T. peanut oil (cooked)
- 6 T. peanut oil

Directions:
1. Clean beef. Remove tendons; cut against grain into shreds. Mix with cornstarch, soy sauce, sha-cha sauce, sugar, ginger and cooked peanut oil.
2. Trim cabbage hearts. Wash and let dry.
3. Heat oil in frying pan. Stir-fry cabbage hearts. Season with a little salt and sugar. Remove to serving plate.
4. Again heat 4 T. oil in frying pan. Stir-fry marinated beef quickly a few times. Spread on cabbage hearts. Serve.

蠔油牛肉　廣東菜
Stir-Fried Beef with Oyster Sauce

材料：12人份

材　　料：嫩牛肉十二兩　　葱白頭五支　　薑五片　　蘇打粉⅙茶匙　　醬油一湯匙　　鹽糖各半茶匙　　豆粉一湯匙　　冷水二湯匙　　熱花生油二湯匙　　花生油二杯

綜合調味：蠔油二湯匙半　　蔴油數滴　　豆粉半茶匙　　冷水二湯匙

做　　法：①首將牛肉橫紋切成薄片，葱白切成一吋長之段備用。
　　　　　②將蘇打粉醬油鹽糖豆粉及冷水加入牛肉碗中拌勻，約半小時後加入熟花生油調和待炒。
　　　　　②將花生油倒入鍋中，以溫油大火將牛肉炒十數下，卽用濾油器撈出鍋中留一湯匙油爆炒葱薑，卽刻傾入綜合調味及已撈出之牛肉片炒數下，卽可盛起，趁熱送席。
　　　　　（此爲火候菜，請用心學習試炒）

Ingredients:
12 oz. beef fillet	5 stalks green onion (white ends only)	5 slices ginger
⅙ t. soda powder	1 T. soy sauce	½ t. salt
½ t. sugar	1 T. cornstarch	2 T. cold water
2 T. cooked peanut oil	2 C. peanut oil	

Seasoning Sauce (combine):
2½ T. oyster sauce	drops of sesame oil	½ t. cornstarch

Directions:
1. Cut beef against grain into thin slices and green onion into 1" lengths.
2. Combine sliced beef with soda powder, soy sauce, salt, sugar, cornstarch and cold water. Let stand 30 min. Blend in cooked peanut oil.
3. Heat oil in frying pan. Stir-fry beef in warm oil, over high heat, 10 times. Remove and drain oil. Leave 1 T. oil in pan. Fry green onion and ginger. Add seasoning sauce and return beef to pan. Stir-fry a few times. Serve hot.

牛肉蘿蔔絲　　家常菜　　材料：12人份
Stir-Fried Shredded Beef and Turnip

材　料：牛肉絲五兩　蘿蔔一小個（二元）　青蒜葉段一支　薑絲一片酌加豆粉　醬油鹽糖及花生油

做　法：①首將牛肉絲拌入薑絲豆粉醬油糖及冷的熟花生油，蘿蔔去皮切絲備用。
②油鍋燒熱，先爆香白頭，倒下蘿蔔煸炒，並加沸水滾爛後酌加鹽糖及蒜葉，即可盛起，鍋中油燒熱，倒下牛肉絲急炒數下，即刻傾下已熟之蘿蔔絲拌炒一下，即可供食。

Ingredients:
- 3 oz. shredded beef
- 1 stalk green garlic stalk (cut into 1½" sections)
- a little cornstarch
- 4 T. peanut oil
- 1 small turnip
- 1 slice ginger (shredded)
- soy sauce, salt and sugar to taste

Directions:
1. Blend beef with ginger, cornstarch, soy sauce, sugar and cold cooked peanut oil. Pare turnip and shred.
2. Heat oil in frying pan. Fry white garlic ends. Add turnip and stir-fry a few times. Add boiling water. Cook till tender. Add salt, sugar and garlic stalk leaves. Remove.
3. Heat oil again. Drop in shredded beef and stir-fry quickly. Add cooked turnip to pan; stir-fry to mix. Remove and serve.

炒腊肉　湖南菜
Stir-Fried Smoked Pork

材料：12人份

材　料：湖南腊肉半斤　青蒜四支　尖紅辣椒二隻　花生油二湯匙
調味品：白醬油一湯匙　鹽糖各¼茶匙
做　法：①首將腊肉略洗切爲大薄片，青蒜撕去老葉洗淨，切長段留用。
②油鍋燒熱，先爆蒜白頭，卽放下腊肉及青蒜葉，加入鹽糖同炒，要使腊肉嫩而蒜青翠，再調下白醬油不停炒着，片刻盛起供食。

Ingredients:	⅔ lb. Hunan smoked pork	4 stalks green garlic stalk
	2 red chili peppers	2 T. peanut oil
Seasonings:	1 T. white soy sauce	¼ t. salt
	¼ t. sugar	

Directions:
1. Clean pork. Cut into big thin slices. Remove tough leaves of garlic stalks. Cut into 1½" lengths.
2. Heat oil in frying pan. Stir-fry white ends of green garlic stalks. Add smoked pork and green garlic leaves. Add salt and sugar. Stir-fry and add white soy sauce. Fry a few minutes longer. Remove and serve.

醬炒靑蟹　杭州菜
Stir-Fried Crabs with Bean Paste Sauce

材料：12人份

材　料：青蟹四隻　葱薑屑各一湯匙　猪油花生油各二湯匙
調味品：黑白醬油各一湯匙　鹽甜醬各二茶匙　糖半茶匙　鹽¼茶匙　酒一湯匙
做　法：①首將青蟹斬去大脚，細細洗淨，每隻去大殼，斬為四塊留用。
②次將油鍋燒熱，放下四湯匙油爆炒薑屑，即將蟹置鍋內略炒，然後下鹽甜醬略爆，再酒下酒及醬油糖滾燒片刻，即加沸水半飯碗滾燒十分鐘，然後加入葱屑一兜，裝盆送席，味極濃香鮮美，酒飯兩宜，誠為秋季之佳餚。

Ingredients:	4 crabs	1 T. chopped green onion	1 T. chopped ginger
	2 T. lard	2 T. peanut oil	
Seasonings:	1 T. black soy sauce	1 T. white soy sauce	2 t. salted bean paste
	2 t. sweet flour paste	½ t. sugar	¼ t. salt
	1 T. wine		

Directions:
1. Remove crab claws. Clean crabs thoroughly. Shell and cut each in four.
2. Heat 4 T. oil in frying pan. Stir-fry ginger. Add crabs and fry, turning constantly. Add salted bean paste and sweet flour paste. Stir to mix. Sprinkle with wine, soy sauce and sugar. Let simmer 2-3 min. Add ½ bowl boiling water. Simmer 10 min. Add green onion. Cook another 30 sec. Remove and serve.

生炒黃蜆　　台灣菜

Stir-Fried Fresh Clams

材料：12人份

　材　料：選購殼黃而大粒之新鮮黃蜆一斤　蒜屑二粒　葱屑一湯匙　薑屑二茶匙　沙茶醬一茶匙
　　　　　花生油三調羹　豆瓣醬、甜麵醬各一茶匙
　調味品：黑醬油一湯匙　白醬油二茶匙　鹽、糖各半茶匙
　做　法：①將黃蜆浸入放點花生油之清水中二、三小時，然後用擦帚擦洗潔淨，瀝水留用。
　　　　　②鍋中把油燒熱，放下蒜屑，葱薑屑及鹹甜醬爆香，然後傾下黃蜆爛炒，同時加入調味品
　　　　　同炒，視黃蜆殼裂，立刻取入盆中，逐只取出，待全取完，加入葱薑屑溜勻，把湯汁澆
　　　　　在已盛盆中之黃蜆內，味特鮮美

Ingredients:　1 & 1/3 lb. fresh clams　　　　　2 cloves garlic (chopped)
　　　　　　　　1 T. chopped green onion　　　3 T. peanut oil
　　　　　　　　1 t. sha-cha sauce　　　　　　 1 t. bean paste
　　　　　　　　1 t. sweet flour paste　　　　　3 slices ginger (chopped)

Seasonings:　1 T. black soy sauce　　　　　 2 t. white soy sauce
　　　　　　　 1/2 t. salt　　　　　　　　　　　1/2 t. sugar

Directions:　1. Add a little oil to 2-3 C. water. Soak clams 2-3 hr. and clean.
　　　　　　　　2. Heat peanut oil in frying pan. Fry chopped garlic, 1/2 green onion, 1/2 ginger, sha-cha sauce, and bean and sweet flour paste. Add clams and seasonings, stirring and turning constantly 1 min. As shells open, take out one by one and place on plate. Fry remaining chopped ginger and green onion in sauce. Pour over clams and serve.

醬爆櫻桃

湖 南 菜   材料：12人份

Stir-Fried Frog Legs with Bean Paste

材　料：田鷄腿一斤　大青椒二只　紅辣椒二只　蒜頭二粒　薑五薄片　鹽甜醬 各二茶匙　醬油一茶匙　酒一湯匙　鹽¼茶匙　豆粉半茶匙　鷄蛋清一湯匙　猪油三湯匙　花生油二湯匙

做　法：①首將田鷄洗淨，斬下雙腿，形似櫻桃，故有此名，將腿置碗內，加入鹽蛋白豆粉拌勻備用。
②先以少油爆炒青椒盛起，又將油鍋燒熱，傾下櫻桃爆炒數下即刻撈出濾去剩油，仍留鍋內放下紅辣椒蒜頭薑片鹽甜醬及酒爆炒片刻，加下三湯匙水煮燒一下，即倒下已炒好之青椒及爆過之櫻桃及醬油兜炒得湯汁濃後盛起，趁熱上席。

Ingredients:
- 1⅓ lb. frog legs
- 2 red chili pepper (diced)
- 5 thin slices ginger
- 2 t. sweet flour paste
- 1 T. wine
- ½ t. cornstarch
- 2 T. peanut oil
- 2 sweet green pepper (cut in cubes)
- 2 cloves garlic
- 2 t. salted bean paste
- 1 t. soy sauce
- ¼ t. salt
- 1 T. egg white

Directions:
1. Clean frogs. Remove legs and mix with salt, egg white and cornstarch.
2. Heat a little oil. Stir-fry green pepper 1-2 min. Remove. Heat remaining oil. Stir-fry frog legs 1 min. Remove. Leave oil in frying pan. Add red chili pepper, garlic cloves, ginger, salt bean paste, sweet flour paste and wine. Stir-fry a few seconds. Then add 3 T. water. Let simmer. Return green pepper and frog legs to pan. Add soy sauce. Stir-fry until sauce is thickened. Serve hot.

滑蛋牛肉　　廣東菜
Stir-Fried Beef with Eggs

材料：12人份

材　料：嫩牛肉四兩　鷄蛋八只　葱屑二湯匙　嫩筋、嫩薑末少許　豆粉二茶匙　熟花生油少許
　　　　花生油十湯匙

調味品：白醬油二茶匙　鹽一茶匙　味精少許

做　法：①首將牛肉橫紋切薄片，加入嫩筋、嫩薑末及清水拌勻，約十分鐘後，加豆粉及白醬油拌勻，隔炒前加入熟花生油少許拌勻，鷄蛋去殼打入碗內，加入鹽及葱屑味精打散備用。
　　　　②炒菜鍋燒熱，倒下花生油，以溫油大火將牛肉倒下炒數下盛起，速卽倒在已打散之鷄蛋內撈勻，卽刻倒下已留油之炒菜鍋內，以大火炒數下，火速盛起，以蕃茄片，黃瓜斜塊飾邊送席。

Ingredients:
4 oz. beef fillet
2 T. chopped green onion
1 t. chopped young ginger
1 t. cooked peanut oil
8 eggs
1 t. tenderizer
2 t. cornstarch
10 T. peanut oil

Seasonings:
2 t. white soy sauce
dash of monosodium glutamate
1 t. salt

Directions:
1. Slice beef thinly; add tenderizer, ginger and water. Mix well and let stand 10 min. Add cornstarch and white soy sauce. Mix. Before frying blend in cooked peanut oil. Beat eggs combined with salt, chopped green onion and M.S.G.
2. Heat oil in frying pan. Fry beef in warm oil, over high heat, tossing constantly. Remove and blend with egg mixture. Leave oil in pan. Pour contents into pan and fry over high heat 10 sec. Remove to serving plate.
3. Garnish with pieces of tomato and cucumber on sides and serve.

蝦仁跑蛋
Shrimp Omelet

杭州菜　　　　材料：12人份

材　料：鷄蛋四只　蝦仁二兩　葱屑一湯匙　猪油四大匙
調味品：鹽半茶匙又¼茶匙　豆粉半茶匙　酒¼茶匙　味精少許
做　法：①首將蝦仁洗淨瀝乾，調入酒，豆粉及¼茶匙鹽拌勻，以一大匙油放鍋內燒熱，將蝦仁過炒盛起待冷備用。
②備碗一只，將鷄蛋打下，加入鹽半茶匙和味精少許打散，再將蝦仁與葱屑調入。
③用平底鍋把油燒熱將蛋汁整碗傾下，視已凝結，火速翻面，使蝦仁包在蛋內迅速盛盆供食。

Ingredients:	4 eggs	2 oz. shrimps (shelled)
	1 T. chopped green onion	4 T. lard
Seasonings:	¾ t. salt	½ t. cornstarch
	¼ t. wine	dash of monosodium glutamate

Directions:
1. Clean and drain shrimps. Mix with wine, cornstarch and ¼ t. salt. Heat 1 T. oil in frying pan. Stir-fry shrimps. Remove and let cool.
2. Beat eggs mixed with ½ t. salt and monosodium glutamate. Stir in shrimps and chopped green onions.
3. Heat oil in skillet. Add egg mixture. Cook until eggs begin to set. Invert quickly. Cook till bottom side is lightly brown. Serve.

炒四季豆　家常菜　　材料：12人份
Stir-Fried String Beans

材　料：四季豆十兩　香腸二條或火腿片一小碟　蝦米一小碟　豬油或花生油三大匙
調味品：白醬油一湯匙　鹽半茶匙　糖¼茶匙
做　法：①首將香腸切斜片，蝦米以溫水泡浸，四季豆撕筋折為二段後洗淨瀝乾。
②油鍋燒熱倒下四季豆和鹽糖拌炒，然後關蓋，開蓋時炒，經過數次，視豆皮有縐紋，卽放下蝦米香腸及白醬油炒勻後，再加下沸水半飯碗，關蓋燜燒片刻視四季豆已軟，盛起供食，請客時也可湊上這一道色香味俱全的菜。

Ingredients: 10 oz. string beans　　2 Chinese sausages or 2 oz. sliced Chinese ham
　　　　　　　2 oz. dried shrimps　　3 T. lard or peanut oil
Seasonings: 1 T. white soy sauce　½ t. salt
　　　　　　　¼ t. sugar
Directions: 1. Slice sausages diagonally. Soak shrimps in warm water. Remove fibers from string beans and cut each in half. Wash and drain.
2. Heat oil in frying pan. Fry string beans; season with salt and sugar. Cover and stir-fry alternately until beans are wrinkled. Add shrimps, sausages and white soy sauce. Stir-fry to mix. Add ½ bowl boiling water. Cover. Braise till beans are tender. Serve.

火腿花菜　　地方菜
Stir-Fried Cauliflower and Chinese Ham

材料：12人份

材　料：花菜一小顆(重約十二兩)　火腿片與蝦米各一小碟　油、花生油二大匙
調味品：白醬油一湯匙　鹽糖各半茶匙
做　法：①首將花菜整個洗淨，然後用刀劈下，撕去梗皮，切作粒花形，再略洗瀝水，蝦米放在濾油器內略洗，即用溫水泡　，均備用。
②鍋中放油燒熱，先倒下花菜煸炒，並加下鹽糖炒數下後，撈下蝦米及火腿片炒數下。即調入白醬油和浸蝦米之水，再略加沸水，然後關蓋滾燒，視花菜已酥，即可盛起供食，吃時花菜以辣豆瓣醬蘸食，味更鮮美，而增進食慾。
附　註：如用肉片炒，肉片應先調入豆粉和白醬油少許，但宜先炒肉片盛起，再炒花菜，待最後再放下肉片即可。

Ingredients: 1 cauliflower (about 12 oz.)　　1-2 oz. sliced Chinese ham
　　　　　　 1-2 oz. dried shrimps　　　　　　2 T. peanut oil

Seasonings: 1 T. white soy sauce　　　　　　½ t. salt
　　　　　　 ½ t. sugar

Directions:
1. Remove hard stem of cauliflower and separate flowerets. Wash and drain. Clean dried shrimps; soak in warm water.
2. Heat oil in pan. Stir-fry cauliflower; add salt and sugar. Add shrimps and ham. Stir-fry a few times. Add white soy sauce, soaking liquid and a little boiling water. Boil, covered, until cauliflower is tender, but still crunchy. Remove and serve. Hot bean paste may be served as dip sauce.

Note: If pork slices are used instead of ham, first mix with a little cornstarch and white soy sauce. Fry pork first, cauliflower next. Combine and serve.

蟹粉芥蘭　廣東菜　材料：12人份
Mustard Green and Crabs

材　料：雌蟹二大只　大芥菜心一斤半　高湯一飯碗　蘇打粉半茶匙　薑二片　猪油五湯匙　豆粉一茶匙（用水調和）
調味品：鹽一茶匙　白醬油一茶匙　糖半茶匙　酒一茶匙半

做　法：①首將菜心切去葉子，削去菜頭洗淨瀝水，切為長塊大小一律留用。
②鍋中燒沸水三飯碗，先加入蘇打粉，然後放下菜心略燙熟，即撈在竹蘿內，用清水沖去蘇打味瀝水備用。
③雌蟹先斬去大脚，細細洗淨，放在盆內，加入薑和半茶匙酒，以大火隔水蒸約十五分鐘，取出剝殼拆取蟹肉，如有蟹膏另放碗內，加入高湯半飯碗打散調稀留用。
④將四湯匙猪油燒熱，先把蟹肉爆炒，加入酒和白醬油炒數下，再將菜心倒下，即加入鹽糖拌炒，然後再傾下高湯半飯碗滾數透，即放下調稀之蟹膏及水豆粉，用鏟子不停地攪動，拘成薄稠狀，最後加入一湯匙猪油，即將菜心盛入細瓷長盆中，再澆上蟹肉蟹膏，趁熱上席。

附　註：『燙菜心如不用蘇打粉，可以鹽糖火煮沸來燙亦可』

Ingredients:
- 2 big female crabs
- 1 bowl meat stock
- 2 slices ginger
- 1 t. cornstarch (mixed with 2 T. water)
- 2 lb. mustard green hearts
- ½ t. soda powder
- 5 T. lard

Seasonings:
- 1 t. salt
- ½ t. sugar
- 1 t. white soy sauce
- 1½ t. wine

Directions:
1. Remove leaves from mustard green hearts. Wash hearts and drain. Cut in lengths.
2. Remove claws from crabs. Wash thoroughly. Place on plate. Sprinkle with ginger and ½ t. wine. Steam above water over high heat about 15 min. Remove shells. Put yolk (if any) in bowl and mix with ½ bowl meat stock.
3. Heat 4 T. lard in frying pan. Stir-fry crab meat. Add wine and white soy sauce. Stir-fry a few times. Add mustard green hearts, salt and sugar. Stir-fry to combine. Pour in ½ bowl meat stock. Let boil. Add crab yolk diluted in meat stock and cornstarch paste. Turn continuously with spatula until sauce thickens. Add 1 T. lard. Place hearts first in serving plate. Pour crab meat and yolk sauce over. Serve hot.

肉末豇豆
Minced Pork with Kidney Beans

家常菜　　　　　材料：12人份

材　料：豇豆半斤（選購青綠色而結實的）　豬腿肉四兩　鷄蛋一只　花生油三湯匙
調味品：白醬油一湯匙　鹽半茶匙又４分之１茶匙　豆粉，糖各４分之１茶匙　味精少許
做　法：①首將豬肉洗淨瀝乾斬碎，調入白醬油一茶匙和豆粉與糖。
②次將豇豆折去兩頭，然後洗淨切爲三、四分長之小段，鷄蛋加鹽與味精打散，均置旁備用。
③用油燒熱，先把豬肉過油一炒盛起，然後倒入豇豆放下鹽糖炒之，時蓋時炒，視豇豆略軟，即倒下肉末，與白醬油，略加沸水燒滾，片刻即調下已打散之鷄蛋攪勻，即可供食，這是一道家常經濟而營養之飯菜。

Ingredients: ⅔ lb. kidney beans　　　　　4 oz. pork (leg part)
　　　　　　　1 egg　　　　　　　　　　　3 T. peanut oil

Seasonings: 1 T. white soy sauce　　　　　¾ t. salt
　　　　　　　¼ t. cornstarch　　　　　　　¼ t. sugar
　　　　　　　dash of monosodium glutamate

Directions:
1. Clean pork and drain water. Mince. Mix with 1 t. white soy sauce, cornstarch and sugar.
2. Remove ends of kidney beans. Wash and cut each into about ½" long pieces. Beat egg seasoned with salt and M.S.G.
3. Heat oil in frying pan. Stir-fry minced pork 1 min. Remove. Stir-fry kidney beans in remaining oil. Add salt and sugar. Cover and stir-fry alternately until beans are somewhat tender. Add pork and remaining white soy sauce. Add a little boiling water. Let simmer. Stir in beaten egg and serve.

蝴蝶蝦　廣東菜
Butterfly Prawns

材料：12人份

材　料：明蝦十二隻　略帶肥的火腿十二薄片（與明蝦同樣大）　生菜葉四張　莞荽三支　胡椒少許　醋、辣、醬油兩小碟　花生油四湯匙
調味品：白醬油兩茶匙　豆粉一湯匙　酒一茶匙　鷄蛋白兩湯匙
做　法：①將生菜與莞荽洗淨，以灰錳養水浸洗，並以冷開水沖洗吹乾備用。
②將明蝦切去頭，剝殼留尾，從背上深深劃到尾邊，抽出泥臟，洗淨瀝乾後以調味品浸漬備用。
③取一片火腿，塗點水豆粉，蓋在每隻明蝦腹面，至尾邊形似蝴蝶，逐隻做完約二十分鐘後，才可下鍋煎。
④備平底鍋一隻，加下花生油二湯匙，排下明蝦六隻，先以火腿面向油略煎，再翻面煎明蝦。此時明蝦尾已豎立，煎至明蝦可以筷子觸入（約二三分鐘），即可取出排列已放生菜葉的細瓷長盆中，蝦身在盆邊，蝦尾向裡，一圈紅尾直立中間，非常美觀，這時，以胡椒粉灑蝦身，莞荽三支飾於蝦尾，誠爲宴客的上菜。

Ingredients: 12 prawns
4 lettuce leaves
dash of pepper
4 T. peanut oil
12 slices ham with a little fat (sliced thinly, same size as prawn)
3 sprigs parsley
2 saucers hot-sour soy sauce

Seasonings: 2 t. white soy sauce
1 t. wine
1 T. cornstarch
2 T. egg whites

Directions:
1. Wash lettuce leaves and parsley. Soak in sodium permanganate solution. Rinse with cold boiled water and let dry.
2. Remove prawn heads; shell, devein and butterfly, leaving tails intact. Clean and drain. Soak in seasonings.
3. Moisten ham slices with a little cornstarch paste. Place on underside of prawn to form "butterfly wings." Let stand 20 min.
4. Heat oil in skillet. Fry prawns six at a time, ham side first; turn and fry prawns until tails stick up and chopstick can penetrate flesh (about 2-3 min.). Arrange prawns, tails inward, on oblong serving plate covered with lettuce. Sprinkle with pepper. Garnish center with parsley. Serve with hot-sour soy sauce as dip.

魚肉蛋捲　　廣　東　菜
Egg Rolls with Fish Meat

材料：12人份

材　料：刺少的魚肉一塊約半斤　肥肉一兩　鷄蛋三只　蝦油一茶匙　豆粉一湯　薑二片　葱二支
　　　　匙　胡椒粉少許　鹽一茶匙　糖酒_士茶匙　肥肉二兩

做　法：①首將魚肉去皮拆骨取肉斬碎肥肉亦斬入，加蝦油豆粉鹽糖酒胡椒粉拌勻備用。
　　　　②鷄蛋去壳加鹽打開，用油在平底鍋內煎攤成鷄蛋餅，把蛋餅舖在菜板上，塗上濕的水豆粉，再將魚肉抹勻在餅上，然後捲成一條鷄蛋捲。
　　　　③用平底鍋放油把蛋捲煎至魚熟。
　　　　④煎好後切成小圓片，排列在盆中，黃白相間好看又好吃。

Ingredients: ⅔ lb. fish meat (with as little bones as possible)
3 eggs
1 T. cornstarch
1 t. salt
¼ t. wine
2 stalks green onion
1 oz. pork fat
1 t. shrimp sauce
dash of pepper
¼ t. sugar
2 slices ginger
2 T. peanut oil

Directions:
1. Skin and bone fish. Mince fish meat with pork fat. Combine with shrimp sauce, cornstarch, salt, sugar, wine and pepper.
2. Beat eggs seasoned with salt. Grease and heat skillet. Add eggs and tilt skillet so that mixture spreads thinly and evenly. Remove to cutting board. Moisten with cornstarch paste. Spread minced fish mixture on egg skin and roll into egg roll.
3. Saute egg roll in skillet till contents are done.
4. Cut in slices and arrange neatly on serving plate. Serve.

雪菜鯽魚　　杭州菜　　　　　　材料：12人份
Bastard Carps and Pickled Mustard Greens

材　料：活鯽魚一斤（約四尾）　新雪裡紅（碎）四湯匙　薑四片　花生油四大匙
調味品：鹽一茶匙半　白醬油二茶匙　黑醬油一茶匙　酒一湯匙　糖半茶匙
做　法：①首將鯽魚刮鱗剖肚，去鰓及內臟，略洗瀝水，在每尾魚背輕割二刀，用鹽敷每尾魚之肚內外，備用。
②油鍋燒熱，先用一塊薑遍擦鍋內，然後放下油，待熱先投下薑片，再放下魚煎微黃，即洒下酒，推魚在一旁，再倒下雪菜略炒，然後將雪裡紅蓋在魚面，調下黑白醬油及糖，加下一點沸水，關蓋滾燒片刻，即可盛起供食。

Ingredients: 1⅓ lb. live bastard carps (about 4)　4 T. newly pickled mustard greens (chopped)
4 slices ginger　4 T. peanut oil

Seasonings: 1½ t. salt　2 t. white soy sauce
1 t. black soy sauce　1 T. wine
½ t. sugar

Directions:
1. Scale fish; remove gills and entrails. Wash slightly and drain. Score two cuts on both sides. Rub fish with salt inside and out.
2. Heat frying pan; rub inside with ginger. Then heat oil until hot. Drop in ginger. Saute fish till tight brown. Sprinkle with wine. Move fish to one side. Stir-fry pickled mustard green in remaining oil. Move fish to center and cover with pickled mustard green. Add black and white soy sauce, sugar and a little boiling water. Cook, covered, 3-4 min. Serve.

辣豆瓣鯉魚　四川菜　Carp with Hot Bean Sauce

材料：12人份

材　料：活鯉魚一尾（重約一斤）　葱薑屑各一湯匙　莞荽三支　酒釀二湯匙　猪油一湯匙　花生油三湯匙　豆粉一茶匙（用三湯匙水調濕）

調味品：醬油一湯匙　鹽一茶匙　糖半茶匙　酒一茶匙

做　法：①首將鯉魚刮鱗去內臟，洗淨瀝乾，然後先灑鹽，再加醬油泡浸約半小時。
②油鍋燒熱，落薑爆香，即投下鯉魚略煎再放下酒和酒釀及辣豆瓣醬糖和浸魚之汁，即傾下高湯二大匙，關蓋燜燒片刻，然後加入葱莞荽及一湯匙猪油，再調下水豆粉，即刻盛起送席。

Ingredients:
- 1 live carp (about 1 ⅓ lb.)
- 1 T. chopped green onion
- 3 sprigs parsley
- 1 T. lard
- 1 t. cornstarch (mixed with 3 T. water to make paste)
- 1 T. hot bean paste
- 1 T. chopped ginger
- 2 T. sweet fermented glutinous rice
- 3 T. peanut oil
- 2 T. meat stock

Seasonings:
- 1 T. soy sauce
- ½ t. sugar
- 1 t. salt
- 1 t. wine

Directions:
1. Scale and clean crap thoroughly. Sprinkle with salt and soak in soy sauce about 30 min.
2. Heat oil in frying pan. Fry ginger and green onion quickly; put in carp and fry on both sides, 3-4 min. Add wine, sweet fermented glutinous rice, hot bean paste, sugar, remaining marinade and 2 T. meat stock. Cook, covered, 3-4 min. Add parsley and lard. Stir in cornstarch paste to thicken and serve.

油淋乳鴿　　　湖　南　菜　　　材料：12人份
Oil Dripped Young Pigeons

材　　料：	乳鴿三只　葱二支　薑二片　花椒½茶匙　蔴油二湯匙　鹽一茶匙
綜合調味：	黑醬油一湯匙　白醬油二茶匙　糖半茶匙　酒一茶匙　胡椒少許　花椒½茶匙
做　　法：	①首將已殺好之乳鴿從背面剪開，取出內臟，棄去脚及腸不用，然後洗淨瀝水放在盆中，先加入一茶匙鹽，再加入綜合調味，至少泡浸一小時，再將葱薑用刀拍碎，放置鴿面。 ②將鴿隔水大火蒸約廿分鐘，離火取出趁熱斬開，先將頭及肫肝墊盆底然後逐只斬成八塊排列入盆，以蒸鴿之湯二大匙澆在鴿塊面上。 ③將鍋燒熱，放下二大匙蔴油，爆炒½茶匙花椒，卽離鍋離火撈出花椒，淋香蔴油於鴿面趁熱上席。

Ingredients:
- 3 young pigeons
- 2 slices ginger (crushed)
- 2 T. sesame oil
- 2 stalks green onions (crushed)
- ¼ peppercorn
- 1 t. salt

Seasoning Sauce (combine):
- 1 T. black soy sauce
- ½ t. sugar
- dash of pepper
- 2 t. white soy sauce
- 1 t. wine
- ¼ t. peppercorn

Directions:
1. Remove pigeon feet; keep heads and giblets. Sprinkle with 1 t. salt. Marinate in seasoning sauce at least 1 hr. Place green onion and ginger on pigeon.
2. Steam pigeons over high heat about 20 min., remove and cut each into 8 pieces. Arrange on serving plate; put heads and giblets beneath. Pour 2 T. stock over pigeons.
3. Heat 2 T. sesame oil in pan. Fry ¼ t. peppercorn, tossing slightly. Discard peppercorn and pour sesame oil over pigeons.

蛤蜊蒸蛋　　家常菜
Steamed Eggs with Clams

材料：12人份

材　料：	蛤蜊（選購重的）十二只（重約十二兩）　火腿小丁一湯匙　鷄鴨蛋各一隻　葱花一支　猪油一湯匙　冷開水少許
調味品：	鹽一茶匙　味精與黑醬油少許
做　法：	①首將蛤蜊浸水約二、三小時，將外殼一一刷洗潔淨瀝水，鷄鴨蛋加鹽和味精放入大碗內打散。
	②備小鋁鍋傾下沸水二飯碗將蛤蜊倒下關蓋片刻，視蛤蜊開殼，卽刻撈在盆內，將湯汁傾入碗內待冷。
	③將全部蛤蜊放在蛋汁中，並加入火腿丁，猪油，葱花，及已冷之蛤蜊湯，再加些冷開水用筷子慢慢使蛋與水攪勻，以大火隔水蒸約二十分鐘開蓋，面洒黑醬油少許，取出趁熱供食。

Ingredients: 12 clams (about 12 oz.)
2 eggs (1 chicken, 1 duck)
1 T. lard
1 T. diced ham
1 stalk green onion (chopped)
cold water (boiled)

Seasonings: 1 t. salt
dash of monosodium glutamate
a few drops black soy sauce

Directions:
1. Immerse clams in water 2-3 hr. Brush and clean outer shells and drain. Beat eggs seasoned with salt and M.S.G. in large bowl.
2. Pour 2 bowls boiling water in pot. Put in clams. Cover 3-4 min. When clam shells open, remove to plate. Save soup and let cool.
3. Put clams into egg bowl; add diced ham, lard, green onion and clam soup. Add a little cold boiled water. Mix well. Steam above water, over high heat, about 20 min. Sprinkle with black soy sauce. Serve hot.

燻 鷄　北平菜
Smoked Chicken

材料：12人份

材　料：肥嫩鷄一隻　鹽三茶匙　小茴香一茶匙　葱一支　薑一片　酒一茶匙

做　法：將肥嫩鷄一隻，全身擦三茶匙鹽，約二小時後，肚內放入茴香一茶匙，葱一支，薑一片，洒下一茶匙酒，在大火上隔水蒸二十分鐘，將鷄取出，以醬油二湯匙，加點蔴油攪勻，塗在鷄的全身，然將鷄放在架上，移至鍋中用茶葉二兩，紅糖二湯匙及木屑少許上去燻，約燻五六分鐘，開蓋塗上醬油，與蔴油再密蓋燻十餘分鐘，視鷄全身透黃，即可取出斬塊，可保持多日不壞。

Ingredients:
- 1 fat young chicken
- 3 t. salt
- 1 t. aniseed
- 1 stalk green onion
- 1 slice ginger
- 1 t. wine
- sesame oil

Materials for smoking:
- 2 oz. black tea leaves
- 2 T. brown sugar
- a little sawdust

Directions:
1. Rub chicken with 3 t. salt. Let stand 2 hr. Put in stomach: aniseed, green onion, ginger and wine. Steam above water, over high heat, 20 min. Brush chicken with 2 T. soy sauce mixed with a little sesame oil.
2. To smoke: Mix black tea leaves, brown sugar and sawdust in pot. Place chicken with plate on top of mixture. Heat pot, covered, to smoke, 5-6 min. Uncover and baste chicken with soy sauce and sesame oil. Cover and heat 10-15 min. longer or until chicken is golden. Remove and cut into pieces.

清蒸河鰻
White Steamed Eel

江 浙 菜　　　　材料：12人份

材　料：肥嫩河鰻一條（重約十兩）　火腿絲香菇絲　嫩薑絲葱段各數條　猪油少許
調味品：白醬油一湯匙　鹽半茶匙　酒一茶匙
做　法：①首將河鰻整條洗淨，然後在頭上斬一刀，破開腹部，取出內臟，在背上斬約一寸多長之段，但腹部不斬斷，盤攏放在盆內，先洒下鹽，再加入酒和白醬油然後一一加入配料備用。
②鍋中水燒沸，將河鰻放入鍋內，隔水蒸約一小時，其間要加蒸水一次，視河鰻已蒸至肉嫩鮮美，取出趁熱送席，亦可洒點胡椒粉。

Ingredients:	1 fresh water eel (10 oz.)	1 oz. shredded Chinese ham
	1 oz. shredded mushrooms	1 oz. shredded young ginger
	1 oz. shredded green onion	
Seasonings:	1 T. white soy sauce	½ t. salt
	1 t. wine	

Directions:
1. Remove head. Cut eel into 1½" sections, but leave underside unbroken. Place in a coil on plate. Sprinkle with salt; add wine and white soy sauce. Put rest of ingredients on top of eel.
2. Boil water in pot. Put in eel with plate and steam about 1 hr. (Add water if water boils dry). Remove after 1 hr., or when eel is tender. Serve hot. (Optional: sprinkle with dash of pepper.)

汽鍋雞
Steamed Chicken

江浙菜　　　　材料：12人份

材　料：嫩雞一隻（重約二斤以內）　火腿十二片　厚冬菇六只　冬筍二支　薑四片　酒一茶匙
　　　　鹽一茶匙　汽鍋一隻（碗店有售）

做　法：①首將已退毛，去內臟的雞洗淨，瀝乾後斬塊，冬菇略洗浸溫水發透後去蒂，一切兩塊。冬筍去殼，修頭後切片，均備用。
　　　　②備汽鍋一隻先放下雞頭、雞腳、雞翅、雞背等墊底，雞胸、雞腿等舖面，然後排上火腿片，元形冬菇及筍片等，面加薑花片；但要排得藝術化些，以增美觀隨即洒下酒一茶匙如有餘下筍片，可墊在雞肉下面。
　　　　③備大鋁鍋一隻，待水滾把汽鍋放下（水在汽鍋中腰），以大火隔水蒸十分鐘後，即刻提出汽鍋，墊下高脚盤一個，再將汽鍋置在盤上，約蒸一小時許，視雞已爛，即刻加鹽一茶匙，再蒸一刻鐘，取出送席。

Ingredients: 2⅔ lb. young chicken　　　　12 slices ham
　　　　　　　6 dried mushrooms　　　　　2 winter bamboo shoots
　　　　　　　4 slices ginger　　　　　　　1 t. wine
　　　　　　　1 t. salt

Directions:
1. Clean chicken and drain. Cut into 1"X1½" pieces. Clean and soak mushrooms in warm water to soften. Stem and cut in half. Peel winter bamboo shoots; remove tough parts and slice.
2. First put chicken head, feet, wings and back in boiler. Next place breast and legs on top. Then arrange ham, mushrooms and bamboo shoots decoratively in over-lapping layers on top of breast and legs. Top with ginger slices. Sprinkle with 1 t. wine. (Put extra slices of bamboo shoots, if any, under chicken.)
3. Fill large pot with water. Bring to boil. Put in boiler (water should reach ½ height of boiler). Steam over high heat 10 min. Remove and put in a rack. Put boiler on rack. Steam about 1 hr. or until chicken is tender. Sprinkle with salt; steam another 15 min. Serve.

臘鯗蒸蛋
Steamed Eggs with Dried Salted Fish

杭 州 菜　　　　材料：12人份

材　料：臘鯗一段（選購尾部上段肉較多）　鷄鴨蛋二只　豬肉三兩　筍半支　葱一支　薑一片
　　　　蒜頭一粒
調味品：白醬油二茶匙　豆粉、鹽、糖各四分之一茶匙　酒一茶匙　豬油少許
做　法：①首將臘鯗洗淨（不刮鱗）瀝乾裝盆中。
　　　　②須將豬肉加筍與葱同斬碎，調入白醬油豆粉與糖備用。
　　　　③臘鯗面拍碎之蒜頭薑絲及少許豬油然後舖上豬肉，又在臘鯗之兩旁打下鷄蛋各一枚，蛋
　　　　　上加鹽，以沸水蒸十分鐘即可。

Ingredients:
- 1 section of salted fish (select fleshy part nearest tail)
- 3 oz. pork
- 1 stalk green onion
- 1 clove garlic (shredded)
- 2 eggs (chicken or duck)
- ½ bamboo shoot
- 1 slice ginger (shredded)

Seasonings:
- 2 t. white soy sauce
- ¼ t. salt
- 1 t. wine
- ¼ t. cornstarch
- ¼ t. sugar
- a little lard

Directions:
1. Clean dried salted fish (do not scale); drain and place on plate. Chop pork, bamboo shoot and green onion; mix together with white soy sauce, cornstarch and sugar.
2. First put crushed garlic clove, shredded ginger and lard on salted fish. Next spread chopped pork on top. Place eggs one on each side of fish. Season eggs with salt. Steam above boiling water about 10 min.

滑油蒸鷄　　廣東菜

Steamed Chicken with Oil

材料：12人份

材　料：	嫩鷄半隻或鷄胸脯一個　香菇三只　香腸一條　筍一小支　葱二支（切斜條）薑二片（切小菱形）　豆粉一湯匙半
調味品：	鹽半茶匙　酒半茶匙　白醬油一湯匙　熟花生油一湯匙
做　法：	①首將鷄洗淨斬小塊後，將鹽與酒拌入備用。 ②香菇洗淨泡發切塊，香腸與筍均切片。 ③將鷄塊在豆粉中逐塊一滾，然後排列盆中，面飾香菇，香腸，筍片，葱，薑等，再澆上白醬油與熟花生油，在沸水中蒸十分鐘，即可供食，亦可給小孩帶便當。

Ingredients:
½ tender chicken or 1 chicken breast
1 Chinese sausage
2 stalks green onions (cut into diagonal strips)
1½ T. cornstarch
3 dried mushrooms
1 bamboo shoot
2 slices ginger (cut into small diamond-shaped slices)

Seasonings:
½ t. salt
1 T. white soy sauce
½ t. wine
1 T. cooked peanut oil

Directions:
1. Clean and cut chicken into 1" squares; marinate with wine and salt.
2. Wash and soak dried mushrooms in warm water to soften; cut in quarters. Slice sausage and bamboo shoot.
3. Coat chicken pieces with cornstarch. Arrange them on a plate neatly. Spread mushrooms, sausage, bamboo shoot and ginger slices over chicken. Pour white soy sauce and cooked peanut oil on top. Steam over boiling water about 10 min. and serve.

牛肉包心菜　　廣　東　菜　　材料：12人份
Beef Wrapped in Cabbage

材　料：包心菜一斤　牛肉半斤　肥猪肉一元　葱二支　薑一片　鹽半茶匙
調味品：黑醬油一湯匙　白醬油一茶匙　鹽糖各半匙　豆粉二茶匙　蔴油少許
做　法：①首將包心菜攀下整張葉（約十二張），洗淨瀝水，牛肉略洗，細切細斬，肥肉葱薑也一同斬入，然後將調味品一一拌勻，並分爲十二堆。
②鍋中燒沸水三飯碗，將包心菜葉投入燙輭，即撈出瀝水待冷。
③將每張菜葉放在菜板上，挑下一堆肉包成長方形，舖在大盤中，逐具包完，用半茶匙鹽洒在菜包上，以沸水用大火，隔水蒸約十五分鐘，即可供食，亦可作便當菜。

Ingredients: 1 head cabbage　　⅔ lb. beef　　2 oz. pork fat
2 stalks green onion　1 slice ginger　3 sprigs parsley
½ t. salt

Seasonings: 1 t. black soy sauce　1 t. white soy sauce　½ t. salt
½ t. sugar　2 t. cornstarch　a little sesame oil

Directions: 1. Peel 12 leaves, each whole, from cabbage.
2. Chop beef, pork fat, green onion and ginger, and mix. Add seasonings, and mix well. Divide mixture into 12 portions.
3. Boil 3 bowls of water in pot and put in leaves 1-2 min. to soften. Remove, drain and let cool.
4. Wrap each portion of beef into oblong shape with leaf. Place on large serving plate; sprinkle with salt. Steam over high heat, 15 min., and serve.

紅豆腐乳扣肉　家常菜

Steamed Pork with Red Bean Curd Cheese

材料：12人份

材　料：上好五花肉一斤半，菠菜半斤（洗淨切長段）紅豆腐乳三小塊　（每塊五角）汁三湯匙（混合搗碎）
　　　　黑醬油二湯匙　酒一茶匙　冰糖四茶匙（碎）　花生油三湯匙

做　法：①首將猪肉刮皮洗淨，放在小鋁鍋內以冷水蓋過肉，在中火爐上燒滾，改用文火煮二十分鐘後端鍋離火待溫取出肉放在菜板上，肉皮貼菜板，用快刀將猪肉切成麻將牌形，最要注意切近肉皮，千萬不可切斷肉皮，此時肉已分塊，而皮茄整塊的。

②將肉放大盤內，把醬油擦遍肉皮，又將豆腐乳之一半糊漿，也擦遍肉皮並浸漬一小時，又一半之豆腐乳糊漿擦在肉內，然後換放粗大碗中，肉皮貼碗，再將冰糖洒加在肉塊上，放在蒸籠內以大火蒸約二小時左右，視肉皮極爛，即可取出，傾去湯汁留用。

③油鍋燒熱，倒下菠菜加點鹽糖炒熟，盛在細瓷盆中墊底，然後將蒸好之肉，倒扣覆出，上又將肉汁放在鍋肉滾得稠濃，澆在肉面，趁熱送席。

Ingredients: 2 lb. high quality fresh bacon (five flower pork)
2/3 lb. spinach (cleaned and cut into 3" sections)
3 cubes red bean curd cheese (mashed and mixed with 3 T. of its sauce)
3 T. sauce of red bean curd cheese　　2 T. black soy sauce
1 t. wine　　4 t. crushed rock sugar
3 T. peanut oil

Directions:
1. Scrape and clean pork skin. Put in pot and cover with water. Bring to boil over moderate heat. Then reduce to low heat and cook 20 min. Let cool slightly. Place pork skin side down on cutting board. Cut pork into mah-jong size but do not penetrate skin.
2. Put pork in large bowl. Rub skin with soy sauce. Rub also with ½ red bean curd cheese. Let stand 1 hr. Rub other ½ red bean curd cheese into meat. Transfer to larger bowl. Place skin side down. Add crushed rock sugar. Steam to over high heat about 2 hr. until skin is very tender. Set sauce aside.
3. Heat peanut oil. Stir-fry spinach. Season with salt and sugar. Fry till done. Spread over serving plate. Invert steamed pork over spinach. Simmer sauce until thick. Pour over pork. Serve.

龍鳳花菇　　　廣東菜　　　材料：12人份

Flower Mushrooms with Minced Pork and Chicken

材　料：花菇廿四粒　鵪鶉蛋一打　雞胸脯一個　猪肉四兩　荸薺四個　煮熟胡蘿蔔廿四小片　莞荽葉廿四張　高湯半飯碗

調味品：白醬油一湯匙　鹽半茶匙　糖四分之一茶匙　酒半茶匙　太白粉一茶匙

做　法：①首將花菇洗淨，以半飯碗溫水泡浸，待發去蒂，加四分之一茶匙鹽，蒸二十分鐘，取出待冷。
②次將雞肉與猪肉合併斬爛，加入調味品及荸薺屑拌勻。
③再將鵪鶉蛋逐一煎成荷包形，舖盆備用。
④每隻花菇以斬爛之肉包在白色面上，胡蘿蔔片裝在肉上，然後舖盆內在沸水中蒸五六分鐘卽可。
⑤將鵪鶉蛋舖在花菇旁，又將莞荽裝在胡蘿蔔片上以增美觀，再澆上稠狀之熱高湯上席。

Ingredients: 24 dried flower mushrooms　　1 doz. quail eggs
　　　　　　　1 chicken breast　　　　　　　4 oz. pork
　　　　　　　4 water chestnuts (chopped)　　24 slices cooked carrot
　　　　　　　24 parsley leaves　　　　　　　½ bowl meat stock

Seasonings: 1 T. white soy sauce　　　　　½ t. salt
　　　　　　　¼ t. sugar　　　　　　　　　½ t. wine
　　　　　　　1 t. cornstarch

Directions:
1. Clean dried flower mushrooms. Soak in ½ bowl water to soften. Remove stems. Add ¼ salt. steam 20 min. and let cool.
2. Chop chicken and pork meat. Mix thoroughly. Add seasonings and chopped water chestnuts. Mix well.
3. Fry each quail egg. Place on plate.
4. Put chopped meat on white side of mushrooms. Top meat with carrot slices. Steam mushrooms above boiling water 5-6 min.
5. Place quail eggs around mushrooms. Garnish carrots with parsley leaves. Thicken stock with a little cornstarch paste. pour over mushrooms and quail eggs and serve.

蟹味青魚　　浙江菜

Steamed Grass Carp with Crab Flavor

材料：12人份

材　　　料：活青魚一尾(重約二斤)　薑二片　酒二茶匙　鹽一茶匙　蕃茄片、香菜葉(飾邊用)
蘸魚之調味：嫩薑末一湯匙　黑醋二湯匙　醬油一茶匙
做　　　法：①首將活青魚刮鱗去內臟洗淨後，斬去頭尾，又將魚從背面對剖留用。
②備大盤一只，將魚用酒兩面擦勻，又擦上鹽，面舖薑二片備用。
③用大鍋把水燒沸，把魚蒸上，片刻停火，將魚燜廿分鐘，取出，邊飾蕃茄片及香菜葉，以醋汁蘸食，味似蟹肉，故有此名。

Ingredients: 1 live grass carp (about 2⅓ lb.) 　 2 slices ginger
2 t. wine 　 1 t. salt
2 tomatoes (sliced crosswise) 　 3 or 4 sprigs parsley

Vinegar Sauce (combine):
1 T. chopped young ginger 　 2 T. brown vinegar
1 t. soy sauce

Directions:
1. Clean fish. Cut off head and tail. Slit back open.
2. Soak fish in wine, first on one side, then on the other. Rub with salt; place ginger on fish.
3. Boil water in large pot. Put in fish to steam. Cover and turn off heat immediately. Keep cover on, 20 min. Remove; garnish with sliced tomatoes and parsley on sides. Dip in vinegar sauce to produce crab flavor.

蜜汁火腿

江浙菜　　　材料：12人份

Chinese Ham with Honey Sauce

材　料：上好火腿一塊（重約一斤）　冰糖五兩（打碎）　大孔蓮藕二節　糯米半飯碗　豆粉半茶匙（用一湯匙水調和）

做　法：①先將火腿整塊去皮洗淨，用清水浸四、五小時，再隔水蒸半小時，待冷切約二分厚，二吋濶、一吋半長之薄塊，順序排列碗中。

②將糯米洗淨，裝入藕孔煮爛切片，舖在火腿上，再洒上碎冰糖，隔水蒸約一小時，取出覆瓷盆中上席。（如無蓮藕，可改用罐頭蓮子或罐頭荔子墊底亦可）

Ingredients: 1⅔ lb. Chinese ham (good quality)　5 oz. rock sugar (crushed)
4 oz. lotus seeds　½ t. cornstarch (mixed with 1 T. water)

Directions:
1. Skin and clean Chinese ham. Soak in water 4-5 hr. Steam over water 30 min. Let cool Cut into 2"x1½"x¼" slices. Arrange in overlapping layers on plate.
2. Soak lotus seeds. Cook till soft. Spread over ham. Sprinkle with crushed rock sugar. Steam over water about 1 hr. Remove and invert on serving plate. (Ham slices are now on top.) Serve.

芙蓉海參
Sea Cucumber Foo Yung

杭州菜　　　　材料：12人份

材　料：海參三、四條（每條切二段）　蝦仁二兩　肥肉一兩　熟胡蘿屑二湯匙　鷄蛋白二個　豆腐四寸見方二塊　豆粉一茶匙　葱一支　薑一片　酒一茶匙　猪油二湯匙　高湯一飯碗　豆粉一茶匙（用二湯匙水調和勾汁用）

調味品：白醬油二茶匙　鹽一茶匙　糖¼茶匙　麻油半茶匙　胡椒少許

做　法：①首將蝦仁與肥肉斬碎，又將豆腐去邊皮用力揿碎，加入綜合調味及蛋白二個，同時將蝦仁與肥肉糊胡蘿蔔屑亦加入拌匀備用。
②將海參加豆粉一茶匙拌匀，用一湯匙猪油燒熱，先爆葱薑，然後倒下海參爆炒，再傾下油和高湯滾燒十分鐘，撈起海參瀝乾留用。
③準備一只粗大碗，將海參倒扣碗底，再放下調好之豆腐糊，隔水蒸二十分鐘，取出覆扣盆中，使海參在盆面，倒出湯汁，然後把油鍋燒熱放下一湯匙猪油，將湯汁倒下，待滾調下水豆粉湯稠澆在海參上送席。

Ingredients:	3-4 sea cucumbers (halved)	2 oz. shrimps (shelled)	1 oz. pork fat
	2 T. chopped carrot (cooked)	2 egg whites	2 cakes bean curd (4"X4")
	1 t. cornstarch	1 stalk green onion (cut into 1½" pieces)	1 slice ginger
	1 t. wine	2 T. lard	1 bowl meat stock
	1 t. cornstarch (mixed with 2 T. water)		
Seasonings:	2 t. white soy sauce	1 t. salt	¼ t. sugar
	½ t. sesame oil	dash of pepper	

Directions:
1. Chop shrimps and pork fat. Rid bean curd of thick skin and crush. Add seasonings and mix with egg whites, chopped shrimps, pork fat and chopped carrots thoroughly.
2. Mix sea cucumbers with 1 t. cornstarch. Heat 1 T. lard in pan; first fry green onion and ginger, then put in sea cucumbers and fry, stirring constantly. Add meat stock. Cook 10 min. Remove sea cucumbers and drain.
3. Place sea cucumbers at the bottom of a thick bowl. Pour bean curd mixture on top and steam 20 min. Invert bowl on serving plate. (Sea cucumbers are now on top.)
4. Pour stock into bowl. Heat 1 T. lard in pan; add stock and bring to boil. Stir in cornstarch paste. Pour sauce over sea cucumbers and serve.

蕃茄蒸豆腐　　家常菜　　材料：12人份
Steamed Bean Curd with Tomatoes

材　料：豬腿肉四兩　豆腐一元半　蕃茄二只　葱一支
調味品：黑白醬油各一茶匙　鹽一茶匙　糖四分之一茶匙　豆粉一茶匙
做　法：①首將豬肉洗淨斬碎，調入黑白醬油，豆粉各半茶匙，及糖四分之一茶匙拌勻備用，蕃茄切丁拌入豆粉半茶匙留用。
　　　　②備一深口瓷盆，將豆腐切丁，排列盆內，洒下鹽一茶匙，黑白醬油各半茶匙，然後先舖上肉末，再放下蕃茄，最後洒下葱花，以大火隔蒸約十五分鐘，這一道色香味俱全的家常菜，熱吃味更鮮美。

Ingredients: 4 oz. pork (upper leg)
2 tomatoes
1½ cakes bean curd (each 4"X4")
1 stalk green onion

Seasonings: 1 t. black soy sauce
1 t. salt
1 t. cornstarch
1 t. white soy sauce
¼ t. sugar

Directions:
1. Clean and mince pork. Blend with ½ t. black soy sauce, ½ t. white soy sauce, ½ t. cornstarch and ¼ t. sugar. Dice tomatoes and mix with ½ t. cornstarch.
2. Dice bean curd and arrange in deep plate. Sprinkle with 1 t. salt, ½ t. black soy sauce and ½ t. white soy sauce. Spread minced pork on bean curd. Top with tomatoes, Sprinkle with chopped green onion. Steam above water, over high heat, 15 min. Serve hot.

西 湖 魚
West Lake Fish

杭 州 菜　　　　　材料：12人份

材　料：購重約半斤之活青魚一尾，薑葱各六條切細絲蒸魚　薑二片　醬油一湯匙　鎮江醋四湯匙　糖三湯匙　酒一湯匙　鹽一茶匙半　高湯七湯匙（即蒸魚之汁）　猪油四湯匙　及藕粉一湯匙（用四湯匙水調和濕一小時）

做　法：①先將魚刮鱗去內臟洗淨，用刀刮開平舖大盆內，加薑酒及一茶匙鹽蒸二十分鐘，起鍋待用。
②次將猪油四湯匙燒熱，加入魚湯及高湯，醬油糖醋及鹽煮片刻，卽調下濕稀之藕粉，用鏟子急速攪勻，使汁水稠勻後加入葱薑絲以數滴蔴油略攪，卽澆在魚面上，趁熱上席。

Ingredients:
- 1 live grass carp (about 2 lb.)
- 6 stalks green onion (shredded)
- 1 T. soy sauce
- 3 T. sugar
- 1 t. salt
- 4 T. lard
- 1 T. lotus root powder or cornstarch (mixed with 4 T. water for 1 hr.)
- 6 ginger roots (shredded)
- 2 slices ginger
- 4 T. Tsen-Chiang vinegar
- 1 T. wine
- 7 T. fish stock (from steamed fish)
- few drops of sesame oil

Directions:
1. Split fish in half; spread out on large plate. Put 2 slices ginger on top; sprinkle with 1 T. wine and 1 t. salt. Steam 20 min.
2. Heat 4 T. lard in pan. Add fish stock (and meat stock if necessary). Add soy sauce, sugar, vinegar and salt. Cook 2-3 min. Blend in lotus root powder paste. Stir till sauce thickens. Add shredded green onion and ginger, and 5-6 drops of sesame oil. Stir. Pour over fish and serve.

竹筒肉

湖南菜　　　　材料：12人份

Steamed Pork in Bamboo Mugs

材　料：竹筒十二個（中華路蒸籠店有售）　猪瘦腿肉（肥肉只可佔有十分之一）十二兩　筍二支　葱三支　蒸籠一個

調味品：白醬油一湯匙　黑醬油三湯匙　鹽一茶匙半　清水三十湯匙

做　法：①首將猪肉去皮略洗瀝水，筍剝殼修去老頭切片蒸十分鐘，均備用。
②又將肉細切細斬，並斬入筍和葱，然後裝大碗內加入調味品和清水攪勻，再分配在每一個竹筒內，約有三四湯匙。
③蒸籠放在鍋中沸水上，將竹筒肉一一排列蒸籠內，以大火蒸約二十分鐘，即可取出分食，其味清香可口。

Ingredients: 12 oz. lean pork (1/10 pork fat allowed)　2 bamboo shoots
3 stalks green onion
12 bamboo mugs (sold at bamboo steamer shop)
1 large steamer

Seasonings: 1 T. white soy sauce　　3 T. black soy sauce
1½ t. salt　　30 T. water

Directions:
1. Clean pork and remove skin. Peel and trim bamboo shoots; slice and steam 10 min.
2. Mince pork together with bamboo shoots and green onion. Blend with seasonings and water. Fill each bamboo mug with 3-4 T.
3. Put large steamer above boiling water. Arrange bamboo mugs in steamer. Steam over high heat, about 20 min.

金菜蒸鴨　　　杭　州　菜　　　材料：12人份
Steamed Duck with Pickled Cabbage

材　　料：肥嫩鴨一只（重約二斤）　香菇四五只（浸發後一切二塊）　筍二支（修去老頭）　金菜四湯匙　薑二片　酒一茶匙
調味品：白醬油一湯匙　鹽一茶匙　糖¼茶匙
做　　法：①首將鴨洗淨瀝乾用小鋁鍋放三飯碗沸水加薑酒把鴨和筍均煮二十分鐘，撈出待冷備用。
②備大細瓷碗一只，將鴨子斬為約一寸見方之塊，筍每只切厚片先將一半筍片墊底二湯匙金菜，然後排上鴨肉，又排上筍片與香菇，排時要講究美觀，然後加上餘下之金菜及調味品，隔水蒸四十分鐘，待好加入煮鴨之沸原汁湯送席。

Ingredients: 1 fat young duck (2⅔ lb.)
4-5 dried mushrooms (soaked in water to soften and halved)
2 bamboo shoots (trim off old part)　4 T. pickled cabbage
2 slices ginger　1 t. wine

Seasonings: 1 T. white soy sauce　1 t. salt
¼ t. sugar

Directions:
1. Clean duck and drain. Cook duck and bamboo shoots in 3 bowls boiling water seasoned with ginger and wine, 20 min. Remove and let cool.
2. Cut duck into 1" squares. Cut bamboo shoots into thick slices. Place ½ bamboo shoots at bottom of large bowl. Add 2 T. pickled cabbage as second layer, duck as third, bamboo shoots and mushrooms as fourth. Arrange decoratively. Top with remaining pickled cabbage and seasonings. Steam above water 40 min. or until duck is tender. Heat duck soup. Pour over and serve.

粉蒸肉

家常菜　　　　　材料：12人份

Steamed Pork in Spiced Rice Powder

材　料：猪腿肉一斤　蒸肉粉半飯碗　檳榔芋或蕃薯一斤
調味品：醬油三湯匙　鹽一茶匙　糖半茶匙　酒半茶匙　五香粉、味精少許　猪油少許
做　法：首將猪肉洗淨瀝乾，切約一寸見方之塊，以調味品泡漬約一、二小時，然後每塊肉在米粉內滾一滾，排列在擦過猪油之大粗碗內，再將芋切塊鋪在肉面，即在中火爐上隔水蒸一小時多，視肉已很爛，取出覆扣盆中送席，可作小孩之便當菜。

Ingredients: 1⅓ lb. pork (leg part)　　　　½ bowl spiced rice powder
1⅓ lb. sweet potatoes

Seasonings: 3 T. soy sauce　　　　½ t. salt
½ t. sugar　　　　½ t. wine
dash of five spices powder　　dash of monosodium glutamate
¼ t. lard

Directions: 1. Wash pork and drain. Cut into 1" squares. Soak in seasonings 1-2 hr. Dredge pork with spiced rice powder and arrange in greased bowl. Place sweet potatoes on pork. Steam above water, over moderate heat for more than 1 hr. or until meat is tender. Remove and invert on serving plate. Serve.

髮菜燉蛋
家常菜　　　材料：12人份

Steamed Eggs with Seaweed

材　　料：雞蛋五隻　髮菜一小團（似胡桃形）　葱屑二湯匙　熟火腿屑二湯匙　雞油丁一湯匙　高湯一飯碗　豆粉一湯匙（用二湯匙高湯調濕）　猪油一湯

調味品：白醬油二茶匙　鹽一茶匙　味精少許

做　　法：①首將髮菜略洗，用温水浸發，再洗數次瀝水留用。
②雞蛋打入碗內，加入白醬油、鹽、味精打散，再調入髮菜高湯及雞油丁續打數下留用。
③備平底粗碗一只，將猪油抹擦碗底及週圍，然後將蛋汁傾入碗內，放入鍋中隔水蒸約二十分鐘，取出覆扣在細瓷大圓盤中，面灑熟火腿屑，盆邊可飾番茄片或曲邊之生菜葉，趁熱送席。

Ingredients:
- 5 eggs
- 4 lettuce leaves
- 2 T. chopped green onion
- 1 T. diced chicken fat
- 1 T. cornstarch (mixed with 2 T. stock)
- 2-3 oz. edible hair-like seaweed (fa-tsai)
- 1 tomato (sliced)
- 2 T. chopped ham (cooked)
- 1 bowl meat stock
- 1 T. lard

Seasonings:
- 2 t. white soy sauce
- dash of monosodium glutamate
- 1 t. salt

Directions:
1. Clean seaweed. Soak in warm water to expand. Clean thoroughly and drain.
2. Beat eggs. Season with white soy sauce, salt and M.S.G. Add seaweed, meat stock and dice chicken fat. Beat a few more times.
3. Grease flat pan on all sides with lard. Pour in egg mixture. Place pan in large pot. Steam above water about 20 min. Remove and invert on round plate. Sprinkle with diced ham. Garnish with tomato slices and lettuce leaves on sides. Serve hot.

富貴雞
Steamed Chicken with Stuffing

江浙菜　　　　材料：12人份

材　料：重約二斤嫩雞一隻　二尺見方玻璃紙一張又一小塊
塞雞肚內之材料：里肌肉絲五元　冬菇絲四只　筍絲二支　熟胡蘿蔔絲半支　葱段二支　嫩薑絲二片　金冬菜三湯匙　或榨菜絲三湯匙
調味品：鹽一茶半匙　酒一茶匙半　白醬油一湯匙　糖半茶匙　味精少許

做　法：①首將雞洗淨瀝水，在雞外抹上一茶匙酒和一茶匙鹽留用。
②次將里肌肉絲加入半茶匙酒和一點豆粉白醬油拌勻，然後將各料放入碗內，再加入調味品攪勻留用。
③將雞放在菜板上，把已攪勻之各絲塞入雞之肚內，用白線將雞開口處縫好備用。
④把玻璃紙舖好，把小塊這張放在大張之中間，然後將雞放在其上，一角一角包緊，再以白線略紮。
⑤大鍋備水，將大碗放入，待沸將雞蒸一小時半，視雞腿略裂，濃香撲鼻，即可離火取出，裝入深口大盆中，碗中之汁，用小碗倒下，一同趁熱送席，然後將玻璃紙打開，小碗之雞汁慢慢淋于雞身，其味之鮮美，與其他之雞，不可相比。

Ingredients: 1 young chicken (about 2⅜ lb.)　2 pc. cellophane wrap (one, 2'X2'; the other, smaller)

Stuffing: 1-2 oz. lean pork (shredded)　4 dried mushrooms (shredded)　2 bamboo shoots (shredded)
½ cooked carrot (shredded)　2 stalks green onion　2 slices young ginger (shredded)
3 T. pickled cabbage　or 3 T. shredded Sze-Chuan cabbage　1 t. cornstarch

Seasonings: 1½ t. salt　1½ t. wine　1 T. white soy sauce
½ t. sugar　dash of monosodium glutamate

Directions:
1. Rub chicken with 1 t. wine and 1 t. salt. Set aside.
2. Mix shredded lean pork with ½ t. wine, cornstarch and white soy sauce. Blend all ingredients with seasonings to make stuffing.
3. Stuff chicken with #2; sew up opening with white thread.
4. Put small cellophane in middle of large one. Place stuffed chicken on top; wrap firmly and tie with white thread.
5. Steam chicken 1½ hr. or until tender. Pour stock into small bowl.
6. Un wrap and pour stock over chicken while serving.

蒸火腿
Steamed Chinese Ham

杭州菜　　　　材料：12人份

材　料：火腿(選購紅色筒骨處中段)五兩　筍一支(約四兩)　毛豆(鮮嫩者)三兩　酒半茶匙

做　法：①首將火腿去皮骨切約一分厚之薄片置旁備用。
　　　　②筍剝殼修去老頭對剖打斜切薄片，毛豆略洗(不可洗去白衣)瀝乾兩樣合一碟內在沸水中以猛火蒸十分鐘取出待冷。
　　　　③另用瓷盆先排列筍片在盆底，然後舖上火腿片，卽洒下酒，上面加翡翠色之熟毛豆，隔水(沸水)亦以猛火蒸四分鐘(不可太久會老)，取出供食，此菜色香味俱全，請客時也可湊上這一道。

Ingredients: 5 oz. Chinese ham　　　　1 bamboo shoot (about 4 oz.)
　　　　　　　1 oz. fresh soy bean　　　　½ t. wine

Directions:
1. Remove ham skin and bone. Cut ham into thin slices.
2. Peel bamboo shoot. Remove tough end. Halve lengthwise and slice diagonally. Wash fresh soy beans (do not remove skin); drain. Put on plate with bamboo shoot. Steam over high heat 10 min. Let cool.
3. Put bamboo shoot slices in overlapping layers on plate. Spread ham on bamboo shoots. Sprinkle with wine and fresh soy beans. Steam over high heat 4 min. Serve.

金銀豬肚
Gold and Silver Pork Stomach

廣東菜   材料：12人份

材　料：豬肚一個(重約一斤半左右)　鷄蛋四隻　薑二片　白醬油一湯匙　鹽一茶匙　酒一湯匙
　　　　豬肚湯約二飯碗　碗豆苗或莞荽一撮　花生油二湯匙　豆粉一茶匙(用二湯匙水調濕)

做　法：①首將豬肚用刀刮去黏液，用花生油二湯匙擦肚，並在水喉石上磨擦，翻覆洗淨。
　　　　②先用一飯碗沸水，放下豬肚，煮約五分鐘後取出，另換開水（蓋過豬肚約五寸），改用文火燉約三小時，視肚已軟，取出待冷，湯汁傾碗內留用。
　　　　③將鷄蛋去殼，放在碗內，加白醬油、鹽、味精調打、再徐徐加入肚湯一飯碗，邊加邊打，使蛋與湯混合，即可灌入豬肚內，然後用線縫肚口，放盆內，以大火隔水蒸約一小時，取出待冷，用快刀切長方塊，排列細瓷長盆中，另用鍋倒下高湯一飯碗，待滾調下水豆粉及豆苗或莞荽，即刻澆在金銀肚上，黃白相間，故有此名。

Ingredients:
- 1 pig stomach (about 2 lb.)
- 2 slices ginger
- 1 t. salt
- 2 bowls pig stomach stock
- 2 T. peanut oil
- dash of monosodium glutamate
- 4 eggs
- 1 T. white soy sauce
- 1 T. wine
- a few sprigs of pea shoots or parsley
- 1 t. cornstarch (mixed with 2 T. water)

Directions:
1. To clean stomach: (1) Scrape off mucous with knife. (2) Scrub with 2 T. peanut oil and rinse under running water. Repeat 3-4 times.
2. Cook stomach in 1 bowl or more of boiling water, 5 min. Discard water. Add fresh boiling water to cover stomach by 5". Reduce to low heat. Cook 3 hr. or until tender. Set stomach stock aside.
3. Mix beaten egg with white soy sauce, salt and M.S.G.; beat into one bowl of stomach stock gradually. Mix well. Pour mixture into stomach and sew up opening. Place in large plate. Steam about 1 hr. over high heat. Remove and let cool. Cut into rectangular pieces and arrange on oblong serving plate. Heat remaining bowl of stomach stock to boil. Blend in cornstarch paste, and pea shoots (or parsley). Pour over stomach. The mixture of yellow and white colors gives this dish its name.

清蒸豬腦
White Steamed Pork Brains

江浙菜　　　　材料：12人份

材　料：豬腦十二個　雞油丁二湯匙　火腿絲、香菇絲各一湯匙　葱花二支
調味品：鹽一茶匙　白醬油四茶匙　酒一湯匙　味精少許
做　法：①首將豬腦浸水片刻，用牙籤挑去血筋，略沖水洗淨。
　　　　②將豬腦一一排列盤中，先洒鹽和酒，然後加其他調味品及火腿絲、香菇絲，面飾雞油丁及葱花，大火蒸十五分鐘，趁熱送席。

Ingredients: 12 pork brains　　　　　　2 T. diced chicken fat
　　　　　　1 T. shredded ham　　　　　1 T. shredded mushrooms
　　　　　　2 stalks green onion (chopped)

Seasonings: 1 t. salt　　　　　　　　　4 t. white soy sauce
　　　　　　1 T. wine　　　　　　　　　dash of monosodium glutamate

Directions: 1. Soak pork brains in water. Use toothpick to remove veins and thin membranes. Wash and drain.
2. Arrange in rows on plate. Sprinkle first with salt and wine, then with white soy sauce, M.S.G., ham shreds and mushroom shreds. Top with chicken fat and green onions. Steam over high heat 15 min. Serve hot.

清蒸鯧魚　　　地　方　菜
White Steamed Pomfret

材　料：鯧魚一尾（重約十二兩）　薑絲火腿絲肉絲葱絲各數條　冬菜數粒　白醬油一湯匙
　　　　酒一茶匙　鹽¾茶匙　猪油一茶匙　味精少許
做　法：①先將魚去鱗洗淨肚內及鰓臟處特別多洗，使無腥味。
　　　　②再將洗淨之魚背上劃成菱形，以鹽輕敷魚之全身及肚內，置大盤內。
　　　　③半小時後將盤內之水倒去放醬油和酒卽以備好之各配料敷于魚上。
　　　　④隔水蒸十分鐘內（水沸始可蒸上）取出時加莞荽上桌，熱吃爲宜，鮮美無比。

Ingredients:
- 1 pomfret (about 12 oz.)
- a few shreds ham
- 1 t. pickled cabbage (diced)
- 1 t. wine
- ¼ t. sugar
- dash of monosodium glutamate (M.S.G.)
- a few shreds ginger
- a few shreds green onion
- 1 T. white soy sauce
- ¾ t. salt
- 1 t. lard

Directions:
1. Scale fish; remove gills and entrails. Wash and clean thoroughly.
2. Score dorsal sides of fish into diamond shapes. Rub salt all over. Put on large plate. Let stand for 30 min.
3. Remove water in plate; add soy sauce and wine to fish. Spread over with shredded ingredients, diced cabbage and lard. Sprinkle with sugar and M.S.G.
4. Steam fish above boiling water 10 min. Remove and garnish with parsley. Serve hot.

霉乾菜扣肉　　杭　州　菜　　材料：12人份

Steamed Pork with Salted Dried Mustard Cabbage

材　料：上好五花肉一斤　霉乾菜一飯碗(碎的)碎冰糖一湯匙　醬油一湯匙　棉白糖四分之一茶匙
　　　　酒半茶匙　花生油二飯碗。

做　法：①首將霉乾菜略洗瀝乾，裝碗內隔水蒸四十分鐘備用。
　　　　②次將豬肉刮皮洗淨，放在小鋁鍋內以冷水蓋過肉在中火上燒滾，改為小火煮二十分鐘後端鍋離火，待溫取出肉，另用一盆放下醬油與棉白糖將肉皮向醬油浸泡一、二小時。
　　　　③用油鍋燒熱，將豬肉以皮向油關蓋炸之，聞劈拍之聲已無，即開蓋取出豬肉投入湯鍋中浸片刻，倒出鍋中之油，然後將霉乾菜在油鍋內拌一拌，再另備一大碗，把肉切約二、三分厚之片，排列碗底（肉皮向碗）先灑下酒，再倒下浸肉之醬油然後舖下霉乾菜，即倒下冰糖上蒸籠蒸至肉爛，覆扣盆中即可供食，又可夾在饅頭或荷葉包內，濃香味美（肉湯留作酸辣湯）。

Ingredients: 1⅓ lb. fresh bacon (five flower pork)
　　　　1 small pkg. salted dried mustard cabbage (mei-kan-tsai)
　　　　2 T. peanut oil

Seasonings: 3 T. soy sauce　　　1 t. wine　　　1 T. crushed rock sugar

Directions:
1. Shave skin of five flower pork. Wash and drain. Cut into 1 inch thick slices. Put in bowl. Soak in soy sauce for 30 min. Wash mei-kan-tsai in strainer. Steam above water about 20 min. Cut in very small pieces.
2. Heat oil in frying pan. Stir-fry pork slices. Sprinkle with wine and soaked soy sauce. Stir-fry to mix. Remove. Stir-fry mei-kan-tsai for a while and pour on top of pork. Steam over medium heat 40 min.
3. Put steamed pork and mei-kan-tsai in pan; cook till sauce is dry. Serve.

冰箱風鷄
Salted Chicken

年菜　　　　　材料：12人份

材　料：退毛除淨光鷄一只，每斤鷄肉用鹽二茶匙　花椒一茶匙　薑二片　高梁酒二茶匙

做　法：①首先將鹽炒熱，放下花椒炒至椒香，鹽成灰色，即可盛起，待冷備用。
②將鷄洗淨瀝水，用花椒鹽遍擦裡外全身，放在盤內醃一天，至晚放進冰箱三夜。
③三夜後，將鷄取出，略洗去花椒及鹽汁，掛起瀝水，再放進冰箱一二天或數日，要吃時放在碗內，面舖薑二片，鷄身內外擦高梁酒二茶匙，以大火隔水蒸二十分鐘取出，撇去湯汁另用，待冷，將鷄肉用手撕條或斬塊供食，香嫩味美。

Ingredients:
- 1 chicken (about 1⅓ lb.)
- 1 t. peppercorn
- 2 t. "Kao Liang" (Chinese gin)
- 2 t. salt
- 2 slices ginger

Directions:
1. Heat salt without oil, stirring constantly. Add peppercorn; stir till fragrant and salt turns gray. Let cool.
2. Rub chicken with mixture of salt and peppercorn; let stand whole day. Put in refrigerator at night to keep for 3 nights.
3. After third night, take out chicken, rinse and drain. Place again in refrigerator for 1-2 days or more, until desired.
4. Put chicken in large bowl. Add ginger on top; Rub inside and outside with "Kao-Liang". Steam over high heat 20 min. Let cool. Tear or cut into pieces. Save chicken stock for other use. Serve cold.

紅燒蹄胖

杭州菜　　　材料：12人份

Stewed Pork Leg in Brown Sauce

材　　料：豬後胖一個（重約一斤半）
調味品：黑醬油五湯匙　白醬油一湯匙　冰糖四茶匙(碎)　酒一茶匙
做　　法：①首將蹄胖拔毛刮皮，洗淨瀝水，以三湯匙醬油泡漬至少半小時。
②先用炒菜鍋把蹄胖放下，先灑下酒，再倒下黑醬油及一湯匙白醬油，翻覆紅透，然後放下沸水與蹄胖，並改用小鋁鍋或砂鍋，在文火爐上燉燒，視蹄胖半爛，再放下冰糖，燒至極爛，湯汁稠濃，即可盛起供食。

Ingredients: 2 lb. pork (upper hind leg)
Seasonings: 5 T. black soy sauce　　　　　　　1 T. white soy sauce
　　　　　　　 4 t. crushed rock sugar　　　　　　1 t. wine
Directions:
1. Pluck hairs on skin. Shave and clean. Marinate in 3 T. soy sauce at least 30 min.
2. Place pork in frying pan; add wine first, then black and white soy sauce. Turn constantly till dark red.
3. Transfer to cooking pot and add boiling water. Stew till half done Add rock sugar. Cook till pork is very tender, and sauce is thick.

洋葱扒鴨
Duck with Onion Sauce

年菜　　　　　材料：12人份

材　料：買二斤重肥鴨一隻　薑三片　洋葱一個　冬菜一湯匙　醬油四湯匙　碎冰糖一湯匙　酒一湯匙　油一湯匙　鹽一茶匙

做　法：①先將鴨洗淨從背上斬開，略吹乾。
②置盤內以醬油二湯匙澆在鴨身內外，約泡浸一小時。
③以一湯匙油置鍋內，將洋葱切寬絲及鹽少許下鍋炒之，片刻盛起，當卽以鴨子在鍋內略煎，並落薑、酒、醬油二湯匙，翻覆燒紅，再下沸水三飯碗及冰糖以文火續燉。
④待鴨半熟，落洋葱與冬菜，煮爛汁濃盛起斬大塊，面澆稠湯味甚濃香可口。如整桌菜宴客，扒鴨整只送席。

Ingredients:
- 1 fat duck (2½ lb.)
- 1 onion (sliced)
- 1 T. white soy sauce
- 1 T. crushed rock sugar
- 1 T. cooking oil
- 3 slices ginger
- 1 T. pickled cabbage
- 4 T. black soy sauce
- 1 T. wine
- 1 t. salt

Directions:
1. Wash duck. Slit open back lengthwise and let dry slightly.
2. Pour 2 T. black soy sauce over duck, inside and out, and marinate about 1 hr.
3. Heat 1 T. oil in pan. Stir-fry onion slices with dash of salt, 2-3 min. Remove. Place duck in pan and sauté on both sides 4-5 min. Add ginger, wine, white and black soy sauce. Cook till duck is brown on all sides. Add 3 bowls of boiling water and rock sugar. Reduce heat and cook.
4. When duck is half done, add onion slices and pickled cabbage. Cook till duck is tender and sauce thickens.
5. Cut duck into large pieces. Pour sauce on top and serve.

咖喱豬舌
Pork Tongue with Curry Sauce

家常菜　　　材料：12人份

材　料：豬舌一個（重約一斤多）　洋芋四個　胡蘿蔔一條　咖喱粉一湯匙半　花生油一湯匙
調味品：鹽一茶匙　白醬油一湯匙　酒一茶匙
做　法：①首將豬舌洗淨瀝乾，洋芋去皮切爲二塊，胡蘿蔔刮去皮亦切二塊，咖喱粉以一湯匙冷水調濕均備用。
②備小鋁鍋一只放下沸水三飯碗，即將豬舌放下待滾，撇去泡沫，將豬舌撈去，刮去白衣，再放在湯內，加下一茶匙酒，改用文火燉約二小時，撈出豬舌待冷，又將洋芋與胡蘿蔔放在湯內煮二十分鐘撈起湯倒在碗內留用，豬舌洋芋等待冷均切塊。
③油鍋燒熱，先放下咖喱醬爆香、然後倒下豬舌與洋芋等同炒，即加入白醬油與鹽，然後傾豬舌湯，關蓋燜煮入味，視汁稠濃，可以盛起供食又可作便當菜。

Ingredients: 1 pork tongue (1⅓ lb.)　4 potatoes　1 carrot
　　　　　　1½ T. curry powder　1 T. peanut oil

Seasonings: 1 t. salt　1 T. white soy sauce　1 t. wine

Directions:
1. Clean pork tongue. Pare and halve potatoes and carrot. Mix curry powder with 1 T. water.
2. Put tongue in pot with 3 filled bowls boiling water. Bring to boil and skim foam and impurities. Scrape off white stuff on tongue. Put tongue back in pot. Add 1 t. wine. Stew over low heat about 2 hr. Remove and let cool. Cook potatoes and carrot in same soup, 20 min. When cool, cut tongue, potatoes and carrot into thick slices.
3. Heat oil in frying pan. Sauté curry powder paste until pungent. Add tongue, potatoes and carrots; stir-fry. Add white soy sauce and salt. Puur in tongue soup. Cook, covered, until sauce thickens. Remove and serve.

油豆腐鷄
Chicken with Oily Bean Curd

上　海　菜　　　　材料：12人份

材　料：肥鷄半只　油豆腐四十只　薑一片　蒜葉二支（拍碎切段）　甜麵醬一湯匙　蘇打粉半茶匙（以半飯碗沸水溶化）　醬油二湯匙　酒一茶匙　鹽一茶匙　冰糖二茶匙　花生油四湯匙

做　法：①首將油鍋燒熱，先爆蒜葉，再加甜麵醬及鷄塊翻覆炒透，然後加酒冰糖及浸鷄之醬油，約滾五分鐘，再加入沸水蓋過鷄約一寸，改用小鋁鍋在文火上燉燒。
②將油豆腐放碗內，倒下蘇打沸水浸片刻，再以冷水漂洗數次，擠去水後，放在鷄上面，並卽洒下鹽，視鷄已爛，卽可供食，亦可作小孩便當菜。

Ingredients:
- ½ young chicken (cut in pieces, 1½"X1")
- 1 slice ginger
- 1 T. sweet flour paste
- 2 T. soy sauce
- 1 t. salt
- 4 T. peanut oil
- 40 pc. oily bean curd
- 2 stalks garlic stalks (crushed and cut into sections)
- ½ t. soda powder (dissolved in ½ bowl boiling water)
- 1 t. wine
- 2 t. rock sugar

Directions:
1. Blend chicken with 2 T. soy sauce. Let stand 30 min. Heat oil in frying pan. Stir-fry garlic stalks. Add sweet flour paste and chicken. Stir-fry, turning constantly. Add wine, rock sugar and soaking soy sauce. Boil 5 min. Add boiling water to cover chicken by 1" and transfer to cooking pot. Continue cooking over low heat.
2. Soak oily bean curd in soda water 1-2 min. Rinse a few times and squeeze out water. Place on chicken; sprinkle with salt. Cook until chicken is tender.

貴妃雞　　江浙菜　　材料：12人份
Braised Chicken Legs and Wings

材　料：嫩雞腿八只　嫩雞膀十只　大葱半斤　冬菇八只　冬筍一斤　醬油二湯匙　酒一湯匙　鹽及冰糖各一湯匙　花生油半杯又一湯匙

做　法：①將每只雞腿一切三，每只雞膀一切二加下醬油及酒浸廿分鐘備用。
②將筍剝殼切塊又將冬菇浸熱切塊。
③將油鍋燒熱加下半杯油候沸即下雞塊爆炒再放下冬菇及筍燒片刻，即盛炒鍋內，再加下鹽及冰糖，並加下開水以蓋雞約半寸燜燉一小時。
④將大葱洗淨切長條，用一湯匙油爆炒，加入雞腿內，燜二十分鐘即可連砂鍋上席。

Ingredients:
- 8 chicken legs
- 10 chicken wings
- ⅔ lb. leeks
- 8 dried mushrooms
- 1⅔ winter bamboo shoots
- 2 T. soy sauce
- 1 T. wine
- 1 T. salt
- 1 T. rock sugar
- ½ cup and 1 T. peanut oil

Directions:
1. Cut each chicken leg into 3 pieces and each wing into 2. Soak 20 min. in soy sauce and wine.
2. Peel and cut bamboo shoots in pieces. Soak mushrooms in water to soften; cut in pieces.
3. Heat ½ C. oil in frying pan to boil. Fry chicken pieces, stirring and turning constantly, 3-4 min. Add bamboo shoots and mushrooms. Stir-fry 2-3 min. longer. Remove contents to earthenware pot. Add salt, rock sugar and boiling water to cover chicken by ½". Braise 1 hr.
4. Cut leeks in 2" lengths. Fry in 1 T. oil 1-2 min. Add to earthenware pot. Cook another 20 min. Serve in earthenware pot.

栗子燒雞
Stewed Chicken with Chestnuts

杭州菜　　　　材料：12人份

材　料：肥嫩鷄一只　栗子半斤　薑二片　花生油二湯匙
調味品：醬油三湯匙　鹽半茶匙　冰糖一茶匙　酒一茶匙
做　法：①首將栗子在大頭上切去一薄片，然後放在冷水中煮二十分鐘，撈出再浸在冷水中片刻後剝去殼和衣留用。
②次將肥鷄洗淨，斬成約一寸見方之塊，以一湯匙半醬油泡浸約半小時
③油鍋燒熱，放下薑片略爆，即倒下鷄塊炒透，然後加入酒和餘下之醬油，翻覆燒紅，再放下冰糖和沸水（蓋過鷄）換小鋁鍋以文火續燉，視鷄已半爛，即將已煮過之栗子倒下，燒煮約半小時，即乘起供食，此爲中秋節時令佳肴。

Ingredients: 1 fat young chicken　　⅔ lb. chestnuts (raw)
　　　　　　　2 slices ginger　　　　　2 T. peanut oil
Seasonings: 3 T. soy sauce　　　　　½ t. salt
　　　　　　　1 t. rock sugar　　　　　1 t. wine
Directions:
1. Cook chestnuts in water 20 min; remove to cold water and soak about 5 min. Remove shell and skin.
2. Cut chicken into pieces 1"X1"; marinate in 1½ T. soy sauce about 30 min.
3. Heat oil in frying pan. Sauté sliced ginger. Add chicken; fry until brown. Add wine and remaining soy sauce; stir and turn constantly. Add rock sugar and boiling water enough to cover chicken; reduce heat and stew until half done. Add chestnuts and cook another 30 min. Serve hot. A favorite dish for Mid-Autumn's Festival.

紅燒圈子
Red Stewed Pork Rings

上海菜　　　　材料：12人份

材　料：豬大腸一副(重約三四斤)，或大腸頭四條　沸水二飯碗　八角桂皮少許　白線數根　麵粉半飯碗　花生油四湯匙

調味品：黑醬油八湯匙　白醬油二湯匙　鹽半茶匙　冰糖一湯匙

做　法：①首將豬腸刮黏液，先以麵粉之一半遍擦腸皮，在水喉石上用力摩擦後，用清水沖洗，再加花生油二湯匙擦洗，然後重以麵粉遍擦，再沖洗一次，又以花生油擦淨，以大量水沖洗（洗豬肚豬腸皆不可用鹽擦，因遇了鹽會使外皮堅硬煮久不軟）然後將腸全部翻面沖洗（翻時用筷子一隻從腸頭挿進卽可翻轉），待潔淨後重翻轉瀝水待用。

②將豬腸每條切約一尺許長，兩頭以白線扎緊（使燒時不會走油），然後放入已有沸水二飯碗之鍋中。待滾將豬腸撈出，傾去鍋中之水，然後再用沸水三碗，把豬腸放入。

Ingredients: 4-5 lb. large intestine of pork
dash of aniseed and kuei-pi (cinnamon bark)
4 T. peanut oil
several white threads
2 bowls boiling water
½ bowl flour
2 slices ginger

Seasonings: 8 T. black soy sauce
½ t. salt
1 T. wine
2 T. white soy sauce
1 T. rock sugar

Directions:
1. Scrape off sticky liquid from intestine. Rub with ¼ bowl flour on hard surface. Wash off with water. Brush 2 T. peanut oil on intestine and again rub with remaining flour. Wash thoroughly. (Do not rub with salt which prevents intestine from tenderizing during cooking.) Turn intestine inside out with a chopstick. Repeat cleaning procedure. Return to original side.
2. Cut intestine into about 1' lengths. Tie two ends together (to prevent oil from escaping). Drop into pot containing 2 bowls boiling water. Cook until boiling. Remove water. Add another 3 bowls boiling water. Add ginger slices. Cook until simmering. Skim foam and impurities. Add 1 T. wine, aniseed and kuei-pi. Reduce to low heat and cook 1 hr. Remove intestine to frying pan. Keep stock in pot.
3. Mix seasonings with intestine. Cook, stirring and turning, till intestine is red. Add stock; cook till simmering. Pour everything back into pot. Cook over low heat until intestine is tender and sauce thickened. Cut into 1" lengths and place in serving plate. Pour sauce over intestines to serve.

紅燒羊肉　　杭州菜　　材料：12人份
Stewed Lamb with Brown Sauce

材　料：羊肉一斤　蘿蔔一斤　薑三片
調味品：醬油二湯匙　酒一湯匙　鹽半茶匙　冰糖二茶匙(碎)
做　法：①首將羊肉洗淨瀝乾塊(比紅燒猪肉大一點)蘿蔔修皮切滾刀切大塊均備用。
②備小鋁鍋一只，放下三飯碗冷水，待沸，將羊肉和薑放下，滾時撇去泡沫，放落蘿蔔與酒改用文火燉燒一小時半，然後改調炒菜鍋，將羊肉鏟入鍋內(湯不倒)加入醬油與冰糖紅透，仍再放小鋁鍋內連湯燉燒，視羊肉已爛，即放下鹽滾燒片刻，視汁稠濃，即可盛起，這樣燒的羊肉，決無羊騷氣(多買羊肉六兩，可作羊肉粉皮)

Ingredients: 1⅓ lb. lamb　　1⅓ lb. turnips　　3 slices ginger
Seasonings: 2 T. black soy sauce　　½ t. salt　　2 t. crushed rock sugar
　　　　　1 T. wine
Directions:
1. Wash lamb. Cut into 1"X1½" pieces. Pare turnips. Cut into pieces same size as lamb.
2. Boil 3 bowls of water in pot. Add lamb and ginger. Cook until simmering. skim foam. Add turnips and wine. Reduce to low heat and stew 1½ hr. Remove lamb to frying pan, but retain soup in pot. Add soy sauce and rock sugar to lamb. Stir till lamb turns brown from soaking. Return to pot and stew till meat is tender. Add salt and let boil until sauce thickens. Remove and serve.

紅燒鱔段

江浙菜　　　材料：12人份

Stewed Eel with Brown Sauce

材　料：肥鱔一斤　火腿豬肉各四兩　蒜頭十粒　薑二片　花生油三湯匙
調味品：醬油二湯匙　鹽半茶匙　酒一湯匙　冰糖一茶匙
做　法：①首將肥鱔殺死，斬去頭，剖出內臟，略洗後切一寸多長之段，火腿與肉均切塊，蒜頭撕衣，均備用。
②油鍋燒熱先爆薑片，然後倒下段鱔爆透，並加酒及火腿肉同炒，再放下醬油冰糖，並沸水約一飯碗多，改用小鋁鍋以文火燉燒，再加入蒜頭，半小時後放鹽，視段鱔極爛，湯汁稠濃，即可供席，可洒胡椒粉。

Ingredients: 1⅓ lb. fat eel　　4 oz. Chinese ham　　4 oz. pork
10 cloves garlic　　2 slices ginger　　3 T. peanut oil

Seasonings: 2 T. black soy sauce　　½ t. salt　　1. T. wine
1 t. rock sugar

Directions:
1. Kill eel. Remove head and entrails. Clean and cut in 1″ long sections. Cut ham and pork in pieces. Skin garlic.
2. Heat oil in frying pan. Stir-fry ginger slices; add eel. Fry, stirring quick!y; add ham, pork and wine; next add soy sauce, rock sugar and about 1 bowl boiling water. Reduce to low heat. Add garlic. Braise 30 min. Season with salt. Cook till eel is tender and sauce thickened. Sprinkle with pepper to serve.

蕃茄燉肉
Stewed Pork with Tomatoes

家常菜　　　　材料：12人份

材　料：排骨肉一斤　蕃茄四只　蒜頭六粒　醬油二湯匙　碎冰糖一湯匙　花生油一湯匙　酒一茶匙

做　法：①先將小排骨肉洗淨切塊置碗內，以醬油一湯匙泡浸約半小時。
②將鍋燒熱，以一湯匙油置鍋內，油熱將肉略炒，再加醬油一湯匙酒一茶匙，翻覆炒數下放開水一飯碗，及冰糖一湯匙以文火續燉。
③煮沸約十五分鐘，即下蒜頭六粒，待肉半爛，即將切塊之蕃茄下鍋，這是一樣最營養的燉肉。

Ingredients: 1⅓ lb. spareribs
6 cloves garlic
1 T. crushed rock sugar
1 t. wine
4 tomatoes (cut into small pieces)
2 T. soy sauce
1 T. peanut oil

Directions:
1. Clean spareribs; cut into pieces. Marinate in 1 T. soy sauce for about ½ hr.
2. Heat 1 T. oil in pan. Stir-fry ribs, 3-4 min. Add 1 T. soy sauce and 1 t. wine; fry and turn 2-3 min. Add 1 bowl of boiling water and 1 T. crushed rock sugar. Simmer over low heat, 15 min. Add garlic.
3. When ribs are half done, add tomatoes. Cook until tender.

鳳爪甲魚　　福州菜　　材料：12人份
Stewed Turtle with Chicken Feet

材　料：甲魚一只（重約十二兩至一斤）　鷄脚十二隻（斬去直骨）　冬菇三四只（浸泡去蒂切塊）
　　　　火腿片一小碟　薑二厚片　酒一湯匙　鹽一茶匙

做　法：①首將甲魚放在地上，用筷子誘其頭伸出，使其用嘴挾住筷子，即速拉出其頸，用利刀斬下頭部，放入小盆中，以沸水燙之，然後，用手刮去外衣，拉去脚爪，再放在荼板上，用剪從腹部軟骨處剪一十字形，取出內臟，如有小蛋，可留同燉食，略洗肚內後瀝水。
　　　　②備小砂鍋一隻，放下沸水七八分，待大滾，再投入甲魚與薑片，並洒下酒，滾後放下鳳爪冬菇塊和火腿片，改用文火燉至甲魚邊緣很爛，再調下鹽，即可盛在細瓷大碗中送席。

附　註：甲魚是一道高貴名菜，要使在燒時湯汁不乾，故用砂鍋來燉，就不易乾湯，食時更清補味美。

Ingredients: 1 turtle (1 lb. – 1⅓ lb., cut in about 1½" squares)
12 chicken feet (cut off upper part)
3-4 dried mushrooms (soaked in water to soften and quartered)
2 oz. sliced Chinese ham　　　　　　　　2 slices ginger
1 T. wine　　　　　　　　　　　　　　1 t. salt

Directions:
1. To kill and clean turtle, see Direction #1, "Stewed Turtle in Brown Sauce."
2. Put turtle in earthenware pot. Cover with boiling water; add ginger and wine. Heat to boil. Add chicken feet, mushrooms and ham. Reduce to low heat and cook until turtle is tender. Season with salt. Remove and serve.

五香肘花

北平菜　　　　材料：12人份

Five-Spices Pork

材　料：猪肘子（蹄膀）一個（重約一斤多）　醬油四湯匙　清酒一湯匙　冰糖二茶匙（碎）
　　　　八角桂皮少許（用紗布袋好）

做　法：①首將蹄膀拔毛刮皮洗淨瀝乾然後將皮對剖把瘦肉整塊取出，挖去肥肉不要。
　　　　②將瘦肉與皮用二湯匙醬油浸漬約二小時然後把瘦肉放在皮內，好好的包起來，用蔴繩捆好。
　　　　③備小鋁鍋一只，將肘花放入，傾下全部醬油及酒和八角桂皮等滾燒紅透，然後放下冰糖和沸水蓋過肘花，改用文火燉燒約二小時，視肘花很爛，汁也稠濃，即耐性盛在盆內，湯留另用，待冷蓋好進冰箱，次日拆線切薄片，排列細瓷盆中，誠爲飲酒之佳肴。

Ingredients: 1⅓ lb. pork (upper leg with skin)　　4 T. soy sauce
　　　　　　　1 T. white wine　　　　　　　　　　2 t. crushed rock sugar
　　　　　　　a little antiseed and kuei-pi (cinnamon bark) (put in cotton bag)

Directions:
1. Pluck hairs and shave pork skin. Wash and drain. Slit skin lengthwise to remove meat. Remove and discard all fat.
2. Soak lean meat and skin in 2 T. soy sauce 2 hr. Wrap lean meat in skin. Bind with strings.
3. Put pork in pot. Add all soy sauce, wine, antiseed and kuei-pi. Simmer till red. Add rock sugar and boiling water to cover pork. Reduce to low heat. Stew 2 hr. until meat is tender and sauce thick. Remove to plate. Save sauce for other use. Refrigerate pork till next day. Remove strings. Cut into thin slices. Serve cold.

鎮江肴肉
Spicy Pork, Tsen-Chiang Style

江蘇菜　　　　　材料：12人份

材　料：豬後腿肉一斤半　鹽二湯匙半　硝一茶匙半（用一湯匙水溶化）　糖花椒各一茶匙半　薑絲一湯匙　加鎮江醋二湯匙　黑醬油一茶匙　另備乾水的青菜葉四張　白淨布一方　重磚二塊

做　法：①首將鹽放在鍋內炒熱，即加入花椒同炒，視鹽黃花椒香盛起，待冷備用
②豬肉以乾布擦淨後，先擦上硝水次將糖擦勻，最後以花椒鹽擦透，放在鋁盆內面蓋青菜葉，上壓重磚二塊
③醃一夜去磚進冰箱，三日後即翻面一次，再醃三日，取出洗淨花椒及鹽水備用。
④備小鋁鍋一只，放下肉塊，以冷水蓋過肉，在中火爐上燒滾，改用文火燉至肉爛。
⑤將白布舖在菜板上，把肉盛在布上，趁熱包好，外面再包上兩層牛皮紙，以布條紮緊，用磚壓成平扁形，約三小時後去磚進冰箱，次日拆開，用刀切約二分厚的肉塊排列細瓷瓶中，與薑絲醋一同送席。

附　註：量匙在向鐵號買，三茶匙為一湯匙。

Ingredients: 2 lb. pork (hind leg)　　　　　2½ T. salt
1½ t. saltpetre (dissolved in 1 T. water)　　1½ t. sugar
1½ t. peppercorn　　　　　　　　　　　　1 T. shredded ginger
2 T. Tsen-Chiang vinegar　　　　　　　　1 t. black soy sauce

Other materials:
4 pc. dry green cabbage leaves　　1 pc. white cloth
2 heavy bricks

Directions:
1. Heat salt in pan; add peppercorn. Stir together till salt is brown and peppercorn pungent. Remove and let cool.
2. Dry pork with cloth. Moisten with saltpetre; rub with sugar and peppercorn-salt mixture. Place on plate and cover with green cabbage leaves. Put bricks on top.
3. Marinate overnight. Remove bricks and refrigerate 3 days. Turn over side and marinate another 3 days. Wash off peppercorn-salt.
4. Place pork in pot and cover with cold water. Cook over medium heat till boiling. Reduce to low heat. Cook until tender.
5. Cover cutting board with white cloth. Place pork on cloth and wrap. Wrap in addition with two layers of brown wrapping paper. Tie firmly with strips of cloth. Crush with brick till flat. Let stand 3 hr. and refrigerate until next day. Unwrap. Cut into ⅙" thick slices and arrange on serving plate. Serve with ginger and vinegar.

紅燒甲魚　　江浙菜　　材料：12人份
Stewed Turtle in Brown Sauce

材　料：甲魚一隻重約一斤多　火腿片一小碟　筍片一支　香菇三、四只　薑四小片　蒜頭四粒切片　猪油或花生油二湯匙

調味品：黑醬油二湯匙　白醬油二茶匙　酒二茶匙　碎冰糖一茶匙

做　法：①將甲魚放在地上用筷子誘其頭伸出，使其嘴挾住筷子，卽速拉出其頸，用利刀斬下頭部，放入水盆內以沸水燙之，然後，用手刮去白衣拉去脚爪，放在枮板上用剪刀從腹部頓骨處剪一十字形，取出內臟，如有小蛋，可留燉食，然後略洗肚內瀝水。

②將甲魚斬塊裝碗加入一湯匙黑醬油及一茶匙酒拌勻備用。

③鍋中放油二湯匙爆香薑片及蒜頭片然後把甲魚傾入煸炒，再加入筍片火腿片及香菇片，一同炒勻再倒下餘下之調味品炒透，放下沸水及冰糖改用小鋁鍋燉燒約半小時後，視甲魚已頓，湯汁稠濃，卽可盛起送席。

Ingredients:
- 1 turtle (about 1⅓ lb.)
- 1 bamboo shoot (sliced)
- 4 slices ginger
- 2 T. lard or peanut oil
- 2 oz. Chinese ham (sliced)
- 3-4 dried mushrooms
- 4 cloves garlic (sliced)

Seasonings:
- 2 T. black soy sauce
- 2 t. wine
- 2 t. white soy sauce
- 1 t. crushed rock sugar

Directions:
1. Kill turtle. (Use a chopstick to provoke it to bite. When neck sticks out, grab and decapitate.) Place in pot and scald with boiling water, 1-2 min. Skim foam and impurities and remove nails. Cut abdomen open crisscross with scissors. Remove entrails. Clean and drain.
2. Cut turtle into 1" squares and place in large bowl. Mix in 1 T. black soy sauce and 1 t. wine.
3. Heat 2 T. peanut oil in frying pan. Fry ginger and garlic; add turtle; turn frequently. Add bamboo shoot, ham, mushrooms and remaining seasonings. Stir-fry till flavor has penetrated. Transfer to cooking pot. Add boiling water and crushed rock sugar, Cook 30 min., or until turtle is tender and sauce thick.

鮮菓銀耳　　湖南菜　　材料：12人份
White Wood Ear with Fruits

材　料：上好白木耳五錢　橘子或櫻桃或枇杷半杯　碎冰糖一杯

做　法：①首將銀耳放在小濾油器內略沖洗，放入大碗中，用溫水三飯碗泡浸一晚，次晨備小砂鍋一只，將銀耳連水傾入，再加下五飯碗水，先用中火燒滾，改用木炭小火燉約五、六小時，然後加入冰糖再燉一小時。

②次將橘子剝去外皮，分成一瓣瓣，再去衣去子，切為二段，如用罐裝櫻桃枇杷亦可，所用鮮果皆在臨上席前加進銀耳內滾一透，即用細瓷湯碗裝盛，趁熱上席。

Ingredients: ½ oz. white wood ear　　½ C. pulps of tangerine, cherry or loquat.
1 C. crushed rock sugar

Directions:
1. Wash white wood ear slightly. Soak in 3 bowls warm water overnight. Put white wood ear with soaking water into earthenware pot. Add 5 more bowls water. Bring to boil over medium heat. Reduce to very low heat. Stew 5-6 hr. Add rock sugar. Stew for another 1 hr.
2. Peel tangerines; break into pieces. Remove skins and seeds of each piece. Cut each plup in half. (Canned cherry and loquat may be substituted.) Parboil fresh fruit in boiling wood ear soup before serving. Serve hot.

鳳採牡丹
Stewed Pigeons & Pork Lung

浙江菜　　　　材料：12人份

材　料：猪肺一個　鴿子二只　薑花片四片　花生油二湯匙
調味品：白醬油一湯匙　鹽一茶匙　酒一茶匙　冰糖一茶匙
做　法：①首將猪肺掛在水籠頭上，用大量水灌入肺內，用手在猪肺上拍動，使其血水流出，視猪肺已呈白色即可取下，以二飯碗沸水，加薑、酒用文火煮頓切塊。
②又將鴿子洗淨瀝水去爪，在煮沸之水中燙一下，取出斬下頭頸，將鴿子斬塊，湯汁留用。
③油鍋爆熱先爆薑花片，再放下鴿塊和猪肺同炒，鴿頭不必燒，調下酒和白醬油、鹽翻覆煸炒，再傾下煮沸之湯及冰糖同燜燉一小時，盛入盤中面挿鴿頭二個，頭之中間挿入紅椒花一個，以增美觀。

Ingredients:	1 pork lung	2 pigeons
	4 slices ginger	2 T. peanut oil
Seasonings:	1 T. white soy sauce	1 t. salt
	1 t. wine	1 t. rock sugar

Directions:
1. Clean pork lung thoroughly. Heat 2 bowls water to boil; add pork lung, ginger and wine. Cook over low heat till tender. Cut pork lung into medium-sized pieces.
2. Remove and discard pigeon feet. Dip pigeons in pork lung stock. Remove and save heads. Cut pigeons into pieces (same size as pork lung). Set aside stock.
3. Heat oil in frying pan. Fry ginger; add pork lung and pigeons. Add wine, white soy sauce and salt. Stir-fry and toss lightly. Add stock and rock sugar. Stew 1 hr. Remove to serving plate. Place pigeon heads on top. Stick a red chili pepper between heads to garnish.

紅燒豬蹄

杭州菜　　　材料：12人份

Stewed Pork Foot in Brown Sauce

材　料：豬前蹄一個（帶有腳的約重二斤）
調味品：黑醬油六湯匙　白醬油一湯匙　冰糖一湯匙半（碎）　酒二茶匙
做　法：①首將豬蹄叫賣肉店對剖斬開（皮不斷）買回細細拔毛，刮洗潔淨瀝水
　　　　②用鋁鍋放下豬蹄，傾下沸水，蓋過蹄約二寸，待滾撇去泡沫，洒下酒，以文火燉燒。
　　　　③視豬蹄半爛，撈出在炒菜鍋內，調入黑白醬油冰糖等紅透，然後再傾下原汁湯，仍倒在小鋁鍋內以文火燉燒，視蹄極爛，湯亦濃香，即可供食。
附　註：豬胖豬蹄，均可以木耳金針菜同燒，但木耳宜早放金針菜則遲一點放下。

Ingredients: 1 pork foot (2⅔ lb.)

Seasonings: 6 T. black soy sauce　　1 T. white soy sauce
1½ T. crushed rock sugar　　2 t. wine

Directions:
1. Let butcher cut pork foot lengthwise in half and crosswise, 1½" thick, without cutting through skin. Pluck hairs on skin; shave and clean.
2. Put pork foot in aluminum pot; pour in boiling water to cover 2" above foot. Bring to boil and skim white foam. Add wine and stew.
3. When pork foot is half-done, remove into frying pan; add black and white soy sauce and rock sugar. Turn and toss till soaked through. Pour soup on top. Return to pot and stew till foot is very tender and sauce is thick.

砂鍋魚頭
Fish Head in Earthenware Pot

地方菜　　　　　材料：12人份

材　料：大魚頭一個（約一斤半）　豆腐一大塊　肉筍香菇均數片　薑二片　葱二支　蒜頭一粒
　　　　醬油二湯匙　酒一湯匙　鹽一茶匙　糖半茶匙　花生油一杯　鹽甜醬各一茶匙

做　法：①首將魚頭括淨魚鱗，剪去魚鰓，洗清後把鹽擦入魚頭，並加醬油酒漬片刻備用。
　　　　②次將油鍋燒熱，投入魚頭用火煎炸十數分鐘（兩面都煎）撈出魚頭留三湯匙油把蒜頭爆
　　　　　香，把魚頭放下，倒入醬油，即盛在砂鍋內，加沸水煮片刻，即下豆腐肉片等用慢火燒
　　　　　一小時，即連砂鍋上席。

Ingredients:
- 1 big fish head (about 2 lb.)
- 5-8 slices pork meat
- 5-8 slices dried mushroom (soaked in water to soften)
- 2 slices ginger
- 1 clove garlic
- 1 T. wine
- ½ t. sugar
- 1 t. bean paste
- 1 cake bean curd
- 5-8 slices bamboo shoots
- 2 stalks green onions
- 2 T. soy sauce
- 1 t. salt
- 1 C. peanut oil
- 1 t. sweet flour paste

Directions:
1. Clean fish head. Rub with salt inside and out. Marinate in soy sauce and wine.
2. Heat oil in frying pan. Fry fish head on both sides 10-15 min. Remove fish head and oil. Fry garlic in 3 T. oil till there is a distinctive aroma. Return fish head and add soy sauce. Add bean paste and sweet flour paste. Remove everything to earthenware cooking pot. Add boiling water and cook 2-3 min. Put in bean curd (cut into large pieces), pork meat, bamboo shoot and mushroom. Cook in low heat 1 hr. Serve in same earthenware pot.

芋芳燒鴨
Duck with Taros

杭州菜　　　材料：12人份

材　料：肥嫩鴨半隻（約一斤重）　芋芳（紅芽的）一斤或（十二兩左右）　嫩薑二兩（切厚片）　猪油二湯匙　酒一茶匙　白醬油一湯匙　鹽一茶匙　碎冰糖半湯匙

做　法：①將鴨洗淨瀝乾放入已沸之三飯碗水中煮開，即加入酒，以文火煮二十分鐘，撈出後待其稍冷斬塊，煮鴨之湯盛碗內留用。

②在炒鍋內燒熱猪油（花生油亦可）爆炒薑片，繼將鴨塊放下略炒，並倒下醬油、鴨湯和冰糖，調炒後改用平底鋁鍋，以文火續燒。（湯需要蓋過鴨塊，如湯不夠，可酌加沸水。）

③待鴨塊半爛時，將切塊之芋芳倒下同煮，至相當穌軟時，再放鹽滾片刻卽盛盆上桌。

Ingredients:　½ young duck (1⅓ lb.)　　1⅓ lb. or less taros (with red buds)
　　2 oz. young ginger (sliced thickly)　2 T. lard
　　1 t. wine　　1 T. white soy sauce
　　1 t. salt　　½ T. crushed rock sugar

Directions:
1. Clean duck and drain. Drop duck into 3 bowls of boiling water; bring to boil. Add wine and cook over low heat 20 min. Remove duck and let cool; cut into pieces. Set soup aside.
2. Heat lard (or peanut oil) in frying pan. Saute ginger; add duck. Stir and turn occasionally. Add white soy sauce, duck soup and rock sugar. Cook over low heat until duck is tender. (Soup must cover duck. Add water if necessary.)
3. When duck is half done, stir in taros; cook until well-done. Sprinkle with salt and let simmer 30 sec. Serve hot.

八 寶 鴨
Stuffed Duck with Eight-Treasures

材料：12人份

材　料：肥鴨一隻　糯米半飯碗　瘦肉丁　火腿丁　蝦米淡菜丁　香菇丁　筍丁　蓮子　花生仁各二湯匙　熟胡蘿花片十數片　熟四季豆數根（一切二斷）　豆粉一湯匙（用三湯匙水調和）　冰糖一湯匙（碎）　薑二片

調味品：白醬油一湯匙　鹽一茶匙半　酒一湯匙　糖半茶匙

做　法：①先將肥鴨洗淨瀝水，在鴨身內外敷鹽一茶匙，約一小時後再燒，蓮子與花生仁用少水煮熟，筍丁蒸十分鐘，瘦肉丁加入豆粉半茶匙和糖及白醬油一茶匙拌勻，糯米洗後浸水約二小時，以水蓋過米約半吋，略滾待冷。

②將八寶與糯米加鹽半茶匙拌勻，然後塞入鴨之肚內以白線縫臀部之口。

③備厚底炒菜鍋，將鴨整隻置沸水中（水至鴨之半身）密蓋以文火燉燒，鴨爛加入熟胡蘿花片及熟四季豆段，並加入碎冰糖與白醬油，片刻後，調下水豆粉拌和，然後盛在細瓷長盆中送席。

Ingredients:
- 1 fat duck
- ½ bowl glutinous rice
- 2 T. lean pork (diced)
- 2 T. Chinese ham (diced)
- 2 T. each dried shrimps and soysters (chopped)
- 2 T. dried mushrooms (diced)
- 2 T. bamboo shoots (diced)
- 2 T. lotus seeds
- 2 T. peanuts
- 10-15 slices cooked carrot (carved)
- 5-8 cooked string beans (cut each in two)
- 2 slices ginger
- 1 T. cornstarch (mixed with 3 T. water)
- 1 T. crushed rock sugar

Seasonings: 1 T. white soy sauce　　1½ t. salt　　1 T. wine　　¾ t. sugar

Directions:
1. Clean duck and drain. Rub 1 t. salt on duck and let stand 1 hr. Cook lotus seeds and peanut until soft. Steam bamboo shoots about 10 min. Mix diced meat with ½ t. cornstarch, 1 t. sugar and 1 t. white soy sauce. Soak glutinous rice, about 2 hr.; water should cover ½" above rice. After 2 hr., cook and bring to boil for few minutes. Let cool.
2. Mix 8 treasures thoroughly with glutinous rice and ½ t. salt, and stuff in duck; sew opening with white thread.
3. Put duck in pot with boiling water to cover half its body. Cook, covered, over low heat until tender. Add carrot slices, string beans, crushed rock sugar and white soy sauce. Cook 2-3 min. Blend in constarch paste. Serve.

煮干絲　　江蘇菜
Boiled Bean Curd Noodles

材料：12人份

材　料：干絲四兩　筍絲一支　香菇三只　肉絲或火腿絲一小碟　小蝦米二湯匙(用溫水泡浸)
　　　　猪油一湯匙　　芹菜段三四支　高湯一大碗　蘇打粉四分之一茶匙

做　法：①首將小蘇打粉用一飯碗沸水溶化，傾入干絲，泡約五分鐘，倒在濾油器內，以冷水沖淨
　　　　蘇打粉味，肉絲調入一茶匙白醬油和豆粉糖各四分之一茶匙拌勻，置旁備用。
　　　　②將高湯傾入小鋁鍋內，待沸放下筍絲，香菇絲及蝦米滾片刻，即倒下干絲同煮約十五分
　　　　鐘，然後加入調味品，並川下肉絲及芹菜段與味精，調味可口後，即可盛起供食。

Ingredients: 4 oz. bean curd noodles
　　　　　　　3 dried mushrooms
　　　　　　　2 T. dried small shrimp (soaked in warm water)
　　　　　　　1 large bowl meat stock
　　　　　　　1 T. lard
　　　　　　　1 bamboo shoot (shredded)
　　　　　　　1 small saucer shredded pork (or ham)
　　　　　　　3-4 celery stalks
　　　　　　　¼ t. soda powder

Seasonings: 1 t. white soy sauce
　　　　　　　¼ t. sugar
　　　　　　　¼ t. cornstarch
　　　　　　　dash of monosodium glutamate

Directions:
1. Dissolve soda powder in a bowl of boiling water. Soak bean curd noodles in soda water about 5 min. Drain water; flush off soda smell with cold water.
2. Marinate shredded pork in seasonings except M.S.G. Set aside for use.
3. Pour stock into pan and boil. Add shredded bamboo shoot, mushrooms and shrimp, and boil 3-4 min
4. Add bean curd noodles and boil 15 minutes. Add all seasonings. Add shredded pork, celery (cut in 1½" sections) and M.S.G.

醬肉
Pork in Soy Sauce and Bean Paste

北平菜　　材料：12人份

材　料：五花肉一斤　黃酒一湯匙
調味品：甜麵醬二湯匙　醬油三湯匙　碎冰糖二茶匙　八角桂皮少許　沸水約一飯碗
做　法：①首將五花肉整塊洗淨略吹乾，用甜麵醬揉擦四週，約醃二小時，然後置鍋內加上醬油冰糖五香，黃酒用中火燒滾片刻，然後加沸水以慢火煮燒一小時左右即可。
②煮爛盛起待冷切片，可作便當菜，湯汁可留作吃麵用。

Ingredients: 1⅓ lb. fresh bacon (five flower pork)　　1 T. rice wine
Seasonings: 2 T. sweet flour paste　3 T. soy sauce　2 t. crushed rock sugar
a little aniseeds and cinnamon bark (kuei-pi)　1 bowl (appr.) boiling water
Directions:
1. Clean fat pork meat and let dry. Brush with sweet flour paste on both sides. Let stand 2 hr. Put in pan; add soy sauce, rock sugar, aniseed and "kuei-pi" and rice wine. Bring boil over moderate heat. Add boiling water, reduce heat, and cook about 1 hr. or until meat is tender.
2. Remove and let cool. Slice and serve cold.

麻婆豆腐
Ma-Po's Bean Curd

四川菜　　材料：12人份

材　料：豆腐二元（每元六格的）　猪肉末二兩　青蒜二小支　高湯半飯碗　花生油二大匙　辣油二湯匙　花椒末半茶匙　豆粉一茶匙（用一湯匙水調濕）

調味品：黑醬油二湯匙　白醬油一茶匙　辣豆腐醬一湯匙　鹽半茶匙　味精少許

做　法：①首將豆腐用刀割片，猪肉末調入一茶匙黑醬油和少許豆粉糖拌勻。
②用一湯匙油燒熱，將肉末略炒盛起，再加入油二湯匙，先爆香蒜白頭，即傾下豆腐，調下醬油、鹽、辣豆瓣醬，翻覆紅一下，再倒下已炒過之猪肉末，加入沸水或高湯，關蓋滾片刻，然後放下青蒜葉滾香，再拘下水豆粉溜勻，即盛盆中，面澆辣油，並洒下花椒末，即可送席。

Ingredients: 2 cakes bean curd (about 4"X4" each)　2 oz. minced pork
2 stalks garlic stalks　½ bowl meat stock
3 T. peanut oil　2 T. chili pepper oil
½ t. peppercorn powder　1 t. cornstarch (mixed with 1 T. water)

Seasonings: 2 T. black soy sauce　1 t. white soy sauce
1 T. hot bean paste　½ t. salt
dash of monosodium glutamate

Directions:
1. Cut bean curd into slices. Mix minced pork with 1 t. black soy sauce, cornstarch and sugar.
2. Heat 1 T. oil. Stir-fry pork. Remove. Heat another 2 T. oil. Saute white garlic ends. Add bean curd; season with black soy sauce, 1 t. white soy sauce, salt and hot bean paste. Stir-fry a few times. Add pork to pan; add also boiling water or meat stock. Cook, covered, 2-3 min. Add green garlic leaves. Stir in cornstarch paste. Remove to serving plate. Sprinkle with chili pepper oil and peppercorn powder Serve.

紅燒烏賊
Red Simmered Cuttlefish

寧波菜　　　材料：12人份

材　料：烏賊一斤（選白嫩而堅硬者卽新鮮）　五花肉六兩　扁尖（又名筍乾）二兩　蒜頭七八粒　薑二片

調味品：醬油二湯匙　冰糖（碎）一茶匙　酒二茶匙　鹽半茶匙　花生油二湯匙

做　法：①首將烏賊去皮洗淨瀝乾切塊，五花肉亦洗淨切塊裝盆放下一湯匙醬油浸漬片刻。
②次將扁尖略洗，以溫水泡軟撕開切段，蒜頭整粒剝皮置旁備用。
③油鍋燒熱先落薑片爆香，倒下烏賊塊與肉塊炒透，卽洒下酒及全部醬油，翻覆燒紅先倒下泡扁尖之水一滾，卽盛小鋁鍋內，再加下沸水關蓋過肉約一寸，待滾卽放冰糖，扁尖和蒜頭，以文火續燉，候肉爛湯稠盛起送席，亦可供小孩帶便當之佳肴。

Ingredients: 1⅓ lb. fresh cuttlefish
2 oz. dried bamboo shoots
2 slices ginger
6 oz. fresh bacon (five flower pork)
7-8 cloves garlic

Seasonings: 2 T. soy sauce
2 t. wine
2 T. peanut oil
1 t. crushed rock sugar
¼ t. salt

Directions:
1. Remove membranes from cuttlefish. Clean and drain. Cut into 1"X1½" pieces; Cut pork into same size as cuttlefish. Mix together with 1 T. soy sauce. Let stand 4-5 min.
2. Wash dried bamboo shoots. Soak in warm water to soften. Rip lengthwise and cut in sections. Save water. Peel garlic cloves.
3. Heat oil in frying pan. Sauté ginger. Add cuttlefish and pork. Stir-fry, mixing thoroughly. Add wine and soy sauce. Fry till reddish brown. Add soaking water. Bring to boil. Transfer contents to pot. Add boiling water to cover meat by 1". Bring to boil. Add rock sugar, dried bamboo shoots, and garlic. Stew over low heat until both cuttlefish and pork are tender and sauce is thick. Serve.

四 狀 元
Four Gentlemen

廣 東 菜　　　　材料：12人份

材　料：乾醃魚頭尾各一個（洗淨斬塊）　猪腿肉半斤（切塊）　豆腐干二元（切塊）　青蒜葉四兩（切段）　薑二片　花生油二湯匙

調味品：白醬油二湯匙　鹽半茶匙　冰糖半茶匙　酒一茶匙

做　法：①首將油鍋燒熱，放下薑片爆香，即倒下鹹魚之頭尾塊，略炒下酒，放下沸水三飯碗，改用小鋁鍋以文火續燉，約十五分鐘，即倒落肉塊及豆干，待滾，再調入白醬油與鹽糖。
②俟肉半爛，放落蒜白頭，不久，即下青蒜葉，片刻盛起，熱吃味更鮮美。

Ingredients:
- 1 dried salted fish head (cleaned and cut into pieces)
- 1 dried salted fish tail (cleaned and cut into pieces)
- 2 dried bean curd (cut into pieces)
- 2 slices ginger
- 2/3 lb. pork leg (cut into pieces)
- 4 oz. garlic stalks (cut into sections)
- 2 T. peanut oil

Seasonings:
- 2 T. white soy sauce
- ½ t. rock sugar
- ½ t. salt
- 1 t. wine

Directions:
1. Heat oil in frying pan. Stir-fry ginger. Add salted fish. Stir-fry a few times. Add wine, and 3 bowls boiling water. Transfer contents to small pot. Stew about 15 min. Add pork and dried bean curd. Let boil. Season with white soy sauce, salt and sugar.
2. Put garlic white ends when meat is half-tender. Cook until tender. Add garlic leaves. Cook a few minutes longer. Serve hot.

花生燉肉
Pork and Peanut Stew

家常菜　　　　　　材料：12人份

材　料：煮用花生仁一斤（千萬勿買炒的花生煮不爛）　豬腿肉或小排骨十二兩
調味品：黑醬油五湯匙　冰糖一湯匙　酒一茶匙
做　法：①首將豬肉洗後瀝水，切約五分見方之塊，以二湯匙醬油泡漬半小時再用。
　　　　②再將花生洗淨，放入小鋁鍋內，加下冷水蓋過花生約二寸，待滾卽撈下已泡醬油之肉塊及酒同燉，以文火燉至一小時後，卽傾入餘下之黑醬油、白醬油、冰糖等，燉至湯稠肉爛，花生極穌，卽可供食，亦可作小孩便當菜。

Ingredients: 1⅓ lb. tenderable peanuts　　12 oz. pork leg or spareribs
Seasonings: 5 T. black soy sauce　　1 T. rock sugar
　　　　　　　1 t. wine
Directions: 1. Cut pork into 1″ squares. Marinate in 2 T. soy sauce 30 min.
　　　　　　　2. Wash peanuts. Put in small pot. Add cold water to cover peanut by 2″. Bring to boil. Add pork and wine. Stew over low heat, 1 hr. Add remaining black soy sauce, white soy sauce and rock sugar. Cook until pork and peanuts are tender.

紅燒划水
Fish Tails in Brown Sauce

江浙菜　　　　材料：12人份

材　料：活青魚尾三、四個(重約十二兩)　薑二片切絲　葱三支切條　鹽半茶匙　醬油二湯匙
　　　　豆粉一茶匙　酒二茶匙　糖半茶匙　豆瓣醬甜麵醬各一茶匙　花生油四湯匙　猪油一湯匙

做　法：①先將魚尾洗淨每個約切三、四條，以鹽醬油、豆粉、酒、糖泡浸入味。
　　　　②起油鍋紅熱落薑絲放魚尾油煎落鹽甜醬及醬油汁與沸水略滾最後加入葱條及一湯匙猪油
　　　　　即可起鍋，宜熱吃。

Ingredients: 3 or 4 fish tails (about 1 lb., from live grass carps)　2 pc. ginger (shredded)
　　　　　　　3 stalks green onions (cut into 1½" pieces)　½ t. bean paste
　　　　　　　½ t. sweet flour paste　4 T. peanut oil
　　　　　　　1 T. lard

Seasonings: ½ t. salt　1 t. cornstarch (mixed with water)
　　　　　　 2 t. wine　½ t. sugar
　　　　　　 2 T. soy sauce

Directions: 1. Clean fish tails. Cut each into 3 or 4 long strips lengthwise; marinate in seasonings.
2. Heat oil in frying pan. Fry ginger first; add fish tails. Add both bean and sweet flour pastes, soy sauce and a little boiling water. Bring to boil. Add green onion and lard. Serve hot.

醃魚燒肉
Braised Pork with Dried Salted Fish

杭 州 菜　　　　材料：12人份

材　料：豬腿肉一斤　醃魚六兩（米魚乾，鰻魚乾，黃魚乾均可）　薑二片　花生油一湯匙
調味品：醬油二湯匙　冰糖二茶匙　酒一茶匙
做　法：①首將豬肉洗淨瀝乾，切塊後以醬油泡漬約二十分鐘，醃魚洗淨斬塊備用。
②油鍋燒熱放落薑片爆香，再倒下醃魚塊及半茶匙酒燜炒幾下卽盛起留用，然後把豬肉倒下略炒，卽放餘之酒同時傾入沸水一飯碗半，卽換小鋁鍋以文火續燉，視肉半爛，卽倒落已煎過之醃魚，燜燉半小時，視湯汁稠濃卽可盛起供食，此菜可保數日，誠爲夏日之開胃佳肴。

Ingredients: 1⅓ lb. pork leg (foreleg)
6 oz dried salted fish (dried salted yellow fish or sea eel.)
2 slices ginger　　　　　　　　　　　　1 T. peanut oil
Seasonings: 2 T. soy sauce　　　2 t. rock sugar　　　1 t. wine
Directions:
1. Clean pork and drain. Cut in 1″ squares. Marinate in soy sauce 20 min. Clean fish and cut in same size as pork.
2. Heat oil in fry pan. Stir-fry ginger, then add fish and ½ t. wine. Stir-fry a few times and remove. Add pork; stir-fry lightly. Add remaining wine and 1½ bowl boiling water. Transfer to small pot. Cook over low heat till pork is half-done. Add fish. Cook 30 min. longer. When sauce thickens, remove and serve.

咖喱鷄
Braised Chicken with Curry Sauce

廣東菜　　　　　材料：12人份

材　料：肥鷄一只（重約一斤多）　洋葱四兩　馬鈴薯半斤　蕃茄半斤　胡蘿蔔一只　咖喱二湯匙（用二湯匙水調濕）　鹽一茶匙　花生油四湯匙

做　法：①將鷄洗淨斬塊，馬鈴薯削去皮，一半切成斜刀塊，一半切成小薄片，蕃茄用滾水泡後削去皮，除去子，同洋葱與胡蘿蔔都切成小薄片留用。
②油鍋燒熱，加下二湯匙油，先將鷄塊爆透盛起，再放下油，先炒洋葱，隨卽加入咖喱粉炒片刻，再將爆過之鷄塊及胡蘿蔔蕃茄馬鈴薯全部倒下攪炒，然後盛在小鋁鍋內，改用文火續燉，約一小時後加入鹽再燜煮半小時，卽可盛起供食。

Ingredients: 1 fat chicken (about 1⅜ lb.)　4 oz. onion
⅔ lb. potato　⅔ lb. tomato
1 carrot　2 T. curry powder (mixed with 2 T. water)
1 t. salt　4 T. peanut oil

Directions:
1. Clean chicken. Cut into 2"X1" pieces. Peel potatoes. Halve. Cut one half into pieces at different angles. Cut other half into thin slices. Blanch tomatoes to peel skins. Remove seeds. Cut tomatoes, onions and carrot into small thin slices.
2. Heat 2 T. oil in frying pan. Stir-fry chicken pieces a few minutes. Remove. Heat remaining oil. Stir-fry onions, then add curry powder. Stir-fry a few times. Add chicken, carrots, tomatoes and potatoes. Stir-fry to combine. Transfer contents to small pot. Braise over low heat 1 hr. Season with salt. Braise another 30 min. Serve.

油豆腐塞肉　廣東菜　　材料：12人份
Pork Meat Stuffed Oily Bean Curd

材　料：三角形油豆腐十五只（每只二角）　猪肉六兩　笋半支　葱二支　金鉤十五只　花生油二湯匙
　　　　豆粉二湯匙（用二湯匙水調濕）

調味品：醬油一湯匙半　　鹽半茶匙　　糖半茶匙

做　法：①首將猪肉洗淨加入笋葱同斬碎，調入半湯匙醬油和一茶匙豆粉及鹽糖拌勻備用。
　　　　②次將油豆粉洗淨，瀝乾每只在當中劃開，裡面擦點水豆粉，然後逐只將肉塞進，又在肉
　　　　　面嵌入金鉤一只然後塗上一點水豆粉備用。
　　　　③花生油燒熱將油豆腐之肉面逐只投入鍋中煎片刻，再把醬油倒入，然後改用小鋁鍋以沸
　　　　　水加至剛蓋過油豆腐，以文火燉至汁乾，盛起供食，味甚濃鮮。

Ingredients: 15 pc. triangular oily bean curd　　6 oz. pork
　　　　　　　1 T. chopped bamboo shoots　　2 stalks green onion (chopped)
　　　　　　　15 dried shrimps　　2 T. peanut oil
　　　　　　　2 T. cornstarch (mixed with 2 T. water)

Seasonings: 1½ T. soy sauce　　½ t. salt　　¼ t. sugar

Directions:
1. Clean pork. Mince. Mince bamboo shoot and green onion. Combine with pork and mince together. Add ½ T. soy sauce, 1 t. cornstarch, salt and sugar. Mix well.
2. Wash oily bean curds; drain. Slit open center, rub inside with a little cornstarch paste and stuff with meat. Stick 1 dried shrimp in each meat filling with cornstarch paste.
3. Heat oil in frying pan. Put in oily bean curds, filling side down. Saute a few minutes. Add soy sauce. Transfer contents to small pot; fill with boiling water to cover. Stew over low heat until sauce is dry. Serve.

葷素菜
Meat and Vegetables

家常菜　　　　　　材料：12人份

材　料：豬後腿肉十二兩　白蘿蔔一斤　紅蘿蔔二條　青梗菜一斤　豆粉一茶匙　花生油四湯匙
調味品：黑白醬油各一湯匙　鹽一茶匙　糖半茶匙
做　法：①首將豬後腿肉略洗瀝水，依皮切到瘦肉，成小手指形之長條，加入黑醬油和豆粉拌勻，紅白蘿蔔均去皮，亦切長條，青梗菜攀去老葉，洗淨瀝水後，也切成長條均備用。
②先把二湯匙油燒熱，倒下青菜，加少許鹽糖炒片刻，盛起置旁備用。
③鍋中再放油二湯匙，先倒下肉條爆炒，然後，倒下紅白蘿蔔同炒，再調入白醬油和糖拌炒，卽加入沸水一飯碗，以文火滾燒，視肉皮已頓，卽放下鹽同煮，並倒下已炒過之青梗菜兜滾，卽可供食。

Ingredients: 12 oz. pork (hind leg)　　1⅓ lb. turnips　　2 carrots
1⅓ lb. green cabbage　　1 t. cornstarch　　4 T. peanut oil

Seasonings: 1 T. black soy sauce　　1 T. white soy sauce　　1 t. salt
½ t. sugar

Directions:
1. Clean pork and drain. Cut, retaining skin, into small-finger lengths. Blend with soy sauce and cornstarch. Pare turnips and carrots; cut into small-finger lengths. Remove old leaves from cabbage. Clean and drain. Cut same lengths as the rest.
2. Heat 2 T. oil. Add cabbage; season with salt and sugar. Stir-fry and remove.
3. Heat another 2 T. oil in frying pan. Stir-fry pork 1-2 min.; add turnips and carrots. Blend in white soy sauce and sugar. Add 1 bowl boiling water. Simmer over low heat until pork skin is tender. Add salt and cabbage. Cook until bubbly and serve.

紅燜雙童 　　湖　南　菜　　　材料：12人份
Red Braised Chickens

材　料：童子雞二只每只重約五百公分（去脚去內臟不用）　芥蘭菜二扎　葱二支　薑一片　花椒半茶匙　醬油四湯匙　酒一湯匙　麻油五湯匙　花生油三湯匙　糖一湯匙　鹽半茶匙

做　法：①首將雞洗淨放大盤內加下醬油浸漬約半小時。
②將鍋燒熱，傾下麻油燒熱，撈出雞放下爆煎，翻轉再爆片刻，卽加下浸雞之醬油及酒、葱、薑滾數下，卽盛起轉放入大砂鍋中，同時放下二茶匙半糖，半茶匙花椒，半茶匙鹽及一杯沸水以文火燜二小時，另將三湯匙花生油燒熱，放下芥蘭菜急炒數下，加下鹽糖各半茶匙及少許水炒幾下卽盛起一半在細瓷盆之一邊，中間盛放雞，二只須相反方向，另一邊又盛另一半之芥蘭菜，最後淋上濃香之雞汁卽趁熱送席。

Ingredients:
- 2 young chickens (about 1 lb. each) (discard feet and entrails)
- 2 stalks Chinese broccoli
- 2 stalks green onion (remove root ends)
- 1 slice ginger
- ½ t. peppercorn
- 4 T. soy sauce
- 1 T. wine
- 5 T. sesame oil
- 3 T. peanut oil
- 1 T. sugar
- ½ t. salt

Directions:
1. Marinate chickens in soy sauce 30 min.
2. Heat sesame oil in frying pan; put chickens in and fry on all sides till lightly brown. Add remaining marinade, wine, green onion and ginger. Cook 30 sec. and remove contents to earthenware pot. Add 2½ t. sugar, ½ t. peppercorn, ½ t. salt and 1 C. boiling water. Cook, covered, 2 hr. over low heat.
3. Heat 3 T. oil; fry broccoli for few seconds, turning frequently. Add salt, sugar (each ½ t.) and 2 T. water. Cook another 2 min.
4. Place broccoli on two ends of serving plate and chickens in center, each facing the other way. Pour stock over chickens and broccoli.

羊肉粉皮
Lamb and Bean Thread Sheets

杭州菜　　　材料：12人份

材　料：羊腿肉六兩　粉皮二十張(四元)　薑一片　青蒜葉一支　花生油一湯匙　胡椒少許
調味品：醬油一湯匙　鹽半茶匙　糖¼茶匙　酒一茶匙
做　法：①首將羊肉洗淨，瀝乾用沸水加薑酒在小火爐上煮軟，撈出待冷切片，湯汁留用。
②粉皮切寬條浸水洗後瀝去水份留用。
③油鍋燒熱，把羊肉略炒卽傾下湯汁約二飯碗半，先調下醬油和鹽糖，待沸，將粉皮放下，再丟青蒜葉一滾，卽可盛起，而洒胡椒粉供食。

Ingredients:	6 oz. lamb leg	20 bean thread sheets (fung-pi)	1 slice ginger
	1 stalk garlic stalk	1 T. peanut oil	dash of pepper
Seasonings:	1 T. soy sauce	½ t. salt	¼ t. sugar
	1 t. wine		

Directions:
1. Clean lamb and drain. Put ginger and wine in boiling water. Drop in lamb. Cook over low heat until tender. Let cool and slice. Set soup aside.
2. Cut bean thread sheets into wide strips. Wash and drain.
3. Heat oil in frying pan. Stir-fry lamb. Add 2½ bowls soup. Blend in soy sauce, salt and sugar. Bring to boil. Add bean thread sheets and garlic stalk. Bring to boil again. Sprinkle with pepper and serve.

鷄絲燴翅

廣東菜　　材料：12人份

Shredded Chicken and Spark's Fin

材　料：圓翅餅一個重約二兩半　鷄湯一大碗　生鷄絲半飯碗　鷄蛋清半飯碗　白醬油一湯匙　火腿一小碟　鹽一茶匙　味精少許　藕粉四湯匙（用五湯匙水調和）

做　法：①首將翅餅用溫水浸五小時後用，用沸水加一塊薑煮二十分鐘，然後取出洗數次後，瀝水留用，浸再用沸水加一塊薑燒十五分鐘取出瀝水留用。
②把鷄絲調一茶匙白醬油和一湯匙蛋清拌勻備用。
③把鷄湯加魚翅同煮，卽放鹽和白醬油，然後加拌好的鷄絲，用湯匙不停地攪勻，同時加入先用水調稀好之藕粉，及味精攪到濃稠，再加入打發泡之鷄蛋清，卽盛大碗內面瀝火腿絲上席。

Ingredients: 2½ oz. shark's fin　　1 large bowl chicken soup
½ bowl shredded chicken (uncooked)　½ bowl egg white
1 small saucer ham (shredded)　1 t. salt
1 T. white soy sauce　dash of monosodium glutamate
4 T. lotus root powder (mixed with 5 T. water)

Directions:
1. Soak shark's fin in warm water 5 hr. Fill pot with boiling water. Drop in fin and ginger. Cook 20 min. Wash several times. Cook again in boiling water with ginger 15 min. Remove and drain.
2. Mix shredded chicken with 1 t. white soy sauce and 1 T. egg white.
3. Put shark's fin in chicken soup. Bring to boil. Add salt, white soy sauce and shredded chicken. Stir continuously. Add lotus root paste M.S.G. Blend till sauce thickens. Stir in egg white (beaten until fluffy). Sprinkle with shredded ham and serve.

鷄茸粟米
Minced Chicken and Corn

廣東菜　　材料：12人份

材　料：鷄胸脯一個　鷄蛋白二個　粟米一罐　高湯一中碗　豆粉一湯匙（用二湯匙水調濕）
調味品：白醬油一茶匙　糖¼茶匙　鹽一茶匙
做　法：①首將鷄胸去皮拆骨取肉斬碎，調入白醬油和糖拌勻，鷄骨加水燉爲高湯備用。
　　　　②將蛋白加一點鹽和味精打發泡，調入鷄肉內拌勻，卽爲鷄茸。
　　　　③把高湯倒在鍋內燒沸，加入鹽及整罐玉米（連湯），煮約五分鐘，卽將水豆粉加入湯內，立刻用湯匙攪勻，視湯汁稠濃，卽可加入調好之鷄茸，但鷄茸在加入前要再搗一下，免得成塊。
附註—如果用鮮玉米，宜先用蘿蔔絲刨子擦碎，並先以水煮頓，始可應用。家常吃可以里肌肉代替鷄胸。

Ingredients: 1 chicken breast　　2 egg whites　　1 can corn paste
　　　　　　　1 medium bowl meat stock　　1 T. cornstarch (mixed with 2 T. water)
Seasonings: 1 t. white soy sauce　　¼ t. sugar　　1 t. salt
Directions:
1. Remove bones and skin of chicken breast. Mince meat. Mix with white soy sauce and sugar. Cook chicken bones in water to make meat stock.
2. Beat egg whites seasoned with salt and M.S.G. until fluffy. Mix into minced chicken.
3. Heat meat stock in pot to boil. Add salt and can of corn paste. Cook 5 min. Stir in cornstarch paste until soup thickens. Add chicken. Stir to avoid lumping.

Note: If fresh corn is used, corn should be grated, then cooked until soft. Lean pork can be used instead of chicken breast if cooking just for the family.

羊腰腦羹
Lamb Kidney and Brain Soup

杭州菜　　材料：12人份

材　料：羊腰腦各二付　冬筍片一支　香菇四只（泡發後切片）　火腿片一小碟　韭黃段數根
　　　　高湯一中碗　豆粉二茶匙　酒一茶匙　猪油一湯匙
調味品：白醬油一湯匙　鹽一茶匙　藕粉一湯匙　用四湯匙水調濕拘汁用
做　法：①首將羊腦浸在清水中，撕去血絲瀝乾切厚片，羊腰撕去白衣，洗淨切片，與羊腦同置碗中，加入豆粉和酒拌勻。
　　　　②油鍋燒熱，先爆筍片和香菇片，然後傾入高湯，待沸，倒下火腿白醬油和鹽，關蓋滾燒片刻，先調下藕粉拘汁，最後川下羊腰腦略滾，卽放下韭黃段一兜，卽刻盛在細瓷碗中送席。

Ingredients:
- 2 each lamb kidney and brain
- 4 dried mushrooms (softened in water and sliced)
- 2 oz. blanched Chinese leeks (chiu-huang) (cut into 1½" length)
- 1 medium bowl meat stock
- 1 t. wine
- 1 bamboo shoot (sliced)
- 1 small saucer sliced ham
- 2 t. cornstarch
- 1 T. lard
- 1 t. salt

Seasonings:
- 1 T. white soy sauce
- 1 T. lotus root powder (mixed with 4 T. water)

Directions:
1. Soak lamb brains in water. Remove veins and thin membranes. Drain. Cut into thick slices. Remove white veins from kidneys. Clean and slice. Combine with brains, cornstarch and wine.
2. Heat oil in frying pan. Stir-fry bamboo shoots and mushrooms. Add meat stock. Let boil. Add ham, white soy sauce and salt. Boil, covered, for a few minutes. Stir in lotus root powder paste. Add brains and kidney. Let boil. Add blanched Chinese leeks. Remove immediately. Serve.

鮮蠔羹
Fresh Oyster Soup

家常菜　　材料：12人份

材　料： 鮮蠔半斤　洋芋胡蘿蔔各一個（切小片蒸熟）　碗豆仁或碗豆莢（切三段）二兩　薑一片　瘦肉二兩（切小片）　韭黃數根（切段）　豬油二湯匙

調味品： 白醬油一湯匙　鹽一茶匙　豆粉一茶匙　酒一茶匙　胡椒粉少許　豆粉一湯匙（用二湯匙水調濕拘汁用）

做　法： ①首將蠔用鹽洗淨瀝乾加下豆粉、酒、薑片拌勻備用，次將瘦肉加少許白醬油及少許豆粉拌勻。

②用豬油先炒肉片，繼下洋芋、胡蘿蔔碗豆等，即倒下沸水一中碗，待滾即調入鹽和白醬油，繼下鮮蠔，燒開後放韭黃及水豆粉，面灑胡椒粉，熱吃味美，這是一道色香味俱全之營養羹湯。

Ingredients: ⅔ lb. fresh oyster　　1 potato (cut into small slices and steamed)
1 carrot (cut into small slices and steamed)　2 oz. snow peas (podded or cut into 3 pieces)
2 oz. lean pork (cut into small slices)　2 oz. blanched Chinese leeks (chiu-huang) (cut into pieces)
2 T. lard　　1 slice ginger　1 t. cornstarch

Seasonings: 1 T. white soy sauce　1 t. salt　1 T. cornstarch (mixed with 2 T. water)　1 t. wine
dash of pepper

Directions:
1. Wash fresh oysters with a little salt. Rinse and drain. Blend in cornstarch, wine and ginger. Mix lean pork with white soy sauce and cornstarch.
2. Heat lard in frying pan. Stir-fry pork. Add potato, carrot, and snow peas. Pour in 1 medium bowl boiling water. Let boil. Add salt and white soy sauce. Add oysters. Let boil again. Add blanched Chinese leeks and cornstarch paste to thicken. Sprinkle with pepper. Serve hot.

蝦球羹
Shrimp Balls Soup

杭州菜　　　材料：12人份

材　料：炸好之蝦球三十粒　筍片一支（蒸十分鐘）　香菇三、四只（泡後切片）　胡椒少許　火腿片一小碟　韭黃少許（切斷）　高湯一中碗　藕粉一湯匙（用二湯匙水調和）

調味品：白醬油一湯匙　鹽半茶匙

做　法：①首將高湯煮沸，放下筍片，香菇片，火腿片等滾燒然後加入調味品，待滾，即下蝦球兜燒，再放下韭黃，並調下水藕粉攪勻盛起，面洒胡椒粉送席。

Ingredients: 30 fried shrimp balls　1 bamboo shoot (steamed 10 min.)
3-4 dried mushrooms (soaked to soften and sliced)
2 oz. sliced Chinese ham　1 oz. blanched Chinese leeks (chiu-huang) (cut in sections)
1 bowl meat stock　1 T. lotus root powder (mixed in 2 T. water) or cornstarch
dash of pepper

Seasonings: 1 T. white soy sauce　½ t. salt

Directions: 1. Boil meat stock. Add bamboo shoots, mushrooms and Chinese ham. Cook until simmering. Blend in seasonings; let simmer. Add shrimp balls and cook 1 min. Add blanched Chinese leeks. Stir in lotus root powder paste. Sprinkle with pepper and serve.

干貝羹
Scallop Soup

杭州菜　　材料：12人份

材　料：干貝一兩　冬菇二只（浸發去蒂切絲）　熟火腿絲二湯匙　韭黃六七根　豬油一湯匙　豆粉一湯匙（用三湯匙水調濕）

調味品：白醬油一湯匙　鹽一茶匙

做　法：①首將干貝略洗，放入碗內以溫水蓋過干貝約三寸浸泡二三小時，然後以中火隔水蒸約一小時，取出除去湯汁留用，以手將干貝慢慢撕散，置旁備用。
②鍋中將油燒熱，先爆炒冬菇絲，再加入干貝汁和七分碗之沸水，（以盛干貝羹之碗）待滾，倒下干貝絲，關蓋滾燒片刻，再放下火腿絲一兜，再調下水豆粉與韭黃段，視湯汁呈薄稠狀，即可盛在細瓷碗中送席。

附　註：干貝羹內亦可加一點蒸熟之筍絲。

Ingredients: 1 oz. scallops
2 dried mushrooms (soaked in water to soften; stemmed and shredded)
2 T. cooked ham (shredded)　6-7 stalks blanched Chinese leeks (chiu-huang)
1 T. lard　　1 T. cornstarch (mixed with 3 T. water)

Seasonings: 1 T. white soy sauce　1 t. salt

Directions:
1. Wash scallops slightly and put in bowl. Add warm water in bowl to cover scallops by 3". Let stand 2-3 hr. Steam above water over medium heat about 1 hr. Remove. Save stock. Tear scallops into shreds with hands.
2. Heat oil in frying pan. Stir-fry shredded mushrooms. Add scallop stock and 7/10 soup bowl boiling water. Bring to boil. Add scallop shreds. Cook, covered, 3-4 min. Add shredded ham. Stir in cornstarch paste to thicken and blanched Chinese leeks. Serve.

Note: Cooked bamboo shoot shreds may also be added.

什錦豆腐
Ten Prceious Bean Curd

江浙菜　　　材料：12人份

材　料：四吋見方豆腐二塊　豬肉小片　筍小片　蝦米　蘑菇片　木耳　金針菜毛豆（蒸十分鐘）一小碟　鷄蛋一只　韭黃少許　豬油三湯匙　高湯一中碗　豆粉二湯匙（用四湯匙水調濕）

調味品：醬油一湯匙　鹽一茶匙　糖四分之一茶匙

做　法：①首將豆腐切小薄片留用，肉片以少少醬油豆粉拌勻備用。
②鍋中放二湯匙豬油，先加入肉片蘑菇片燴炒一分鐘，再放下蝦米，木耳金針毛豆等拌炒，然後傾下高湯滾燒，卽倒下豆腐，加入調味品，關蓋滾片刻，再調下水豆粉及一湯匙豬油，最後加入韭黃及打散之鷄蛋，使湯汁已稠成薄羹，卽可盛起供食。

Ingredients:
- 2 cakes bean curd (4"X4")
- 2 oz. sliced bamboo shoots
- 2 oz. sliced mushrooms
- 2 oz. lily buds
- 1 egg
- 3 T. lard
- 2 T. cornstarch (mixed with 4 T. water)
- 2 oz. sliced pork
- 2 oz. dried shrimps
- 2 oz. wood ears
- 2 oz. fresh soy beans (steamed 10 min.)
- 1 oz. blanched Chinese leeks (chiu-huang)
- 1 bowl meat stock

Seasonings: 1 T. soy sauce　　1 t. salt　　¼ t. sugar

Directions:
1. Cut bean curd into small thin slices. Mix sliced pork with a little soy sauce and cornstarch.
2. Heat 2 T. lard in frying pan. Stir-fry sliced pork and mushrooms, 1 min. Add dried shrimps, wood ears, lily buds, bamboo shoots and fresh soy beans. Combine. Add meat stock and let boil. Add bean curd and seasonings. Simmer, covered, 3-4 min. Blend in cornstarch paste and 1 T. lard. Add blanched Chinese leeks and egg (beaten). Cook until sauce thickens slightly and serve.

芙蓉黃魚參

杭州菜　　　材料：12人份

Yellow Fish & Sea Cucumber Foo Yung

材　料：海參三條　黃魚一尾（如無黃魚，馬頭魚，石斑魚、鱸魚等均可代替凡魚肉嫩者皆可）
　　　　雞蛋白三、四個　高湯一大碗　葱一支　薑一片　火腿末葱薑屑各一湯匙　豆粉一湯匙
　　　　豬油二湯匙　藕粉三湯匙（烹調一小時前以五湯匙水調濕）

調味品：白醬油一湯匙　鹽二茶匙　糖半茶匙　酒二茶匙　胡椒粉少許

做　法：①首將海參洗淨，直紋切做二塊，再每塊切爲斜片，以一茶匙豆粉和一茶匙酒拌勻，鍋中
　　　　放二飯碗沸水，放下一支葱，一片薑即傾下海參川燒片刻撈起留用。
　　　　②黃魚刮鱗去內臟，洗淨拆骨取肉，打斜切片（皮不要）先加一茶匙鹽，豆粉，白醬油，酒
　　　　，糖及一湯匙蛋白拌勻，留用，蛋白加鹽和味精打發泡，均置旁備用。
　　　　③將高湯加鹽在鍋內燒滾，放入海參煮半小時，繼川下黃魚片，待開片刻，再加入豬油澆
　　　　上蛋白，即盛大碗內，面灑火腿末與葱薑屑，及胡椒粉，趁熱送席。

Ingredients: 3 sea cucumbers　　1 yellow fish (or any fish with tender meat)　　3-4 egg whites
　　　　1 large bowl meat stock　　1 stalk green onion　　1 slice ginger
　　　　1 T. chopped Chinese ham　　1 T. chopped green onion　　1 T. chopped ginger
　　　　1 T. cornstarch　　2 T. lard　　3 T. lotus root powder (mixed with 5 T. water 1 hr. before cooking)

Seasonings: 1 T. white soy sauce　　2 t. salt　　½ t. sugar
　　　　2 t. wine　　dash of pepper

Directions:
1. Clean sea cucumbers. Cut in half lengthwise. Cut each half in slices diagonally. Combine with 1 t. cornstarch and 1 t. wine. Fill pot with 2 bowls boiling water. Add green onion and ginger. Parboil sea cucumber 2-3 min. Remove and drain.
2. Scale fish; remove entrails, bones and skin. Cut into slices. Mix with 1 t. salt, cornstarch, white soy sauce, wine, sugar and 1 T. egg white. Beat remaining egg whites seasoned with salt and M.S.G. until fluffly.
3. Bring meat stock seasoned with salt to boil. Add sea cucumbers to cook 30 min. Add fish. Cook until simmering. Add lard, egg white and lotus root powder paste. Remove to large bowl. Sprinkle chopped ham, chopped green onion and pepper on top. Serve hot.

槽溜魚片

北平菜　　　材料：12人份

Fish Slices with Pai-Tsao Sauce

材　　料：活青魚中段半斤　冬筍二支　香菇或鮮蘑數只　火腿片或豬肉片一小碟　韮黃少許　高湯或沸水一中碗　豬油二湯匙　味精、胡椒粉少許　薑二片（拍碎）
魚片調料：豆粉一茶匙　白醬油一湯匙　鹽半茶匙　酒一茶匙　二片碎薑　味精少許
綜合調料：黑醬油一湯匙　鹽半茶匙　醋一湯匙　糖二茶匙　豆粉一湯匙　（加清水一湯匙）
做　　法：①首將青魚去鱗洗淨瀝水，然後切爲二分厚之薄片，放盆內加入調味品拌勻備用。
　　　　　②筍去殼對剖切片，香菇洗淨以溫水泡發亦切片，火腿或豬肉均切片，如用豬肉則須以少許水豆粉白醬油拌和。
　　　　　③取鍋燒熱放下豬油二湯匙，先下筍片爆炒，繼下肉片，香菇略炒，卽倒下高湯或沸水滾片刻，再放下已調好之魚片，待沸加入綜合調味及韮黃。視湯呈稠狀，卽刻盛起，面洒胡椒粉，熱吃味更鮮美。

Ingredients: about ⅔ lb. fish (middle part of any fresh water fish)
2 winter bamboo shoots　　3-4 mushrooms (dried or fresh)　1 small saucer sliced pork or ham
1 oz. blanched Chinese leeks (chiu-huang) (cut into 1" sections)　1 bowl meat stock or boiling water　2 T. lard
dash of monosodium glutamate and pepper powder　　2 slices ginger

Seasonings for marinating fish:
1 t. cornstarch　　　1 T. white soy sauce　　½ t. salt
1 T. wine　　　　　　2 slices ginger (chopped)　dash of M.S.G.

Seasonings Sauce (combine):
1 T. black soy sauce　　½ t. salt　　2 t. sugar
1 T. cornstarch (mixed with 1 T. water)　2 T. vinegar

Directions:
1. Cut fish in thick slices and marinate.
2. Peel bamboo shoots; cut in halves lengthwise and slices. Clean mushrooms and slice. (If pork is used, marinated in cornstarch and soy sauce.)
3. Heat 2 T. oil in frying pan. Fry bamboo shoots; add pork and mushrooms tossing quickly. Add meat stock and simmer 3-4 min. Add marinated fish, stirring at same time. Add blanched Chinese leeks and seasoning sauce. Remove at once when sauce thickens. Sprinkle with pepper and serve hot.

菠菜羹
Chopped Spinach Soup

家常菜　　　材料：12人份

材　料：瘦肉絲半飯碗　菠菜半斤　猪油一湯匙半　豆粉一湯匙（用三湯匙水調濕）

做　法：①首將菠菜揀去老葉修頭後洗淨瀝乾，切為二段，肉絲調入白醬油一茶匙和糖豆粉各四分之一茶匙均備用。
②次將鍋中放下水三飯碗，待沸放下菠菜，川片刻，撈起瀝乾切碎湯傾出在碗內留用。
③油鍋燒熱，即將肉絲略炒，待沸，將調味品放下，即放落菠菜，調入水豆粉盛起，即可供食。

Ingredients: ½ bowl shredded lean pork
1½ T. lard
⅓ lb. spinach
1 T. cornstarch (mixed with 3 T. water)

Seasonings: 1 T. white soy sauce
¼ t. sugar
1 t. salt

Directions:
1. Remove old leaves from spinach and trim roots. Cut spinach in half. Mix shredded pork with 1 t. white soy sauce and ¼ t. sugar.
2. Boil 3 bowls water. Parboil spinach. Remove and drain. Chop spinach. Save water.
3. Heat oil in frying pan. Stir-fry pork, 1-2 min. Add water used to parboil spinach and bring to boil. Add lard, seasonings and chopped spinach. Blend in cornstarch paste. Serve.

蟹粉魚唇　湖南菜
Shark's Lip with Crabs

材料：12人份

材　料：厚軟之魚唇二斤　膏蟹二隻　薑二片　薑末一茶匙　猪油二大匙　高湯一中碗　豆粉一湯匙（用二湯匙水調和）

調味品：白醬油一湯匙　糖半茶匙　酒四茶匙　味精少許　鹽一茶匙

做　法：①首將蟹洗淨瀝水，隔水蒸十五分鐘，取出剝殼取肉留用，魚唇刮去黏液，洗淨瀝水後，切約一寸多長方塊備用。
②鍋中放水約二飯碗，加入薑二片，待沸傾入魚唇，並加酒二茶匙，滾燒十分鐘，撈出瀝水留用。
③鍋中放油二大匙，先爆香薑末，再倒下蟹粉，然後加二茶匙酒，翻覆煸炒一下，再傾入魚唇及高湯，並調下白醬油和鹽糖，關蓋滾燒，視魚唇極軟，即拘下水豆粉和味精少許，使汁呈薄稠，即可盛入深口細瓷大盆中，趁熱送席（並可面飾火腿絲二湯匙，以增美觀）。

Ingredients: 2⅔ lb. soft and thick shark's lip　2 crabs　2 slices ginger
1 t. minced ginger　2 T. lard　1 bowl meat stock
1 T. cornstarch (mixed with 2 T. water)

Seasonings: 1 T. white soy sauce　½ t. sugar　4 t. wine
dash of monosodium glutamate　1 t. salt

Directions:
1. Steam crabs over water 15 min.; remove shells. Clean shark's lip well and cut into pieces (about 1" long).
2. Fill pot with 2 bowls water. Add ginger. Bring to boil. Add shark's lip and 2 t. wine. Simmer 10 min. Remove and drain.
3. Heat 2 T. lard in pan. Saute minced ginger 1 min; add crab meat and 2 t. wine; stir-fry 1-2 min. Add meat stock and shark's lip. Stir in white soy sauce, salt and sugar. Simmer, covered, until shark's lip is tender; add M.S.G. and cornstarch paste. Remove when sauce thickens slightly. Serve hot. (You may garnish with 2 T. shredded Chinese ham.)

全 家 福
Happy Family

江 浙 菜　　　　　材料：12人份

材　料： 豬前腿肉半斤　海參二條　響皮（即油炸肉皮）二元　筍一支　胗肝二副（煮熟切片）　熟豬肚十餘片　蝦六兩　青菜心十餘顆　葱一支　薑一片　酒一茶匙　豆粉一茶匙（以一湯匙水調濕）　高湯二碗　花生油一碗半　豬油四湯匙

調味品： 白醬油一湯匙　鹽半茶匙　糖四分之一茶匙

做　法：
① 首將豬肉洗淨，瀝水後細切粗斬，裝碗內調下醬油一湯匙，雞蛋半只，豆粉一茶匙，糖少許拌匀，海參洗淨整條下半茶匙豆粉，響皮以冷水泡頓切條煮十五分鐘，筍剝殼修頭切片蒸十分鐘，蝦以『鳳尾蝦』作法，青菜心洗淨以鹽糖沸水川片刻備用。

② 次將已調味好之豬肉做成肉圓，入油鍋炸黃盛起。然後倒出油重將肉圓倒下。調下一湯匙醬油及半飯碗沸水關蓋滾燒片刻，連汁盛起留用。海參以一湯匙豬油先爆一支葱一片薑，把海參爆炒，卽傾下酒和一飯碗高湯，滾燒十分鐘，揀棄葱薑，倒去高湯，撈出海參瀝乾直切二條，打斜切片留用。

③ 用豬油燒熱，先倒下海參再放下筍片及響皮略炒，卽傾下高湯一飯碗，待滾，再把胗肝肚片倒下翻覆炒匀，然後倒下肉圓，卽將調味品一一放下，關蓋滾燒片刻，卽調下水豆粉，及青菜鳳尾蝦一兜，盛長瓷盆中送席。

Ingredients:
- 2/3 lb. pork
- 1 oz. crispy pork skin
- 2 chicken gizzards (cooked and cut into slices)
- 10 or more slices stomach (cooked)
- 10 stalks green cabbage hearts
- 1 slices of ginger
- 1 t. cornstarch (mixed with 1 T. water)
- 1½ bowl peanut oil
- 2 sea cucumbers
- 1 bamboo shoot
- 2 chicken livers (cooked and cut into slices)
- 6 oz. shrimps
- 1 stalk green onion
- 1 t. wine
- 2 bowls meat stock
- 4 T. lard

Seasonings: 1 T. white soy sauce　½ t. salt　¼ t. sugar

Directions:
1. Wash pork and drain. Chop and combine with 1 T. soy sauce, ½ egg, 1 t. cornstarch and a little sugar. Wash sea cucumber; mix with ½ t. cornstarch. Soak crispy pork skin till soft. Cut in lengths. Sook in water 15 min. Peel bamboo shoots. Slice and steam 10 min. Prepare shrimps according to "Pheonix Tail Prawns". Wash cabbage hearts. Parboil in boiling water seasoned with salt and sugar.
2. Shape chopped pork into meatballs. Brown in frying pan and remove. Remove oil. Return browned meatballs to pan. Add 1 T. soy sauce and ½ bowl boiling water. Simmer, covered, 3-4 min. Heat 1 T. lard. Sauté green onion and ginger. Add sea cucumbers; stir-fry. Add wine and 1 bowl meat stock. Boil 10 min. Discard green onion and ginger. Cut sea cucumber in half. Slice diagonally.
3. Heat lard in pan. Add sea cucumbers first, then bamboo shoots and crisp pork skin. Stir-fry. Add a bowl meat stock. Bring to boil. Add gizzards and liver and combine. Add meatballs. Add seasonings. Simmer, covered, 3-4 min. Stir in cornstarch paste, cabbage hearts and shrimps. Serve in long plate.

清燴鴨掌
White Braised Duck Feet

北平菜　　　材料：12人份

材　料：鴨腳二十四只　粗鹽二茶匙　熟冬筍片二支　香菇六只（洗後用溫水泡發去蒂切塊）　高湯一碗　牛豆粉一茶匙（用二湯匙水調和）　豬油二湯匙

調味品：白醬油一湯匙　鹽一茶匙　酒一茶匙

做　法：①首將鴨腳洗淨瀝水，用粗鹽揉搓後再沖洗潔淨，然後放入鍋內，加入冷水，蓋過鴨腳煮半小時，撈出拆骨後備用。

②油鍋燒熱，先爆香菇及筍片，然後傾下高湯及酒，待滾放下鴨掌，用文火滾二十分鐘，再調下水豆粉，拘成薄稠狀，然後盛入深口瓷盆中，趁熱送席。

附　註：照此材料，在調水豆粉前，先放入鮑魚片，即成『鮑魚鴨掌』，此菜要湊入高貴的酒席上。

Ingredients: 24 duck feet　　　　　　　　　　　　2 t. salt
　　　　　　 2 bamboo shoots (sliced and cooked)
　　　　　　 6 dried mushrooms (soaked with warm water to soften, stemmed and quartered)
　　　　　　 1½ bowl meat stock　　　　　　　1 t. cornstarch (mixed with 2 T. water)
　　　　　　 2 T. lard

Seasongings: 1 T. white soy sauce　　　　1 t. salt　　　　1 t. wine

Directions: 1. Clean duck feet and drain. Rub with salt. Wash again. Fill pot with water to cover duck feet. Boil 30 min. Remove bones.

2. Heat lard in frying pan. Stir-fry mushrooms and bamboo shoots first. Add meat stock and wine. Let boil. Add duck feet. Simmer over low heat 20 min. Stir in cornstarch paste until sauce thickens. Serve hot.

Note: Add slices of abalone before stirring in cornstarch paste to make another dish, "Duck Feet with Adalone"

清燴蹄筋
Pork Tendon in Thick Sauce

江浙菜　　材料：12人份

材　料：已發好之蹄筋十二兩　熟筍片及火腿片各一小碟　冬菇四、五只（用温水泡浸後切片）
　　　　碗豆苗十數支（用小青菜亦可）　猪油二湯匙　鮮湯三飯碗

調味品：白醬油一湯匙　鹽半茶匙　糖┼茶匙　酒一茶匙　味精少許　豆粉一茶
　　　　匙（用一湯匙水調和）

做　法：①首將蹄筋洗淨放鍋內加鮮湯一碗半煮沸加下一茶匙酒約煮十餘分鐘，將蹄筋撈出傾去汁不要。
　　　　②燒油鍋倒下蹄筋冬菇及筍片炒數下，卽加入調味品及鮮湯，燜煮片刻，卽下火腿片略滾，然後調下水豆粉，卽放下碗豆苗一兜盛起送席。

Ingredients: 12 oz. softened pork tendon　　2 oz. cooked bamboo shoots (sliced)
2 oz. sliced Chinese ham　　4-5 dried mushrooms (soaked in warm water to soften, and slice)
10 stems pea shoots (or small green vegetable with leaves)
2 T. lard　　3 bowls meat stock

Seasonings: 1 T. white soy sauce　　½ t. salt　　¼ t. sugar
dash of monosodium glutamate (M.S.G.)　　1 t. cornstarch (mixed in 1 T. water)

Directions:
1. Put pork tendon in pan. Add 1½ bowl meat stock and bring to boil. Add 1 t. wine and cook about 10 min. Remove stock.
2. Heat oil in frying pan. Fry pork tendon, sliced mushrooms and bamboo shoots, and turn few rounds. Add seasoning sauce and meat stock. Cook, covered, 1-2 min.; add sliced ham. Stir in cornstarch and add pea shoots. Cook 1 min. longer and serve.

干貝三色球　　廣東菜　　　　　材料：12人份
Scallops with 3 Colored Vegetables

材　料：干貝一兩半　白蘿蔔一斤　胡蘿蔔二條　鮮綠大碗豆仁一小碗　高湯一中碗　豬油一湯匙　水豆粉一茶匙

調味品：白醬油一湯匙　鹽一茶匙　酒少許

做　法：①首將干貝略洗放入碗內，以溫水蓋過干貝約三寸，浸泡二三小時，然後加點酒以中火隔水蒸約一小時，取出除去湯汁留用，以手將干貝慢慢撕散，置旁備用。

②白蘿蔔胡蘿蔔修去皮後，用挖球型挖出圓球用高湯煮軟後，加入碗豆仁同煮軟，撈出三色球留用，湯汁另裝備用。

③備鍋燒熱，傾下高湯及干貝和干貝汁，待沸，加入豬油並倒下三色球及白醬油和鹽，滾燒片刻，再調下水豆粉，呈薄稠狀，即盛入深口細瓷盆中送席，此菜色香味俱全，宴客席上也可湊用。

Ingredients: 1½ oz. scallops　　1⅓ lb. turnip　　2 carrots
1 small bowl snow peas (shelled)　1 bowl meat stock　1 T. lard
1 t. cornstarch blended with water

Seasonings: 1 T. white soy sauce　　1 t. salt　　few drops wine

Directions:
1. Soak scallops in warm water (cover 3" above scallop), 2-3 hr. Steam 1 hr. with a little wine. Drain and save stock. Tear scallops into shredds.
2. Pare carrots and turnips. Use melon ball scoop to make small balls. Cook in meat stock until tender, add peas and cook till soft. Drain and save stock.
3. Heat vegetable stock, scallops and scallop stock in cooking pan. Bring to boil. Add lard and all vegetables. Season with salt and white soy sauce. Cook 3-4 min. and stir in cornstarch. When sauce is slightly thickened, remove and serve.

燴 八 寶
Simmered Eight-Treasures

湖南菜　　　　　　材料：12人份

材　料：白蘿蔔半斤　胡蘿蔔二條　洋芋半斤　荸薺八隻　鮮蔴菇二兩　青菜心十餘顆　金針二元　木耳三元　高湯三飯碗　鷄油或猪油三大匙　豆粉二湯匙(用四湯匙水調濕)
調味品：白醬油一湯匙　鹽一茶匙　糖半匙　味精少許

做　法：①首將金針木耳用溫水浸泡後整理洗淨瀝乾留用。胡蘿蔔刮皮在高湯內煮十五分鐘，白蘿蔔去皮後與胡蘿蔔均修為橄欖形。荸薺削皮後一切二塊。洋芋去皮切得和荸薺同樣大小。鮮蔴菇在洗米水中洗淨。青菜心洗淨在鹽糖水中川片刻均備用。
②白蘿蔔荸薺洋芋合併放下二飯碗沸水煮軟（荸薺不會軟的）。
③把高湯傾入鍋內煮沸，即放下金針、木耳、鮮蔴菇同滾，十分鐘後，即將白蘿蔔、胡蘿蔔、荸薺洋芋倒下同煮，待滾將調味品一一傾下，約煮十分鐘，即放下鷄油與青菜心，待滾後調下水豆粉和味精，視汁呈薄稠狀，即盛在深口之細瓷大盤中送席，色美味精，非常可口。

Ingredients:
- ⅔ lb. turnips
- 8 water chestnuts
- 1 oz. lily bud
- 3 T. lard or chicken fat
- 2 carrots
- 2 oz. fresh mushrooms
- 1 oz. wood ear (mu-erh)
- 2 T. cornstarch (mixed with 4 T. water)
- ⅔ lb. potatoes
- 10-12 green cabbage hearts
- 3 bowls meat stock

Seasonings: 1 T. white soy sauce　1 t. salt　½ t. sugar
dash of monosodium glutamate

Directions:
1. Soak lily buds and wood ears in warm water to expand; drain. Pare carrots. Cook in meat stock 15 min. Pare turnips. Cut both turnips and carrot into olive shapes. Pare water chestnuts. Cut in half. Pare potatoes. Cut same size as water chestnuts. Wash mushrooms in rice water. Wash green cabbage hearts. Dip in salt-sugar water.
2. Cook turnips, water chestnuts and potatoes in 2 bowls boiling water until turnips and potatoes are soft. (Water chestnuts will not soften.)
3. Heat meat stock to boil. Add wood ears, lily-buds and mushrooms. Boil 10 min. Add turnips, carrots, water chestnuts and potatoes. Bring to boil. Add seasonings. Cook about 10 min. Add chicken fat and green cabbage hearts. Again bring to boil. Stir in cornstarch paste and M.S.G. Remove when sauce thickens. Serve.

金銀荷包
Gold and Silver Pouches

家常菜　　　　材料：12人份

材　料：雞蛋二隻　千張六張　豬肉半斤　熟胡蘿蔔半條　葱二支　芹菜半斤（折葉切長段）　蘇打粉4茶匙　豬油一湯匙　花生油二湯匙。

調味品：白醬油二茶匙　鹽一茶匙　糖4茶匙　豆粉半茶匙　黑醬油一茶匙

做　法：①首將豬肉細切細斬，胡蘿蔔與葱屑亦斬入，然後加入白醬油，糖，豆粉及半茶匙鹽拌勻，千張放下蘇打粉沸水半飯碗浸泡，視千張已呈白色，即可冲洗瀝水。雞蛋加點鹽和味精打散，均備用。
②備小鍋放點油，傾下一湯匙蛋汁，攤為小圓片，挑點肉，把蛋皮摺攏半張，然後用筷子在肉下挾緊，成為荷包形，即為金荷包，可做十二個。又將千張一切二塊，每塊挑點肉在中間，肉的週圍途點水豆粉，把千張也摺攏半張，用手在旁塗點水豆粉，捏成荷包形，即為銀荷包，逐只做完，與金荷包合放一盤，隔水蒸約十分鐘取出，銀荷包印出紅色胡蘿蔔，真美觀。
③油鍋燒熱，倒下芹菜段加鹽爆香，即刻推在鍋旁，再倒下金銀荷包，又把芹菜蓋面，並移下沸水半飯碗，關蓋滾燒片刻，即將芹菜盛在長盤底，金銀荷包各裝一端送席，食時蘸點大衆香醋，味更鮮美。

Ingredients: 2 eggs
⅔ lb. pork
2 stalks green onion
¼ t. soda powder
2 T. peanut oil
6 bean curd wrappers (pai-yeh)
½ carrot (cooked)
⅔ lb. celery (cut celery stalks into 1½" pieces)
1 T. lard

Seasonings: 2 t. white soy sauce　　1 t. black soy sauce　　1 t. salt
¼ t. sugar　　½ t. cornstarch

Directions:
1. Chop pork, carrot and green onion. Combine. Add white soy sauce, sugar, cornstarch and ½ salt. Mix well. Dissolve soda powder in ½ bowl boiling water. Soak bean curd wrappers until they turn white. Wash under running water and drain. Beat eggs. Season with salt and M.S.G.
2. To make gold pouch, heat a few drops of oil in small frying pan and pour in 1 T. beaten egg. Tilt and rotate pan to form thin round layer. Cook until bottom sets, but upper surface is still moist. Place filling in center. Fold egg skin in half; pinch edge together with chopsticks to seal.
To make sliver pouch, cut each bean curd wrapper in half. Place filling in center of each half. Moist filling with cornstarch paste and fold bean curd wrapper in half. Press edges together to seal, using cornstarch paste as sealing agent.
Place together with gold pouches on plate. Steam above water about 10 min.
3. Heat oil frying pan. Stir-fry celery quickly. Season with salt. Move to one side. Add gold and silver pouches. Cover with celery. Add ½ bowl boiling water. Simmer, covered, for a while. Spread celery over long plate. Put gold pouches and silver pouches on top, each on one side.

稀露海參

江浙菜　　　　材料：12人份

Sea Cucumber with Minced Pork

材　料：海參一斤　豬肉六兩(斬碎)　葱四支(三支切長條)　薑一片　酒一茶匙　豆粉一茶匙　豬油三湯匙　高湯二飯

調味品：黑醬油一湯匙　白醬油一茶匙　鹽半茶匙　糖半茶匙　豆粉二茶匙半（用二湯匙水調濕）

做　法：①買已發好之海參一斤，洗淨瀝乾，以一茶匙豆粉拌勻，用一湯匙豬油爆香一支葱，一片薑，將海參整只放下略炒，卽放一茶匙酒，並加入高湯一飯碗滾燒十分鐘，取起倒入竹籮內瀝去湯汁，並揀去葱薑不用，再將海參直紋切做兩塊，再打斜切塊留用。

②次將肉末調入一茶匙醬油和半茶匙豆粉，及半茶匙糖。

③用豬油二湯匙燒熱，先倒了肉末爆炒，然後放下海參略炒，再將調味品一一調入略滾，卽傾下高湯一飯碗滾燒片刻，調下水豆粉及條葱，盛盆送席。

Ingredients: 1⅔ lb. sea cucumber
4 stalks green onion (cut 3 stalks into 1½" pieces)
1 t. wine
3 T. lard
6 oz. pork (minced)
1 slice ginger
1 t. cornstarch
2 bowls meat stock

Seasonings: 1 T. black soy sauce
½ t. salt
2 t. cornstarch (mixed in 2 T. water)
1 t. white soy sauce
½ t. sugar

Directions:
1. Blend sea cucumber with 1 t. cornstarch. Heat 1 T. lard; fry 1 stalk of green onion and ginger. Add whole piece of sea cucumber and fry 1 min. Add wine and 1 bowl meat stock. Cook 10 min. Remove and drain. Discard green onion and ginger. Cut sea cucumber in half lengthwise; cut each half into pieces at different angles.
2. Combine minced pork with 1 t. soy sauce, ½ t. cornstarch and ¼ T. sugar.
3. Heat 2 T. lard; sauté #2.; Add sea cucumber, stir and toss a few times. Mix in rest of seasonings. Let boil; blend in 1 bowl meat stock, cornstarch and pieces of green onion. Serve hot.

酸辣海參
Hot and Sour Sea Cucumber

四川菜　　材料：12人份

材　料：烏參十二兩　豬肉四兩半　薑末一湯匙　白醋二湯匙　辣油一茶匙　蔥一支　薑一片　酒一茶匙　高湯一中碗　豬油或花生油二湯匙　豆粉一茶匙(用一湯匙水調濕)
調味品：黑白醬油各一湯匙　糖四分之一茶匙　鹽半茶匙　味精少許
做　法：①首將海參洗淨切寬絲，用半茶匙豆粉拌勻，豬肉斬碎，加入一茶匙黑醬油和糖拌勻，均備用。
②鍋中加水二飯碗，投入一支蔥，一片薑，一茶匙酒，待沸，將海參倒下川片刻，然後撈出海參，揀去蔥薑不用。
③鍋中放油二湯匙燒熱，先把豬肉炒一下盛起，再加入剩油，先爆薑末，再倒下海參炒一下，即調下黑白醬油，鹽及味精翻覆炒勻，再傾入高湯一滾，然後放入已炒過之肉末，再調下白醋和水豆粉溜勻，即可盛入深口瓷盆中，面澆辣油送席。

Ingredients:
- 12 oz. sea cucumber
- 2 T. white vinegar
- 1 slice ginger
- 2 T. lard or peanut oil
- 4½ oz. pork
- 1 t. hot sauce
- 1 t. wine
- 1 t. cornstarch (mixed with 1 T. water)
- 1 T. minced ginger
- 1 stalk green onion
- 1 medium bowl meat stock

Seasonings:
- 1 T. black soy sauce
- ½ t. salt
- 1 T. white soy sauce
- dash of monosodium glutamate
- ¼ t. sugar

Directions:
1. Clean sea cucumber and cut into wide shreds. Mix with ½ t. cornstarch. Mince pork. Mix with 1 t. soy sauce and sugar.
2. Fill pot with 2 bowls water. Add green onion, ginger and wine. Bring to boil. Parboil sea cucumber 3-4 min. Discard green onion and ginger.
3. Heat 2 T. oil in frying pan. Saute pork 2-3 min. Remove. Saute ginger in remaining oil. Add sea cucumbers; stir and turn a few times. Add white soy sauce, black soy sauce, salt and M.S.G. Stir-fry to mix. Add meat stock. Let simmer. Add pork. Blend in vinegar and cornstarch paste. Sprinkle with hot sauce and serve.

醋溜魚片　　杭州菜　　材料：12人份
Fish Slices with Vinegar

材　料：米魚中段一斤　白糟汁一飯碗（不易買到糟汁可以酒釀半飯碗代替）　木耳三湯匙（乾）　蒜頭二瓣　豆粉二茶匙（用三湯匙水調濕）　猪油或花生油一斤　鷄油一湯匙

調味品：蝦油一湯匙　鹽一茶匙半　糖二茶匙　酒一茶匙

做　法：①首將木耳用溫水泡發後，整理洗淨瀝水，蒜頭剝衣切薄片，均備用。
②將魚肉剖為二片，去皮拆骨然後直切約二吋長一吋多寬之魚塊，放入碗內，加入一湯匙鹽及一湯匙水豆粉和味精拌勻備用。
③油鍋燒熱，不待沸時，即將魚塊在熱油猛火中溜一下，用濾油器撈出，把油傾出，鍋中只留一湯匙，先爆香蒜片，再倒下木耳炒數下，即加入酒釀，鹽半茶匙及其餘之調味品，並移下沸水半飯碗，滾燒片刻，再調入剩餘之水豆粉溜勻後，即倒下魚片及一湯匙鷄油一兜，即刻盛起，趁熱送席。

Ingredients: 1⅜ lb. middle section of tender large fish.
3 T. dried wood ears.
2 t. cornstarch (mixed with 3 T. water)
1 T. chicken fat (melted)
1 bowl pai-tsao sauce (½ bowl sweet fermented glutinous rice may be substituted if pai-tsao sauce is unavailable.)
2 cloves garlic
3-4 C. lard or peanut oil
dash of monosodium glutamate

Seasonings: 1 T. shrimp sauce
2 t. sugar
1½ t. salt
1 t. wine

Directiong: 1. Soak wood ears in warm water to expand. Wash and drain. Peel garlic. Cut in thin slices.
2. Cut fish in two horizontally. Remove skin and bones. Cut into 2"X1" pieces. Combine with 1 t. salt, 1 T. cornstarch paste and M.S.G. Mix well.
3. Heat oil in frying pan over high heat. Fry fish 30 sec. Remove and drain. Leave 1 T. oil in pan. Sauté garlic; add wood ears. Stir-fry a few times. Add sweet fermented glutinous rice, ½ t. salt and other seasonings. Add ½ bowl boiling water. Simmer 3-4 min. Blend in remaining cornstarch paste. Add fish and 1 T. chicken fat. Stir to mix. Serve hot.

溜黃菜
Stirred Egg Yolk

北平菜　　　　材料：12人份

材　料：鷄蛋黃六個　高湯一飯碗（如用涼開水須加點味精）　荸薺屑六只　熟火腿屑與熟嫩碗豆仁一小碟　猪油六湯匙　豆粉一湯匙（以二湯匙高湯調濕）

調味品：鹽一茶匙　酒一茶匙

做　法：①首將蛋黃和高湯調勻，荸薺屑鹽酒均加入再打，然後加入已調濕之水豆粉。

②猪油倒鍋內燒沸，把調好之蛋一齊傾入，趕緊不停地溜勻，使蛋與油溶合變濃，略開一下，即可盛入深口細瓷盆中，面飾已熟之火腿屑與碗豆仁，色香味俱全，爲款待高朋佳餚。

Ingredients: 6 egg yolks　1 bowl meat stock (or boiled water with flavor essence)
6 chopped water chestnuts
1 saucer cooked Chinese ham (shredded) and cooked snow peas.
6 T. lard　1 T. cornstarch (mixed with 2 T. meat stock)

Seasonings: 1 t. salt　1 t. wine

Directions:
1. Mix egg yolks and meat stock. Add chopped water chestnuts, salt and wine. Beat mixture. Stir in cornstarch paste.
2. Heat lard in frying pan till boiling. Pour in egg mixture. Stir thoroughly and continuously until thick. Let simmer. Pour into deep plate and garnish with shredded ham and snow peas.

溜黃豆腐
Bean Curd with Egg Yolks

北平菜　　材料：12人份

材　料：雞蛋黃四只　中嫩豆腐二元(每元六格的)　肉鬆二湯匙　熟火腿屑　蝦米屑各一湯匙　豆粉一湯匙　高湯十二湯匙　花生油五大匙　鹽一茶匙　味精少許

做　法：①首將豆腐去邊皮，放在大碗內搗碎，然後加入蛋黃四只，鹽和味精，用筷子四只，調打得極勻而細膩，再加入已加高湯四湯匙之水豆粉及餘下之高湯，再繼續調打均勻留用。
②油鍋燒熱，放下油五大匙燒沸，卽刻傾下已調好之蛋黃豆腐，用鏟子不停地溜勻，俟中間略滾，卽盛在深口細瓷盆中，面灑肉鬆、火腿屑、蝦米屑等，趁熱送席。

Ingredients:　4 egg yolks
　　　2 T. fried pork meat (jo-sung)
　　　1 T. chopped dried shrimps
　　　12 T. meat stock
　　　1 t. salt
　　　2 cakes bean curd
　　　1 T. chopped Chinese ham
　　　1 T. cornstarch
　　　5 T. peanut oil
　　　dash of monosodium glutamate

Directions:
1. Cut off sides of bean curd; put into a large bowl and crush. Add egg yolk, salt and M.S.G.; beat until fine. Add cornstarch (mixed with 4 T. stock) and rest of stock. Beat and mix until smooth.
2. Heat pan and add 5 T. oil. When oil is hot, put in mixture. Use spatula to stir mixture evenly in pan. When the center of mixture starts to boil, pour in deep bowl. Sprinkle with jo-sung, chopped ham and shrimp. Serve piping hot.

炸溜黃魚
Stirred Fried Yellow Fish

杭州菜　　　材料：12人份

材　　料：	新鮮黃魚一尾（重約一斤四兩）	鹽一茶匙半	酒一湯匙	蝦仁	熟火腿丁	熟筍丁	熟
	胡蘿蔔丁　洋葱丁　碗豆仁各二湯匙	麵粉六湯匙	胡椒少許	炸油半鍋			
綜合調味：	醋三湯匙　糖四湯匙　醬油二湯匙　蕃茄汁二湯匙　高湯一飯碗　麵粉一湯匙

做　法：①首將黃魚刮鱗去內臟，洗淨瀝乾後，用刀在魚背肉厚處稍割開，然後用鹽胡椒及酒擦遍魚身內外，掛起吹約二小時後，用麵粉塗遍魚之全身內外備用。
②將油放鍋以大火燒得極沸，即將魚投入油炸，須炸至兩面鬆黃，撈出濾去油後，盛放細瓷長盤中候用。
③將鍋中油傾出，留回五湯匙在鍋內，先炒蝦仁盛起，然後爆炒洋葱丁和碗豆仁，隨即加入熟火腿丁，筍丁，胡蘿蔔丁，約炒二分鐘，即傾下綜合調味汁及蝦仁，用鏟子溜匀，視湯汁濃稠，即盛起澆舖黃魚面上，趁熱送席。

Ingredients:
- 1 fresh yellow fish (about 1⅔ lb.)
- 2 T. shrimps (shelled)
- 2 T. diced carrots (cooked)
- 6 T. flour
- 1½ t. salt
- 2 T. diced ham (cooked)
- 2 T. diced onions (cooked)
- dash of pepper
- 1 T. wine
- 2 T. diced bamboo shoots (cooked)
- 2 T. snow peas (shelled and cooked)
- 4 C. cooking oil or oil to fill ½ frying pan

Seasoning Sauce (combine):
- 3 T. vinegar
- 2 T. tomato sauce
- 4 T. sugar
- 1 bowl meat stock
- 2 T. soy sauce
- 1 T. flour

Directions:
1. Scale fish and remove entrails. Clean and drain. Score on both sides 3-4 times. Rub fish with mixture of salt, pepper and wine, inside and out. Suspend about 2 hr. on hook or nail to dry. Coat with flour inside and out.
2. Heat oil over high heat till boiling. Deep-fry fish on both sides till brown. Remove and drain oil. Place on oblong plate.
3. Leave 5 T. oil in pan. Fry shrimps. Remove. Sauté diced onion and snow peas. Add diced ham, bamboo shoots and carrots. Stir-fry about 2 min. Add seasoning sauce and shrimps. Stir until sauce thickens. Pour contents on fish. Serve hot.

鹽焗蝦
Salted Shrimps

廣東菜　　　　材料：12人份

材　料：鮮紅大蝦一斤　薑二片　葱白頭二段　蒜屑一小粒　太白粉四茶匙　花生油一斤
調味品：再製鹽一茶匙　酒一茶匙　味精六分之一茶匙
做　法：①首將大蝦剪鬚，洗淨吹乾，隔炸十分鐘前，灑下太白粉留用。
②備大碗一只，放入蒜屑、鹽、酒、味精拌勻，置旁備用。
③把油鍋燒熱，先放下薑片，葱段，再投入已洒麵粉之紅蝦，以大火炸之，約炸五分鐘，視蝦殼已酥，卽用濾油器撈出，速卽倒入調味好之大碗中，用盤密蓋，以兩手上下搖動使鹽味透入蝦殼面，再燜片刻，卽開盤蓋，傾入盆中卽可供食，盆邊飾炸好之蝦片及淸色菜以增美觀。

Ingredients: 1⅓ lb. large shrimps (unshelled)　　2 slices ginger
　　　　　　　2 stalks green onion (keep white ends only)　1 clove garlic (minced)
　　　　　　　4 t. cornstarch　　3-4 C. peanut oil

Seasonings: 1 t. salt　　1 t. wine
　　　　　　　⅙ t. monosodium glutamate

Directions: 1. Trim and clean shrimp. Let dry. Dip in cornstarch.
2. Mix garlic, salt, M.S.G. and wine thoroughly in large bowl.
3. Heat oil in frying pan. Add ginger and green onion; deep-fry shrimps about 5 min. over high heat until light brown. Strain oil and remove shrimps to large bowl containing garlic mixture #2. Cover tightly and shake 1 min. For seasonings to permeate, cover another 3-4 min. Garnish with fried shrimp chips and lettuce on sides of serving plate.

鹽焗雞

廣東菜　　材料：12人份

Pan Baked Chicken with Salt

材　料：用約一斤半肥嫩雞一隻　細鹽二斤　錫紙半張　花椒半茶匙　薑一片　酒半茶匙
　　　　花生油半茶匙　雞油二湯匙

做　法：①首將雞洗淨吹乾，以一茶匙半鹽洒雞身內外，再以花椒薑酒塞肚內，即以錫紙包好。
　　　　②取舊鍋擦上花生油，復以一斤鹽舖鍋底，將包好之雞放在鹽上，然後雞上又蓋一斤鹽，
　　　　　再加密蓋，以文火燒約四十五分鐘即熟。
　　　　③取出拆紙裝盤，待冷斬塊排列盤中，面澆雞油與雞汁，香嫩味美，誠為飲酒之佳餚。

Ingredients: 2 lb. fat and young chicken
　　　　½ t. peppercorn
　　　　½ t. wine
　　　　2 T. chicken fat
aluminum foil to wrap chicken

2⅔ lb. salt
1 slice ginger
½ T. peanut oil
chicken stock

Directions:
1. Clean chicken. Let dry. Sprinkle with 1½ t. salt inside and out. Sprinkle inside with peppercorn, ginger and wine. Wrap with aluminum foil.
2. Grease an old pan. Cover bottom with 1⅓ lb. salt. Put wrapped chicken on salt. Cover with another 1⅓ lb. of salt. Cook, covered, over low heat about 45 min.
3. Unwrap and let cool. Cut into pieces 2"X1". Sprinkle with chicken fat (melted) and chicken stock. Serve.

鶉蛋豬肚湯
Pork Stomach Soup with Quail Eggs

湖南菜　　材料：12人份

材　料：重約一斤餘之豬肚一個　鶉蛋二打　酒半湯匙　鹽一茶匙　白醬油一湯匙

做　法：①鶉蛋煮熟去殼裝在碗內待用。
②豬肚用刀刮黏液，用花生油在水喉石上磨擦，翻覆洗淨，多洗為要。
③先用少些水煮沸下肚，約煮五分鐘取出切四塊，沸水倒去，另用開水，以文火燉三、四小時爛切肚條再加鹽加鶉蛋上桌，這湯最富營養滋補。

Ingredients: 　1 pork stomach (about 1⅓ lb.)　　2 doz. quail eggs
　　　　　　　　3 slices ginger　　　　　　　　　　½ T. wine
　　　　　　　　1 t. salt　　　　　　　　　　　　　1 T. white soy sauce

Directions:　1. Boil eggs and shell.
2. Clean stomach thoroughly by scraping off sticky liquid with knife and rub on hard surface with peanut oil inside and out. Wash off with water. (see step 1., Stewed Pork Rings)
3. Cook pork stomach in boiling water enough to cover about 5 min. Remove and cut into 4 pieces. Discard used boiling water. Cook stomach again in boiling water (about ¾ pot), covered, over low heat, 3-4 hr. or till tender. Remove and cut each piece into 2" strips. Return stomach to soup and add quail eggs. Sprinkle with salt and serve.

淡菜鷄湯　　　江浙菜　　　材料：12人份
Chicken Soup with Dried Oysters

材　料：肥嫩鷄一隻　淡菜二、三十粒　火腿一小塊　薑二片　鹽一茶匙　酒一茶匙

做　法：①首將淡菜洗淨，以温水泡浸，使淡菜略軟，拔去鬚根備用。

②將鍋中水燒沸，放下已洗淨之鷄，待沸撇去泡沫，放入薑酒並淡菜火腿及浸淡菜之水，滾後再用文火燉燒，候鷄爛，淡菜軟，卽調下鹽滾片刻，先將鷄盛在碗中，火腿切片與淡菜盛在鷄上，然後澆上鷄湯，此湯營養鮮美，誠爲宴客之上品。

Ingredients:
- 1 fat young chicken
- 1 piece (about 2 oz.) Chinese ham
- 1 t. salt
- 1 t. wine
- 20-30 dried oysters
- 2 slices ginger
- 2 t. white soy sauce

Directions:
1. Soak dried oysters in water to soften.
2. Boil water in cooking pot; add chicken and bring to boil. Remove foam and impurities. Add ginger, wine, softened oysters, Chinese ham and water used for soaking oysters. Bring to boil, reduce heat and cook until tender. Season with white soy sauce and salt; let boil 2 min. Remove chicken to soup bowl; slice ham and place with oysters on top of chicken. Pour soup over contents and serve.

蛋豆腐　江浙菜
Egg Bean Curd Soup

材料：12人份

材　料：雞鴨蛋三只　肉絲筍絲蝦米各二湯匙　青菜或生菜數支　蕃茄二只
調味品：醬油一湯匙　鹽一茶匙　猪油一湯匙　豆粉一湯匙　味精少許

做　法：①首將雞鴨蛋放在中號碗內，加少鹽打碎，然後加一湯匙水豆粉及開水，蒸二十分鐘，卽成蛋豆腐劃成小塊備用。
②次將油鍋燒熱，炒筍絲肉絲及蝦米，再倒下高湯或水燒滾，卽放落調味品及蛋豆腐，再下蕃茄、味精燒片刻，卽放下青菜一滾，盛起供食。

Ingredients: 3 eggs (chicken or duck)
2 T. shredded bamboo shoots
3-4 leaves green cabbage or lettuce
meat stock or water
2 T. shredded pork
2 T. dried shrimps
2 tomatoes
2 T. peanut oil

Seasonings: 1 T. soy sauce　　1 t. salt　　1 T. lard　　1 T. cornstarch
dash of monosodium glutamate

Directions:
1. Beat eggs seasoned with salt in a medium-sized bowl. Add 1 T. cornstarch paste and water. Blend well. Steam 20 min. Cut egg bean curd into small squares.
2. Heat peanut oil. Fry shredded bamboo shoots, pork and dried shrimps. Add meat stock or water. Bring to boil. Add seasonings, egg bean curd, then tomatoes and M.S.G. Cook 2-3 min. Add green cabbage. Let boil. Remove and serve.

金銀魚圓
Gold and Silver Fish Balls Soup

杭州菜　　　　材料：12人份

材　料：活鰱魚或鰻魚十兩　生豬油丁二湯匙　豆粉一湯匙（用二湯匙水調濕）　清水十二湯匙　鹽一茶匙　酒一茶匙
鷄蛋黃二個　魚圓配料　筍二支（切絲蒸十分鐘）冬菇三、四只（洗淨浸發後切絲蒸十分鐘）豌豆苗十數支
已蒸熟火腿細長絲一湯匙

做　法：①首將魚洗淨去皮骨，用刀背輕拍去小骨，仍用刀背斬拍，直至魚肉鬆爛，再用刀鋒斬細，然後加入已斬碎之生豬油合斬。
②將魚泥放在大碗內，加入水豆粉及少許鹽，以竹筷六隻打攪，隨打隨加，直至清水與鹽加完，再調打約廿分鐘，金魚圓照此材料則加蛋黃二個。
③用湯鍋倒下清水然後把量匙弄濕，再盛起一圓匙魚肉，使成圓子形，一一丟入冷水中，逐只做完，即關蓋在文火爐上燒，俟滾，卽開蓋洒下酒撇去面浮渣泡，卽撈出浸冷水中，另備細瓷碗一只，將筍絲香菇絲墊碗底，然後將用高湯煮過之金銀魚圓盛上，留下一點高湯川下豌豆苗卽盛在魚圓上，再在豆苗上洒下火腿絲，這一道色香味俱全之佳肴，極爲高朋歡迎。

Ingredients:
- 10 oz. live carp or sea eel
- 1 T. cornstarch (mixed with 2 T. water)
- 1 t. salt
- 2 egg yolks
- 3-4 dried mushrooms (soaked in water to soften, shredded and steamed 10 min.)
- 10 sprigs pea shoots
- 2 T. raw lard (diced fine)
- 12 T. water
- 1 t. wine
- 2 bamboo shoots (shredded and steamed 10 min.)
- 1 T. ham (cooked and shredded)

Directions:
1. Clean and remove fish skin and bones. Beat fish meat with back of knife until soft. Mince. Mix with lard. Continue mincing until mixture is fine.
2. Put mixture in bowl; add cornstarch paste and a little salt, a little at a time to combine. Use 3 pairs of chopsticks to beat and mix until all have been blended. Continue beat another 20 min. Stir in egg yolks.
3. Fill pot with water. Make fishballs and put into pot. Cook, covered, over low heat to boil. Add wine. Remove foam. Remove fishballs and soak in cold water.
4. Put bamboo shoots and mushrooms shreds in soup bowl. Place fishballs (cooked in meat stock) on top. Parboil pea shoots in fishball soup. Spread over fishballs. Sprinkle ham over pea shoots. Pour over soup. Serve.

蓮鍋湯　四川菜
Soup with Lotus Leaves

材料：12人份

材　料：曝醃肉（半肥瘦的）五兩　白蘿蔔一斤　薑一塊（形似大拇指）　葱四支　花椒半茶匙
調味品：白醬油一湯匙　酌加鹽
做　法：①首將醃肉略洗，蘿蔔修皮直切薄片，薑一塊在頭部直切二刀不斷，葱整條洗淨均備用。
②備炒菜鍋將花椒小火炒二下，使香而不焦，立即傾入清水一大碗，待滾將曝醃肉整塊放下，加一茶匙酒，滾十分鐘即撈出，亦切為大薄片，連同蘿蔔片放入花水中，以小火去燉，同時放下葱薑，約煮二十分至半小時即可再調白醬油及鹽，此湯清甘濃香，別有滋味。
附　註：此湯要使蘿蔔片頓而不碎，醃肉不太爛，荷花蓮梗均在其中。

Ingredients: 5 oz. salted pork (half fat and half lean)　1⅛ lb. turnip
1 pc. ginger (thumb-shaped)　4 stalks green onions
½ t. peppercorn

Seasonings: 1 T. white soy sauce　salt to taste

Directions: 1. Clean salted pork. Pare turnip and cut into thin round slices ("lotus leaves"). Cut 2 gashes in top end of ginger.
2. Heat peppercorn in frying pan, over low heat, until pungent (do not let scorch). Add bowl of water and bring to boil. Put in pork and add 1 t. wine; simmer 10 min. Remove pork and cut into big and thin slices. Stew with sliced turnip over low heat. Add green onion and ginger. Cook 20 or 30 min. Season with white soy sauce and salt.

燕皮荷包湯
Yen-Pi Soup

福 州 菜　　　　材料：12人份

材　料：燕皮（雜貨舖有售）六元　豬肉五元　蕃茄一只　豌豆苗一撮　高湯一大碗　白醬油一湯匙　鹽一茶匙

做　法：①首將豬肉洗後斬碎調入豆粉及少許白醬油拌勻，燕皮切爲餛飩皮樣，蕃茄切爲眉月形，均備用。
②把燕皮用冷水拍潮濕，挑點肉在燕皮中，用手捏一把，形似荷包，逐只包好，排列盤中候用。
③把高湯傾入鍋中燒滾，加入調味品，再將燕皮荷包倒下，關蓋約滾十分鐘，盛在湯碗中，鍋中留湯半碗，倒下眉月形之蕃茄滾片刻，再川下豌豆苗一兜，卽盛在燕皮荷包上，趁熱供食，味極鮮美。

Ingredients:　4 oz. yen-pi (meat sheet, sold in Chinese grocery stores)
　4 oz. pork (minced)　　1 tomato　　　　pinch of pea shoots
　1 large bowl meat stock　1 T. white soy sauce　1 t. salt
　1 t. cornstarch

Directions:
1. Mix chopped pork with cornstarch and white soy sauce. Cut yen-pi into won-ton skin size, about 3"X3". Cut tomatoes into crescents.
2. Moist yen-pi with cold water. Wrap 1 t. pork in each yen-pi (Squeeze together ½" sides of yen-pi to wrap). (See picture above)
3. Boil meat stock; add seasonings. Drop in yen-pi dumplings. Cook, covered, about 10 min. Remove, but leave half bowl of soup in pot. Cook tomatoes and let simmer. Add pea shoots. Let boil 1-2 min, and pour over yen-pi dumplings. Serve hot.

鵲橋湯
Pigeon Soup with Winter Melon

廣東菜　　　　　　材料：12人份

材　料： 鴿子或鵪鶉二只　冬瓜一斤（切成約一寸半寬之大半圓形，如拱橋狀）　火腿一塊（約四兩）
　　　　　薑二片　酒一茶匙　鹽一茶匙　白醬油一湯匙

做　法： ①首將鴿子或鵪鶉悶死後，退毛，去內臟洗淨瀝乾，火腿以溫水洗淨備用
　　　　　②把水放鋁鍋內燒滾先放下鴿子及一片薑待滾撇去泡沫加下酒，改用文火續燉，約半小時後放下火腿，視鴿子已爛，放下冬瓜燉軟，（不可太爛）即調下鹽和白醬油，然後將冬瓜盛在細瓷長大碗中央，兩旁各放鴿子一隻，火腿切片，裝在橋上，倒下鮮湯，這是一道味極清香而又精緻的湯。也是七月初七的時令菜。

Ingredients: 2 live pigeons (or quails)
　　　　　　　1 slice winter melon (about 1⅓ lb., 1½" thick, use only half to form bridge)
　　　　　　　4 oz. Chinese ham　　2 slices ginger　　1 t. wine
　　　　　　　1 t. salt　　1 T. white soy sauce

Directions:
1. Kill pigeons. Pluck feathers and remove entrails. Clean and drain. Wash ham in warm water.
2. Place pigeons and ginger in pot with boiling water to cover; bring to boil. Skim foam and impurities; add wine. Simmer over low heat, 30 min. Add ham; cook till pigeons are tender. Add winter melon and cook till soft. Add salt and white soy sauce.
3. Place winter melon in center of an oblong soup bowl, with two pigeons one on the other end. Slice ham and place on winter melon "bridge." Pour in delicious soup and serve.
4. This soup is served usually on July 7 lunar calendar.

柴耙鴨湯
Soup with Duck Sheaves

湖 南 菜　　　　材料：12人份

材　料：嫩鴨一只　鴨肫五只　火腿二兩　嫩筍尖二兩　鴨腸四付　鹽二湯匙　酒一茶匙　薑二片

做　法：①首將鴨腸用刀切開，刮去髒污，用半湯匙鹽擦洗，再在水喉石上摩擦沖洗數次，瀝水後每付腸剪成五段備用。

②將鴨肫每只切成四、五塊，筍尖洗淨用開水泡軟撕開切段備用。

③再將嫩鴨拆骨切二吋長四分濶薄片火腿與鴨肉同樣大小，然後將每二片鴨肉一片火腿，一片鴨肫三段筍尖用腸逐個扎住，連鴨骨薑同放大半鍋沸水以文火燉湯，待開下酒約燉二小時加鹽再煮半小時即成，盛時鴨骨不要，將每扎鴨肉一一盛入細湯碗內加湯上席。

Ingredients: 1 young duck　　5 duck gizzards　　2 oz. Chinese ham
2 oz. dried bamboo shoots　　4 duck intestines

Seasonings: 2 T. salt　　1 t. wine　　4 slices ginger

Directions:
1. Cut intestines lengthwise; clean and rub with ½ t. salt; wash thoroughly and drain. Cut into 5 sections.
2. Cut each gizzard into 4 or 5 pc. lengthwise. Soak dried bamboo shoots in hot water to soften; tear apart; then cut into sections.
3. Remove bones from duck. Slice duck and ham thinly, 2"X¼". Tie up every 2 slices of duck, 1 slice of Chinese ham, 1 slice of gizzard and 3 pieces of bamboo shoots with intestine to form bundle.
4. Put duck bones, ginger and all bundles in cooking pot with boiling water. Cook over low heat. When boiling, add wine and stew 2 hr. Add salt; cook another 30 min. Serve without bones.

鯉魚湯　廣東菜
Carp Soup

材料：12人份

材　料：活鯉魚一尾（重約十二兩至一斤）　猪油花生油各一大匙　薑二片　芹菜二支或荽菜一撮
調味品：白醬油一湯匙　鹽一茶匙　酒一湯匙
做　法：①首將活鯉魚刮去魚鱗，剖腹後取出內臟，略洗瀝水，（活魚不必多洗），在魚身內外敷鹽半茶匙，約廿分鐘後始可燒。
②鍋中油燒熱，先投下薑片爆香，再放下鯉魚略煎，即洒下酒及沸水一大碗，待滾後倒在小鍋中，改用文火約燉一小時，再調下白醬油和鹽，此時湯已呈乳白色，川下已切段之芹菜一滾，如用荽菜，俟盛在碗內，再入即可。吃時魚肉可以醮檸檬汁或香醋蘸食，味極鮮美。

Ingredients: 1 live carp (about 12 oz.-1⅓ lb.)　　1 T. lard
1 T. peanut oil　　2 slices ginger
2 stalks celery or 4 sprigs parsley

Seasonings: 1 T. white soy sauce　　1 t. salt　　1 T. wine

Directions:
1. Scale carp. Slit abdomen to remove entrails. Clean carp inside and out with ½ t. salt. Let stand 20 min. before cooking.
2. Heat peanut oil. Stir-fry ginger slices first. Then add carp. Sauté a few minutes. Sprinkle with wine and 1 large bowl boiling water. Let boil. Remove to smaller pot. Cook over mild heat 1 hr. Season with white soy sauce and salt. Soup should appear milkish white. Add shredded celery. Let simmer and remove. If parsley is used, add before serving. Carp may be served with lemon sauce or vinegar as dip.

蓮藕排骨湯
Lotus Roots and Spareribs Soup

家常菜　　　　　　　材料：12人份

材　料：排骨十二兩　蓮藕一斤　以仁米(中藥舖有售)一茶匙
調味品：白醬油二湯匙　鹽一茶匙
做　法：①首將排骨略洗瀝水，蓮藕刮衣，每節切斷，用刀平拍碎，然後切約一吋多長之後，以仁米洗淨均備用。
②備中號鍋一只，加入半鍋水，放下蓮藕，以中火燒滾（蓮藕應用冷水燉，否則就用沸水），改用文火燉煮約半小時，加入排骨和以仁米，待滾洒下酒，約燉二小時，視蓮藕已軟加入調味品，卽可供食，清涼可口，誠為夏季美味之湯菜。

Ingredients: 12 oz. spareribs　　　　　　　　　　　　　　1⅓ lb. lotus roots
　　　　　　　1 t. i-jen-mi (seeds of Job's tear) (sold at Chinese drugstores)
Seasonings: 2 T. white soy sauce　　　　　　　　　　　　1 t. salt
Directions: 1. Wash spareribs and drain. Peel lotus roots, and crush to flatten. Cut in 1" sections. Wash i-jen-mi.
2. Fill medium pot with ½ pot water. Add lotus roots. Bring to boil over medium heat. Reduce to low heat and cook 30 min. Add spareribs and i-jen-mi. When water boils, add wine. Stew about 2 hr. longer. or till lotus roots are tender. Add seasonings. Remove and serve.

酸辣湯
Hot and Sour Soup

四川菜　　　　　材料：12人份

材　料： 雞鴨血一圓塊（教友可以雞肝代替）　切長寬絲　四寸見方豆腐二塊　亦切長寬絲　猪肉絲三兩（以少少醬油、豆粉、糖拌勻）　筍絲一支　木耳半飯碗（已發好切絲）　蝦米二湯匙　雞蛋一只　芫荽三支（切碎）　肉湯一大碗　豆粉一湯匙（用四湯匙冷水調和）

調味品： 醬油一湯匙　鹽一茶匙　醋二湯匙　胡椒半茶匙　糖四分之一茶匙

做　法： ①首將猪油二湯匙燒熱，先爆炒筍絲，即倒下肉絲炒數下，再傾入肉湯，待滾加入雞血、豆腐、木耳、蝦米，然後將醬油鹽也放下，關蓋滾燒片刻，再倒下醋與胡椒粉，即勾下水豆粉，再加入一湯匙猪油後，慢慢傾下已加味精打碎之雞蛋，而飾芫荽一撮，盛起送席。

Ingredients: 1 pc. congealed chicken or duck blood (cut into long strips) (Chicken liver may be substituted.)
2 cakes bean curd (each cake, 4"X4"; cut into long strips)
3 oz. shredded pork (mixed with a little soy sauce, cornstarch and sugar)
1 bamboo shoot (shredded)　　½ bowl wood ear (soak in water to soften and shredded)
2 T. dried shrimps　　1 egg (beaten)
3 sprigs parsley (chopped)　　1 large bowl meat stock
1 T. cornstarch (mixed with 4 T. cold water)

Seasonings: 1 T. soy sauce　　1 t. salt　　2 T. vinegar　　½ t. pepper　　¼ t. sugar

Directions: 1. Heat lard in frying pan. Fry shredded bamboo shoots. Add shredded pork. Stir-fry a few times. Pour in meat stock. Bring to boil. Add chicken blood, bean curd, wood ears and dried shrimps. Add soy sauce and salt. Simmer, covered, 2-3 min. Sprinkle with vinegar and pepper. Stir in cornstarch paste to thicken. Add 1 T. lard. Pour in slowly beaten egg seasoned with M.S.G. Stir well. Garnish with parsley.

醃燉鮮　　江浙菜　　材料：12人份
Salted & Fresh Pork Stew

材　料：醃腿肉十二兩　鮮腿肉十二兩　筍一斤
調味品：冰糖一茶匙酒一茶匙鹽半茶匙
做　法：①首將醃肉用溫水洗淨切為約一寸長之塊，鮮肉洗淨亦切為與醃肉同樣大小，筍剝殼切為滾刀塊留用。
②備小鋁鍋一只將醃肉放下，傾下冷水二飯碗，在中火爐上燒滾，改為文火煮約半小時，再放落鮮肉與筍及冰糖，視醃肉皮軟，即加鹽滾燒片刻，盛起供食，此菜，亦可加百葉節，也可燒為湯。

Ingredients: 12 oz. salted pork leg   12 oz. fresh pork leg   1⅓ lb. bamboo shoots
Seasonings: 1 t. rock sugar   1 t. wine   ½ t. salt
Directions:
1. Wash salted pork in warm water. Cut into 1" pieces. Wash fresh pork. Cut as salted pork. Peel bamboo shoots. Cut into pieces at different angles.
2. Put salted pork in small pot. Add 2 bowls water. Bring to boil. Reduce to low heat. Stew 30 min. Drop in fresh pork, bamboo shoots and rock sugar. Cook until salted pork skin is soft. Add salt. Simmer a few more minutes and remove. For additional delight, cook with bean curd wrapper knots (pai-yeh-chieh). This dish can be made into soup by adding water.

蕃茄牛利湯

Beef Tongue and Tomato Soup

廣東菜　　材料：12人份

材　料：牛利（牛舌）一個（重約一斤半）　蕃茄一斤（約十數只）　薑三片　莞荽一撮
調味品：白醬油一湯匙　鹽一茶匙半
做　法：①首將牛舌洗淨，一切三段待湯鍋水沸，放下牛舌滾片刻，撈起牛舌刮去白衣，然後仍置湯鍋內以文火燉燒約二小時，視牛舌已爛撈出待冷切片。
②蕃茄洗淨一切二塊備用，牛舌切好，再度放入湯中燒，滾後放下蕃茄，調入白醬油和鹽，再燉片刻，盛在細瓷海碗中，蕃茄在上，牛舌在下，面飾莞荽一撮，這道色香味俱全，而營養價值很高的鮮美湯菜，頗受賓客歡迎。

Ingredients: 1 beef tongue (2 lb.)　　1 1/3 lb. tomatoes
3 slices ginger　　sprigs of parsley
Seasonings: 1 T. white soy sauce　　1 1/2 t. salt
Directions:
1. Clean beef tongue. Cut into three parts and place in pot of boiling water. Boil 3-4 min. Take out and scrape off white coating. Replace in pot and boil in low heat for 2 hr. till tender. Remove and let cool. Cut into slices.
2. Cut tomatoes in halves.
3. Put tongue slices into pot again and bring to boil. Add tomatoes, white soy sauce and salt. Cook over low heat, 3-4 min. and remove to soup bowl. Place tongue slices at bottom and tomatoes on top. Garnish with parsley.

河州肉片湯　四川菜
Sliced Pork & Cucumber Soup

材料：12人份

材　料：豬瘦肉五兩　粗形小黃瓜半斤　高湯一中碗
調味品：白醬油一湯匙　鹽一茶匙　豆粉半茶匙　糖少許
做　法：①首將瘦肉洗淨，切大薄片，加入白醬油一茶匙，豆粉半茶匙，糖少許拌勻，小黃瓜修去薄皮切約二寸多長之段，再橫切很薄片均留用。
②將高湯燒沸，調入鹽和二茶匙白醬油，先放下黃瓜片一滾，卽投下薄肉片，見沸卽刻盛起供食，此湯淸甘鮮美，亦爲川菜中之一味。

Ingredients: 5 oz. lean pork　　　　⅔ lb. cucumber
1 bowl (middle size) meat stock

Seasonings: 1 T. white soy sauce　　½ cornstarch
pinch of sugar　　1 t. salt

Directions:
1. Cut meat in big slices, mixed well with soy sauce, cornstarch and sugar. Peel cucumber and cut into 2″ sections. Slice thinly lengthwise.
2. Boil meat stock; add remaining soy sauce and salt. Drop in sliced cucumber. Cook 1 min.; add sliced pork. Let simmer. Remove and serve.

龍鳳雙爪盅
Dragon & Pheonix Feet Soup

廣 東 菜　　　材料：12人份

材　　料：小猪脚一隻（對剖斬小塊）　鷄脚十二只（斬去直骨）　冬菇四只　筍一支　高湯一碗
調味品：酒　白醬油　鹽　味精少許
做　　法：首將猪脚（龍）和鷄爪（鳳），洗淨瀝水後，裝入瓷盅內，又將冬菇和筍片排列面上，放得美觀些，再加入酒，隔水蒸約二小時，待頓，放入調味品，待爛，加入熱高湯送席。

Ingredients: 1 pork foot (symbolic of dragon) (cut in half lengthwise and cut each half into small pieces)
12 chicken feet (symbolic of pheonix) (remove upper parts)
4 dried mushrooms (soak in water to soften)
1 bamboo shoot (sliced)　　　　　　　　　1 bowl meat stock

Seasonings: a little wine, white soy sauce, salt and monosodium glutamate.

Directions: 1. Clean feet and drain. Put in a deep bowl. Arrange sliced mushrooms and bamboo shoots attractively on surface, and sprinkle with wine. Steam about 2 hr. or until half done. Add seasonings, and continue to steam until well done. Pour hot meat stock over contents to serve.

蟹粉麵　　江浙名點心
Noodles with Crab Meat

材　　料：梭子蟹二隻　薑末一湯匙　豬油四大匙　酒二茶匙　高湯一飯碗
調 味 品：白醬油一湯匙　鹽半茶匙　糖四分之一茶匙
麵的材料：粗圓麵一斤　高湯半小鍋　豬油或花生油半飯碗　鹽半茶匙　黑醬油二湯匙　白醬油一湯匙　味精少許
做　　法：①首將蟹洗淨瀝水，加入二片薑和一茶匙酒，隔水蒸二十分鐘取出（蒸蟹之汁留用），剝殼取肉略斬碎備用。
②油鍋燒熱，放下薑末爆香，然後倒下蟹粉煸炒，加入酒一茶匙及高湯蟹汁調味品滾燒片刻，卽調入一茶匙水豆粉拘成薄稠，成爲蟹粉糊，盛起備用。
湯　　水：①鍋中燒沸水半鍋，將麵放下，用筷子撥散一滾，立刻撈在冷水中沖涼，放在濾油器內濾水（此時麵半生不熟）。
②鍋中油燒熱，然後傾下高湯及蟹汁，並落醬油及鹽等，待滾將麵放下一滾，卽撈分配好之碗內倒下湯及蝦爆鱔或蟹粉糊，亦可洒椒粉，味甚鮮美可口。

Ingredients: For crabs:
- 2 crabs
- 2 t. wine
- 1 T. minced ginger
- 1 bowl meat stock
- 2 slices ginger
- 1 T. cornstarch
- 4 T. lard

For noodles:
- 1⅛ lb. noodles
- 2 T. black soy sauce
- ½ small pot meat stock
- 1 T. white soy sauce
- ½ bowl lard or peanut oil
- dash of monosodium glutamate
- ½ t. salt

Seasonings: 1 T. white soy sauce　½ t. salt　¼ t. sugar

Directions:
1. Clean srabs and drain. Add 2 slices ginger and 1 t. wine. Steam 20 min. Remove. Save stock. Remove shells and mince meat.
2. Heat oil in frying pan. Stir-fry ginger 1-2 min. Add crab meat. Add 1 t. wine, meat stock, crab stock and seasonings. Cook 2-3 min. Stir in 1 t. cornstarch blended with water to make thin paste. Stir until contents turn to mash.
3. Boil ½ pot water. Add noodles. Stir with chopsticks to loosen strands. Cook until water boils. Remove and rinse under running water. Drain.
4. Heat oil in frying pan. Add meat stock, rest of crab stock, soy sauce and salt. Bring to boil. Add noodles and cook until done. Remove to large soup bowl. Pour soup and crab mash over noodles. Sprinkle with pepper and serve.

八寶飯
Eight Precious Rice

江浙名點心

材　料：糯米二飯碗　豆沙一飯碗　桂元肉(即龍眼肉)　蓮子　紅棗各數粒　白沙糖六大匙　猪油六大匙　紅綠絲少許　豆粉一湯匙(用二湯匙水調濕)

做　法：①首將糯米洗淨以冷水蓋過米約半寸，浸泡二三小時，然後蒸熟，加入二湯匙糖拌勻備用。
②次將紅棗洗淨浸水後煮軟去核，蓮子同煮均乾湯。
③備一海碗放下猪油擦遍碗之四週，將桂元肉紅棗蓮子在碗底排成圖案形，然後放下一些糯米飯，加些猪油與糖，然後加下豆沙，舖在糯米飯之外圈，再加猪油與糖，再加入糯米飯，不可太滿，蒸了會發脹。
④放好後隔水蒸約一小時多，取出覆扣大瓷盤中。
⑤備鍋傾下一飯碗水，加點糖煮沸，調下水豆粉變稠狀，即澆在八寶飯上，最後洒下紅綠絲上席。

Ingredients: 2 bowls glutinous rice　　1 bowl sweet red bean paste (dou-sa)
3-4 red dates　　3-4 lotus seeds
3-4 lung-gan-jo (dried dragon eye meat)　　6 T. granulated sugar
6 T. lard　　dash of candied red papaya
dash of candied green papaya　　1 T. cornstarch (mixed with 2 T. water)

Directions:
1. Wash glutinous rice. Soak with water to cover ½" above rice 2-3 hr. Steam till done. Add 2 t. sugar and mix.
2. Wash dates. Soak and boil with lotus seeds until tender. Remove pits. Cook until no water is left.
3. Grease deep bowl with lard. Arrange lung-gan meat, dates and lotus seeds at bottom decoratively. Cover with glutinous rice first, lard and sugar next. Spread sweet red bean paste around glutinous rice. Again cover with glutinous rice with lard and sugar on top.
4. Steam above water 1 hr. or longer. Invert contents of bowl to serving plate.
5. Fill pot with 1 bowl water. Add a little sugar and bring to boil. Stir in cornstarch paste until thick. Pour over Eight Precious Rice. Garnish with candied red and green papaya.

片兒川　　江浙名點心
Noodles in Sliced Pork Soup

「片兒川」是一道麵食，也算是杭州的名點心，故特介紹如下：

材　料：瘦肉片五兩　冬筍片二支　新雪裡紅（切碎的）半飯碗　粗圓麵十兩　花生油或猪油五湯匙　沸水一大碗

調味品：醬油二湯匙　白醬油一湯匙　鹽半茶匙　豆粉半茶匙　糖四分之一茶匙　味精少許

做　法：①首將肉片加入醬油一茶匙，及豆粉和糖拌勻，筍片蒸十分鐘均備用。
②先用一湯匙油在鍋中燒熱，將雪裡紅炒數下盛起再用四湯匙油燒熱把肉片放下翻數下盛起，鍋中剩下之油將筍片炒數下，然後傾下沸水或高湯，換用鋁鍋滾燒片刻，再把已炒過之雪裡紅倒下，然後將調味品一一加入，稍滾即可。
③另備鍋傾下沸水將麵條投入關蓋燒滾，撈出以冷水沖洗瀝乾，然後倒在片兒川之湯中燒煮，再將炒好之肉片川下，加點味精，用筷子翻動，視麵已入味，即可盛起，盛時麵在碗下，肉片筍片均倒在麵上，味鮮而香，實爲最開胃之麵食。

Ingredients: 5 oz. pork fillet (sliced)　2 bamboo shoots (sliced)
½ bowl pickled mustard green (chopped)　10 oz. round noodles
5 T. peanut oil or lard　1 large bowl boiling water or meat stock

Seasonings: 2 T. soy sauce　1 T. white soy sauce
½ t. salt　½ t. cornstarch
¼ t. sugar　dash of monosodium glutamate

Directions:
1. Combine sliced pork with 1 t. soy sauce, cornstarch and sugar. Steam sliced bamboo shoots for 10 min.
2. Heat 1 T. oil in frying pan. Stir-fry pickled mustard greens. Remove. Heat another 4 T. oil. Stir-fry pork. Remove. Fry bamboo shoots in remaining oil a few minutes. Add boiling water or meat stock. Transfer contents to pot. Let boil a few minutes. Add pickled mustard greens and seasonings. Let boil and remove.
3. Drop noodles in pot of boiling water. Let boil, covered. Remove and rinse in running water. Drain. Drop into soup and cook until tender. Add pork and M.S.G. Stir to blend in flavor. Remove. Place sliced pork and bamboo shoots over noodles in serving bowl. Serve.

蓮藕粥
Lotus Root Congee

江浙名點心

蓮藕粥是江南的名點心，我特介紹給諸位嚐一嚐。

材　料：大孔蓮藕二大節　糯米二飯碗　紅糖半斤　棉白糖半飯碗

做　法：①首將糯米洗淨瀝乾，蓮藕刮外衣，切去頭上一片，將乾糯米裝入孔內，用筷子一只將米塞緊，然後加蓮頭上一片用牙籤挿入，放到鋁鍋的冷水中去煮，改用文火，燉至蓮藕半爛，然後將糯米倒入同煮，視蓮藕已爛撈出，放入紅糖，粥已稠濃，即可供食，蓮藕切片以棉白糖蘸食。（此份量可供十五人吃）

Ingredients: 2 large segments lotus root (with big holes)　　2 bowls glutinous rice
⅔ lb. brown sugar　　½ bowl powdered sugar

Directions: 1. Wash glutinous rice and drain well. Scrape lotus skin. Cut a slice from top part. Stuff lotus root with glutinous rice through holes. Cover with top slice and stick on with toothpick. Place in pot filled with water. Bring to boil. Reduce to low heat. Cook until lotus root is half-tender. Add remaining glutinous rice. Cook until whole lotus root is tender. Remove lotus root; stir in sugar. Continue cooking until congee is thick. Cut lotus root into slices. Serve with powdered sugar as dip. (15 servings)

蝦肉餛飩
Shrimp-Pork Won-Tons
江浙名點心

我知道餛飩人人會做,可是調味不同,我編此稿,請主婦們嚐嚐我做『蝦肉餛飩』的調味。

材　料：猪後腿肉半斤　鮮蝦半斤(以半茶匙鹽水洗淨)　薄餛飩皮約一○○張　薑末一茶匙葱屑一湯匙(這材料可供四人吃)

肉的調味：白醬油一湯匙　黑醬油,豆粉,鹽各半茶匙　糖士茶匙　鶏蛋半只(加味精打散)

蝦的調味：酒鹽豆粉各半茶匙　水豆粉,豆粉二湯匙,以二湯匙水調濕

做　法：①首將蝦去殼抽泥臟用鹽水洗淨瀝乾後每只對劃二片,加入薑末及調味品拌勻,約半小時後備用。
②猪肉洗淨瀝水後細切細斬,加入葱屑及調味品攪勻,約半小時後備用。
③左手心舖餛飩皮,右手持筷先挑點肉,再挑半只蝦放在肉上,然後將皮子捲二次,在右角下塗點水豆粉,包貼在左角上,即成為蝦肉餛飩,逐只包完,投入沸水中去煮滾片刻,即用濾油器撈在每只大湯碗內,湯的調味,醬油、猪油或鶏油、蔴油、葱花或紫菜榨菜屑隨心所欲可也。

Ingredients: ⅔ lb. pork (hind leg)　⅔ lb. shrimps　100 thin won-ton skin
1 t. chopped ginger　1 T. chopped green onion

Marinade for pork:
1 T. white soy sauce　½ t. black soy sauce　½ t. cornstarch
½ t. salt　¼ t. sugar　½ egg (seasoned with salt and beaten)

Marinade for shrimps:
½ t. salt　½ t. wine　½ t. cornstarch
2 T. cornstarch (mixed with 2 T. water)

Directions:
1. Shell shrimps and remove black lines. Wash with salted water and drain. Cut into halves lengthwise. Mix with chopped ginger and seasonings. Let stand ½ hr.
2. Mince pork. Mix with chopped green onion and seasonings. Let stand ½ hr.
3. To wrap, hold won-ton skin in palm of left hand with lower corner toward you. Place ½ t. of pork filling slightly below center of skin. Top with shrimp. Fold lower corner over filling. Fold again. Brush a bit of cornstarch on front of triangle's right corner and back of left corner. Twist both corners back. Bring moistened surfaces together and pinch to seal.
4. Drop won-tons into boiling water. Cook till they float. Remove to large soup bowl containing soup seasoned with soy sauce, lard or chicken fat, sesame oil, chopped green onion or laver and chopped Szechuan cabbage.
5. To fry, parboil won-tons. Rinse with cold water. Let dry. Fry in hot oil until brown on both sides.

小籠包　江浙名點心
Steamed Small Meat Pastries

材　料：麵粉一斤（約四飯碗）　發粉半茶匙　猪油一湯匙　糖一茶匙（以二湯匙沸水溶化）　猪腿肉十二兩　高湯一飯碗半　洋菜三湯匙（剪碎）　葱三支　薑三片　嫩薑絲一小碟　香醋三湯匙　醬油一湯匙　小蒸籠二屜白布二塊

調味法：白醬油二湯匙　鹽半茶匙　糖和味精各四分之一茶匙

做　法：①首將洋菜以半碗水浸泡一小時，放在高湯內以文火煮化，調入白醬油一湯匙及味精少許，盛在碗內待冷進冰箱。
②次將發粉用少水溶化，麵粉二飯碗裝盆加入猪油糖水及發粉水撈勻，再加點清水搓揉後，成為粉糰，面蓋乾白布並加蓋放溫暖處待發，另二碗麵粉，則裝盆約以一碗沸水調勻，揉為粉糰，面蓋濕白布待冷，俟發麵膨大，再與燙麵混合在麵板上搓揉極勻，再裝盆蓋布加蓋待發，然後才可以做。
③把猪肉洗淨瀝水去皮細切細斬，裝在碗內，加入葱薑屑及一湯匙白醬油和鹽糖味精等拌勻，然後將洋菜凍切小粒，約一飯碗，隨包拌入備用。
④將麵板灑點乾麵粉，把已發的麵粉糰撈出在板上搓揉並切為小段，用滾麵棒擀為中間較厚邊沿較薄之麵皮，約四十餘張，用左手指托包子皮右手用筷子挾肉餡放在包子皮上，左手略為窩攏，右手將包皮四週捏成細摺，令上口合攏即成一個包子。
⑤包子做好，排列在麵板上或竹攤上（圓形的以竹編成）面蓋乾白布，然後放入小蒸籠內，在沸水鍋中蒸十分鐘，即好，連蒸籠上桌，以嫩薑絲泡醬油及大眾香醋蘸食，非常鮮美。

Ingredients: 1⅓ lb. flour (about 4 bowls)　　1 t. yeast　　1 T. lard
　　　　　1 T. sugar (dissolved in 2 T. boiling water)　12 oz. pork leg　1½ meat stock
　　　　　3 T. agar-agar (scissored into short pieces)　3 stalks green onion (chopped)　3 slices ginger (chopped)
　　　　　1 small saucer young ginger shreds　　3 T. vinegar　　1 T. soy sauce
　　　　　2 small steamers (in tier)　　2 pc. white cloth

Seasonings: 2 T. white soy sauce　　½ t. salt　　¼ t. sugar　　¼ t. monosodium glutamate

Directions:
1. Soak agar-agar in ½ bowl water 1 hr. Cook over low heat in meat stock to melt. Add 1 T. white soy sauce and a little M.S.G. Let cool and refrigerate to make gelatin.
2. Dissolve yeast in a little water. Mix with 4 bowls flour, lard and sugar (dissolved in a little water). Add water to make dough. Cover with white cloth. Put in warm place to let rise.
3. Clean pork. Drain and skin. Mince pork meat and combine with green onion, ginger, 1 t. white soy sauce, salt, sugar and M.S.G. Dice agar-agar gelatin finely to fill one bowl. Mix with pork.
4. Sprinkle flour on board. Knead risen dough and shape into long roll. Cut into about 40 small portions. Use roller pin to roll each portion into round skins 2½" diameter (Center should be thicker than side). Put skin on left hand. Place 1 t. filling on skin. Cup left hand. Use right hand to gather edges together by pinching into pleats. Twist pleats together to seal opening.
5. Spread wet cloth over bottom of steamer. Arrange meat pastries on cloth. Steam over boiling water 10 min. Serve in steamers and with ginger shreds soaked in soy sauce and vinegar as dip.

芝蔴湯糰　　　江浙名點心
Sesame Dumplings (Chih-Ma-Tang-Tuan)

材　料：水磨糯米粉一斤　糖豬油丁或凝結豬油八湯匙　黑芝蔴屑十六湯匙　棉白糖二十四湯匙（即二飯碗）

做　法：①首將芝蔴早日洗淨晒乾（倒在篩子內洗），放在鍋內炒香，趁熱用麵棒滾擂細碎，卽放在碗內，加入糖、豬油丁或凝結豬油，用手揉勻，搓成長條，一粒粒摘下來，搓成圓形，約可分三十餘粒。
②次將糯米粉分散，加入一湯匙清水揉勻，做成圓形，一粒包一個芝蔴餡，再搓圓形，排列在已墊濕白布的盤內。
③用小鋁鍋放下半鍋水，待滾將湯糰一一投入，湯糰上浮時，關蓋再滾片刻，卽可盛起供食。

Ingredients: 1⅓ lb. glutinous rice dough　　8 T. sugar
8 T. raw lard (diced) or congealed lard　　16 T. crushed black sesame
24 T. powdered sugar (2 bowls)

Directions:
1. Wash black sesame and let dry by exposing to sunlight. Bake in pan until fragrant. Use roller pin to crush on board while hot. Put in bowl. Mix with sugar, diced fat or congealed lard. Make into long rolls with hands. Pinch off small piece at a time and roll between hands to make small balls (same size as marble balls) (makes about 30 or so).
2. Add 1 T. water to glutinous rice dough. Mix well. Shape into balls same size as fillings. Make balls hollow. Insert filling and seal openings. Roll between hands again to ensure ball-shape.
3. Bring ½ pot water to boil. Drop in dumplings one by one. Cook, covered, until they float. Let boil, uncovered, for a few more minutes. Serve.

炒　　麵　　江浙名點心
Stir-Fried Noodles (Chao-Mian)

『炒麵』看去似乎很普通，但要炒得可口，也並不容易，炒麵的配料隨心所欲，如蝦仁、鷄絲、三鮮……等都可，我介紹的是家常吃的肉絲炒麵，請試試做。

材　料：粗圓麵十兩　肉絲半飯碗　熟筍絲一支　熟胡蘿蔔絲半條　蝦米一小碟　蘑菇十數只黃芽白菜心一小顆　韮黃段半飯碗　猪油或花生油八湯匙　熟花生油二湯匙

調味品：黑醬油一湯匙半　白醬油一湯匙　鹽一茶匙半　豆粉半茶匙　糖¼茶匙　味精少許

做　法：①首將鍋中燒沸水半鍋，把麵放下，用筷子撈散，關蓋待滾，即撈出在冷水中沖凉，然後瀝在籮內，加入熟花生油拌鬆，再拌入一茶匙鹽。
②肉絲加入黑醬油半湯匙及豆粉和糖拌勻，黃芽白菜洗淨瀝水，切細絲均備用。
③用二湯匙油放鍋內燒熱，先倒下肉絲一炒盛起，然後倒下各配料拌炒，加入沸水少許。關蓋滾片刻。盛起再放油四湯匙在鍋內，放下麵，用二只筷子雙手各持一隻翻覆炒透，隨時倒下油，同時調入黑白醬油味精和鹽半茶匙拌炒，使味透入麵內，然後再倒下已炒好之配料拌勻，然再放下韮黃數下，即可盛在大盆內供食。

Ingredients: 10 oz. round noodles　　　　　　½ bowl shredded pork
1 bamboo shoot (cooked and shredded)　½ carrot (cooked and shredded)
1-2 oz. dried shrimps　　　　　　　　　10-14 fresh mushrooms
1 celery cabbage heart　　　　　　　　½ bowl blanched Chinese leek (chiu-huang) (cut in 1½" lengths)
8 T. lard or peanut oil　　　　　　　　2 T. cooked peanut oil

Seasonings: 1½ T. black soy sauce　　　　　　1 T. white soy sauce
1½ t. salt　　　　　　　　　　　　½ t. cornstarch
¼ t. sugar　　　　　　　　　　　dash of monosodium glutamate

Directions:
1. Put noodles in half-pot boiling water. Stir to loosen strands. Cover and bring to boil. Remove and rinse in cold water. Drain. Mix in cooked peanut oil to loosen. Add 1 t. salt.
2. Combine pork with ½ T. black soy sauce, cornstarch and sugar. Wash celery cabbage. Drain and shred.
3. Stir-fry pork shreds in 2 T. hot oil. Remove. Stir-fry all ingredients except blanched Chinese leeks in remaining oil; add a little boiling water. Cook, covered, for a while. Remove.
4. Heat 4 T. oil in frying pan. Add noodles; toss and turn with each hand holding a chopstick. Add oil occasionally. Season with black soy sauce, white soy sauce, M.S.G. and ½ t. salt. Mix thoroughly. Add rest of cooked ingredients. Stir-fry to mix. Add blanched Chinese leeks. Stir-fry a few times. Serve on large plate.

粽子　　江浙名點心
Meat Dumplings in Bamboo Leaves (Chung-Tse)

端陽節是吃粽子的季節，我今介紹肉粽豆沙粽及豆瓣粽。

材　料：糯米二斤　猪後腿肉一斤半　粽葉半斤　捆草一扎

調味品：醬油四湯匙　白醬油二湯匙　糖二茶匙　酒一茶匙　五香粉￼茶匙　鹽半茶匙　味精少許

做　法：①首將猪肉洗淨切約一寸半長之塊加入調味品泡浸一夜，次晨將糯米洗淨泡浸水約一二小時後瀝起泡在已撈出猪肉之醬油中浸約二小時。

②粽葉在前一天剪去頭每張洗淨與捆草泡在滿水中。

③先用二張粽葉放齊。將下半截窩成尖斗形，裝入一大匙喝湯的調羹糯米放進一塊肉。再蓋上一大匙糯米後，將下半截粽葉摺覆過來包成斧頭形。如粽葉不夠可挿進一張。包好後，用草繩兩頭紮緊俟全部包好。放入大鍋之沸水中以大火燒滾即改爲中火煮一小時多後上下翻轉，如水不夠，即加沸水，以文火燜煮約三小時取出供食。

附：『豆沙粽』白糯米泡浸三小時，每只均用二大匙糯米，中間放進豆沙猪油長條一個與肉粽包法相同。

『豆瓣粽』白糯米泡浸三小時，拌進鹽豆瓣加鹽亦與肉粽同樣包，食時蘸棉白糖，比任何粽子好吃。

Ingredients: 2⅔ lb. glutinous rice　　2 lb. pork hind leg

Seasonings: 4 T. soy sauce　2 T. white soy sauce　2 t. sugar
1 t. wine　¼ t. five-spices powder　½ t. salt
dash of monosodium glutamate

Materials for wrapping: ⅔ lb. wide bamboo leaves　　a bunch of straws for binding

Directions:
1. Clean pork. Cut into 1½" long pieces. Combine with seasonings and soak overnight. On the next day, soak glutinous rice in water 1-2 hr. Drain. Remove pork from marinade. Blend marinade with glutinous rice. Let stand about 2 hr.
2. Trim two extremes of bamboo leaves on preceding day. Wash and soak with straws in enough water to cover.
3. Place two bamboo leaves together, stem ends downward. Twist lower end into cone shape. Fill with 1 T. glutinous rice and 1 piece of pork. Add another 1 T. glutinous rice to cover. Fold upper end over filling to wrap. Bind with straws. Drop in boiling water. Heat to boil. Reduce to medium heat. Cook 1 hr. or so. Turn sides. Add more boiling water if necessary. Reduce to low heat and cook 3 hr.

Variations: Red bean paste dumpling: Soak glutinous rice 3 hr. For stuffing use red bean paste and 1" piece of raw lard.

Lima bean dumpling: Soak glutinous rice 3 hr. Mix with lima beans seasoned with salt. Eat with powdered sugar as dip.

炒年糕　　江浙名點心
Stir-fried Year Cakes

『炒年糕』是買寧波年糕來做的，因為它經常有賣，所以不限於過年才吃，平時做一盆炒年糕，配上稀飯，也很可口。

材　料：寧波年糕十條　　猪腿肉或瘦肉六兩　　熟筍絲二支　　熟胡蘿蔔絲半條　　油菜半斤　　韭黃段半飯碗　　猪油或花生油半飯碗

做　法：①將買來乾年糕用清水泡浸，如先切片，也要浸清水中，待要炒時瀝乾水份備用。
②猪肉洗淨瀝水切絲，調入黑醬油一茶匙，豆粉半茶匙和糖¼茶匙拌勻，油菜攀去老葉洗淨切小段，均備用。
③先把鍋燒熱，放入油三湯匙，倒下肉絲，爆炒片刻盛起，然後把油菜倒下，加入鹽半茶匙炒數下，即放下筍絲及胡蘿蔔絲同炒，加點沸水，關蓋略滾，即刻倒下已炒過之肉絲，翻覆炒勻盛起留用。
④重將三湯匙油燒熱，傾下年糕炒之，隨即倒落餘下之黑白醬油，及鹽糖味精，翻覆炒勻，並將炒好配料之湯汁撇去，關蓋燜燒片刻，即倒下配料拌炒，此時年糕已糯，放下韭黃拌炒數下，即可盛起供食。

Ingredients: 10 Ning-po nian-kau　　6 oz. pork leg or lean pork
2 bamboo shoots (cooked and shredded)　　½ carrot (cooked and shredded)
⅜ lb. rape　　½ bowl blanched Chinese leeks (chiu-huang) (cut into sections)
½ bowl lard or peanut oil

Seasonings: 1 T. black soy sauce　　1 T. white soy sauce
1 t. salt　　½ t. sugar
½ t. cornstarch　　dash of monosodium glutamate

Directions:
1. Soak year cakes in water. Slice and dry.
2. Wash and drain pork. Cut into shreds. Combine with 1 t. soy sauce, ½ t. cornstarch and ¼ t. sugar. Mix well. Remove tough stems and leaves of rape. Wash and cut into small lengths.
3. Heat 3 T. oil in frying pan. Stir-fry pork shreds. Remove quickly. Stir-fry rape; season with ½ t. salt. Stir-fry a few times. Add bamboo shoots and carrot shreds. Add a little boiling water. Cover and bring to boil. Add pork shreds; stir and turn constantly to combine. Remove.
4. Again heat 3 T. oil. Add year cakes, black and white soy sauce, salt, sugar and M.S.G. Stir-fry to mix. Add sauce of cooked ingredients. Cook, covered, for a few minutes. Add cooked ingredients. Stir-fry to mix. Year cakes should be soft by this time. Add blanched Chinese leeks. Stir-fry to combine and serve.

桂花金子糕　　江浙名點心
Gold Cakes with Kuei-Hwa (the Osman thus Fragrans)

「桂花金子糕」是糯米做成的點心，美觀而好吃，特介紹給主婦們試做。

材　料：糯米二飯碗　白沙糖四兩　半圓形豆腐皮十二張　豆沙一飯碗　桂花少許　花生油六湯匙。

做　法：①首將糯米放大碗內洗淨後，傾下水一飯碗又二湯匙泡浸約二小時，然後，以大火隔水蒸約四五十分鐘，視糯米已熟，將糖及桂花拌入（如覺太甜糖可酌減）攪勻後取出待冷。

②取豆腐皮一張半，放在菜板上，塗上一點清水使豆腐皮潮濕，即將糯米飯舖上一條，加上一些豆沙，再舖上糯米飯，然後將豆腐皮包起來，包成金條形，每條一切二段，每段似十兩之金條備用。

③用平底鍋放下二湯匙油，一條一條放入油鍋中煎之，可關蓋片刻，再翻面煎黃，時蓋時開，使糕成金黃色，即可盛起每條切為三四塊，排列細瓷盤中，趁熱送席，好吃又好看。

Ingredients:
- 2 bowls glutinous rice
- 12 semicircular bean curd sheets
- dash of kuei-hwa (the osmanthus fragrans)
- 4 oz. white granulated sugar
- 1 bowl sweet red bean paste
- 6 T. peanut oil

Directions:
1. Wash glutinous rice. Soak in 1 bowl and 2 T. water 2 hr. Steam above boiling water, over high heat, 40-50 min. until glutinous rice is done. Blend in sugar and kuei-hwa. Let cool.
2. Put 1 bean curd sheet on cutting board. Moisten with a little water. Spread a layer of glutinous rice; add a layer of red bean paste; add another layer of glutinous rice. Roll bean curd sheet into rectangular shape (like a gold ingot). Cut each in half. Prepare the rest in same way.
3. Heat 2 T. oil in skillet. Fry each "ingot". Cover 2-3 min. Brown other side. Fry until both sides are golden brown. Cut each into 3-4 pieces. Serve hot.

蟹黃燒賣
Crab Shao-Mai

江浙名點心

在中國點心燒賣也算是一色名點心，做起來也並不麻煩，所以我特介紹蟹黃燒賣，給主婦們試做。

材　料：豬腿肉半斤　（瘦六兩肥二兩）筍一隻　青蟹一隻　小鷄蛋一隻　香菜屑葱屑各一湯匙　餛飩皮三十張（切角）蒸熟之火腿屑與川熟之豌豆屑，各二湯匙。

綜合調味：鹽一茶匙　糖半茶匙　豬油一湯匙　蔴油半茶匙　胡椒少許

做　法：①首將蟹洗淨加下一片薑及半茶匙酒以大火蒸約十五分鐘，待冷剝殼取肉，豬肉洗淨切細丁，成榴子形，筍切細丁，蒸十分鐘均備用，
②將各備好之材料置大碗中混合，加入鷄蛋及綜合調味攪勻片刻後，再拌入香菜屑與葱屑，約漬二十分鐘後，取餛飩皮挑肉餡，與糯米燒賣形（請參閱米食類之糯米燒賣），面灑摻勻之火腿屑與豌豆屑，排列蒸籠中，以沸水猛火約蒸七八分鐘，取出排列細瓷盆中供食，這一色精巧的細點，可在宴客席上列為點心一道。

Ingredients:　2/3 lb. pork (leg part) (6 oz. lean; 2 oz. fat)　1 bamboo shoot
　　　　　　　1 crab　　　　　　　　　　　　　　　　　　1 egg
　　　　　　　1 T. chopped coriander or parsley　　　　　1 T. chopped green onion
　　　　　　　30 wonton skins (cut corners)　　　　　　　2 T. chopped ham (cooked)
　　　　　　　2 T. chopped snow peas (parboiled before chopping)

Seasoning Sauce (combine):
　　　　　　　1 t. salt　　½ t. sugar　　1 T. lard　　½ t. sesame oil　　dash of pepper

Directions: 1. Wash crab. Steam over light heat with one slice ginger and ½ t. wine about 15 min. Let cool and remove shell. Wash pork and chop into small dices. Dice bamboo shoots too. Steam 10 min.

2. Mix above ingredients in bowl to make filling. Add egg and seasoning sauce. Mix well. Add chopped parsley and green onion. Let stand 20 min. Place filling on wonton skins. Gather edges together around filling by pleating. Flatten bottom to make a base. Press inward slightly around the middle to make a waist. Mix chopped ham and snow peas. Sprinkle over filling in each shao-mai. Arrange in steamer. Steam above boiling water, over high heat, about 7-8 min. Remove to serving plate and serve.